MODERN AND
AMERICAN DIGNITY

RELIGION AND CONTEMPORARY CULTURE SERIES

Edited by Peter Augustine Lawler

MODERN AND AMERICAN DIGNITY

⁓

Who We Are as Persons, and What That Means for Our Future

Peter Augustine Lawler

Wilmington, Delaware

Lawler, Peter Augustine.
    Modern and American dignity : who we are as persons, and what that means for our future / Peter Augustine Lawler.
    p. cm.
    Includes bibliographical references and index.
    ISBN 978-1-935191-89-6

    1. Human rights—Moral and ethical aspects—United States. 2. Dignity. 3. Biotechnology—Moral and ethical aspects—United States. 4. Bioethics—United States. I. Title.

JC599.U5L38 2010
172—dc22   2010020116

ISI Books
Intercollegiate Studies Institute
3901 Centerville Road
Wilmington, DE 19807-1938
www.isibooks.org
Manufactured in the United States of America

CONTENTS

INTRODUCTION

The closely related essays in this book were all written during my time on President George W. Bush's Council on Bioethics. The Council—especially when it was headed by Leon Kass—was criticized for being a sort of pseudo-Socratic debating society that aimed to illuminate or even encourage moral conflict among Americans rather than reaching consensus based on scientific truth and American principle. It was also criticized for being too worried about the effect that scientific, technological, and biotechnological progress might have on human dignity. Dignity, the criticism went, was used as a code word for stifling science and its benefits with discredited, repressive moral dogmatism. Like Socrates, the Council wasted lots of time humoring opinions that no reasonable person could regard as true.

Those, such critics claim, opposed to the destruction of embryos for research are really about slowing or stopping the scientific progress that's bound to alleviate the suffering and save the lives of millions with an unsubstantiated, nonscientific opinion about the status of the embryo. Similarly, those who want to outlaw abortion must want to impose their religious opinion about who or what a fetus is on women at the expense of the woman's right to choose who she is and how she wants to live.

Those, the critics go on, who fear that biotechnological enhancement might change who we are in some undignified way are worried

1

about nothing. Biotechnology is just the next stage of technological progress, which has already succeeded in all sorts of wonderful ways in increasing human comfort while reducing human drudgery. Does it really make sense to choose unnecessary suffering just to have an opportunity to display your dignity? Nature, without technological improvements, treats particular persons with random cruelty and undignified indifference. The more control we have over nature, the more dignified we can be. When we say dignity, these critics conclude, we do or should really mean autonomy—or personal freedom from nature.

President Obama has appointed an advisory council that will offer him definitive policy guidance based on reasonable consensus; its goal is to use scientific expertise to bring conflict to an end. The president is careful to add that we must respect those who dissent from the consensus. But that doesn't mean that we allow their disagreeable opinions to influence public policy. After all, those opinions are based on religious values that Americans do not hold in common, and they often point toward policies that enforce conformity with sectarian values.

The president said in his March 24, 2009, press conference that his decision to remove limitations on federal funding on embryonic stem cell research was "the right thing to do and the ethical thing to do." He added that "I respect people who have different opinions," although there's no evidence that those opinions are really right or ethical. Consensus, the president's hope is, will triumph when the experts and gifted rhetoricians work together to replace error with truth, or, in the words of Thomas Jefferson, when they successfully displace "monkish [or evangelical or fundamentalist] ignorance and superstition" with "the light of science."

It's easy to object that it is undemocratic to have an expert group determine what our true bioethical consensus is. And surely it is offensive to some of our best citizens to be told that their moral opinions are unscientific and, therefore, illegitimate. They might respond that science doesn't provide us with sufficient guidance about who a human being is. Yet the foundation of our country depends on the real existence of rights and dignity, on the self-evidence of the truth that we are all created equally unique and irreplaceable.

Scientists—be they neuroscientists or neo-Darwinians—characteristically find no scientific evidence for the reality of dignified personal significance, even if some of them regard it as a most useful fiction. They have declared themselves incapable of defending the indispensable truth about who we are. They can offer a variety of hypotheses about why each of us demands personal significance, but they do not really think there is any evolutionary or neuroscientific support for the dignified "I" each of us claims to be. So our scientists, for example, don't really think that the proudly liberated contemporary woman is the autonomous person she claims to be. There's no room, our scientists often think, for personal reality in an impersonal universe.

The experience of the Kass Council was also that there is actually basic disagreement about what even the scientific evidence alone suggests about who we are. That Council was, after all, composed not of religious leaders but of men and women of formidable scientific credentials in a variety of fields. On the embryo issue, Robert George of Princeton argued eloquently that the science of embryology showed beyond any reasonable doubt that the embryo had the same dignified, unique, and irreplaceable status as, say, a teenager. He argued not from revelation but with the ruthless logic of a lawyer for scientific truth. Other members, such as the famous all-around expert Francis Fukuyama (who seems unusually resistant to the charms of revealed religion), claimed that the embryo deserved more respect than a random clump of cells but less than a baby. James Q. Wilson, the preeminent American scholar in public policy, argued from sociobiology that the unborn come to deserve greater protection as they come to look more like us. Kass himself argued that we cannot know for sure that an embryo is a member of the human family, but it deserves the benefit of the doubt. The Council's prominent neuroscientist, Michael Gazzaniga, thought it is clear that what distinguished human beings were brains and hearts. So embryos—having neither—could safely be regarded as material for research. No brain, no heart, no problem is a memorable slogan, but most members of the Council were troubled by its implications for us all.

I have not even begun to do justice to the range of reasonable opinion on the Council. This conflict was a fine example of disagreement at the highest level about the moral and political implications of what the scientific studies show. The dispute was illuminated by something close to genuinely Socratic dialogue, with those involved remaining friends in common pursuit of the truth. Despite great competence and the best intentions, however, no consensus emerged. The disagreement, let me emphasize, has always been over what the scientific evidence really shows about who we are and what we're supposed to do.

The moral conflict that exists in our nation over destroying embryos for research is both reasonable and passionate, and it is based both on different views of the facts we can see with our own eyes and on conflicting human goods. The progress of medical science in alleviating suffering and extending human life does serve the cause of human dignity, but not at the expense of destroying lives or compromising our principled devotion to the significance of every person. On the embryo issue, the conflict may be specific to a certain stage in scientific progress. It is clear now, as the Kass Council reported more than once, that there are some and will be more ways to obtain pluripotent stem cells without destroying embryos. That encouraging fact was curiously absent from our president's statements. Obama's opinion seems to be that research scientists have no obligation to be limited or even inconvenienced by those who disagree with them on the scientific facts about who a person with rights is. Those convinced of the moral status of the embryo by faith or reason do not have to be accommodated, even if accommodating them would be easy to do.

Similarly, one reason among many that it is disquieting to see President Obama so complacent about *Roe v. Wade* is that the real goal of the Supreme Court in that decision was obviously to end public discussion over what or who the fetus or unborn child is. The Court acknowledged that Americans were caught in an intractable disagreement—one neither science nor religion was able to resolve—about when human life begins. Still, the Court concluded that the unborn have no rights which we are bound to recognize; more precisely, they have no rights which the law is even allowed to recognize. The Court, in *Planned Parenthood v. Casey*, eventually let us know that *Roe* is one of a very few "watershed" precedents. For a variety of reasons, its ruling can't be revisited even if it might be in error.

In his 2009 speech at Notre Dame, the president said that supporters and opponents of the pro-life position should extend "the same presumption of good faith" to one another. By doing so, they might "discover at least the possibility of common ground." He went on to say, however, that ultimately "the views of the two camps are irreconcilable" and "health care policies" must be "grounded in clear ethics and sound science, as well as respect for the equality of women."

Women, so this ethical line of thinking goes, must be free to exercise reproductive choice to live equally with men. Men, after all, have always been perfectly free not to have babies, no matter what they do. All persons are equally free to define "one's own concept of existence," the Court explained in *Planned Parenthood,* including one's own place in the universe and "the mystery of human life." Our president didn't take time to explain why he thinks this existentialist ethic of radical personal liberty is compatible with what sound science teaches these days about who we are. The point of science, our scientists often think, is to expunge the illusions that our place in the universe is up to us and that human life—or anything else—is fundamentally mysterious.

Although the president called for a "sensible conscience clause" that would "honor the conscience of those who disagreed with abortion," it's not so clear what honor involves. The president told the students that "the ultimate irony of faith is that it necessarily admits doubt," but the same, for him, is not true of the universal and rationally persuasive principles of scientific ethics. Honor, from their view, means the impotent marginalization of opinions—or personal conceptions of existence—our experts know to be ignorant, immoral, and unjust. Respect for conscience can't actually be honoring the thought that the pro-life position is really both what's required by our dedication to the proposition that all persons are created equal, and in accord with what we now know through science.

Despite our experts, it is clearer than ever that there are both moral and scientific reasons why more and more Americans are not persuaded by our law's sham certainty about the status of the unborn. And surely the president knows that the youth who supported him so strongly are more pro-life than their parents. There is plenty of need for more national dialogue before anyone could reasonably regard this fundamental issue as resolved. As Socrates himself constantly reminded us, for the most reasonable men and women it often remains the case that the fundamental questions, despite our best efforts, remain more obvious than their answers. That is why there needs to be much more room for legislative compromise—for the consent of the morally conflicted governed—which the Court has quite arbitrarily denied us.

When the president admitted, rather cheerfully, that it was "above his pay grade" to determine when, exactly, a being becomes human enough to have rights, he should have concluded that, in the face of such doubt, the necessary decision would have to be made by the American people acting through their legislatures. And the modesty that should flow from uncertainty should lead not just to lip service but to the genuine accommodation of opposing views that comes through compromise. Bush's policy of limiting research destructive of embryos, reversed by Obama, was just such a compromise.

The rule by a consensus discerned and implemented by experts—by judges, bureaucrats, and scientists—might be fine if they were all philosopher-kings who had united in themselves not only technological power but also perfect wisdom. It is obvious, however, that the human power over both nature and human nature is growing faster than is our wisdom about how to use that power for authentically human purposes. Experts very often hide their personal opinions and ideological agendas behind impersonal claims of being guided merely by what the studies say. We can learn from the experts but we shouldn't trust them. These days, people should, above all, distrust meddlesome, schoolmarmish, vain technocrats who want to deprive people of the dignity that comes from deliberating about who we are and how we should live.

Each chapter of this book is meant to contribute to our deliberation about who we are as free, dignified, and purposeful beings. The first chapter, commissioned by the Council, lays out my view of the distinction between the modern and American views of dignity. The second defends the indispensability of speaking of dignity (as opposed to autonomy or rights) today, partly by showing that rights were inadequate for facing the threats to who we are that came from the ideologies of the twentieth century and the biotechnology of the twenty-first. I also show, following the lead of many who wrote for the Council on the issue, that the idea of autonomy—or the identification of our freedom as not being determined by nature—is just too empty to be a source of moral guidance that could subordinate technology to human purpose. That was the core illusion of the Sixties (see chapter 6). That illusion may be the most important reason why the humanities are fading away in America; our higher education is more and more about nothing more than technological productivity (see chapter 3).

The idea of personal autonomy, by itself, points us in the direction of perfect justice that might come with perfect freedom from nature. The autonomous person is not natural or biological. Natural enhancements, from this view, can't transform personhood, but only allow it to flourish more securely as what it is in freedom. Leon Kass is right that those who reduce dignity to autonomy don't reflect on what enhanced personal freedom might do to our loves and longings, to the dignified fulfillment found in doing what comes naturally to self-conscious, embodied, social animals, in freely taking responsibility for being men and women who know they are born to die. Those who think in terms of disembodied personhood don't reflect, for example, on what the separation of sex from procreation in the name of personal security might do to personal identity.

Kass and others have a kind of "Brave New World" concern. In trying to make ourselves more than who we are by nature, we might end up becoming beings who lack what it takes to display our personal dignity. My own view is that there is some Christian wisdom in even today's personal view that we can't make ourselves into something better or worse than who we are as persons. We can't, thank God, reduce ourselves to just another "subhuman" species, and we can't raise ourselves to either the immortal gods or the personal God. The human species is one among a huge number, but it's not just another species. Our personal longings and our personal behavior can't be explained in the way that of the other species can. Those who speak of autonomy are right, at least, in thinking of each of us as a free, unique, and irreplaceable person.

Contrary to extreme fears concerning personal degradation, I really think that in an increasingly enhanced or biotechnological world we will be distinguished by our personal virtue like never before. That means, to begin with, by the bourgeois virtues that lead to personal productivity. But there's no reason to believe that the other virtues—especially those connected with loving caregiving, but also those connected with courage in the face of death and in defense of other persons—will become superfluous. It will be more admirable than ever to risk one's life if it could extend for an indefinitely long time. It will be harder, but still necessary, to face up to every person's inescapable biological finitude in order to live well. The lonely disorientation that comes from being detached from God and nature—and especially from the personal Creator—will become more common. So being a better person in the moral or spiritual sense will be tougher and more of an advantage.

Thinking realistically about personal virtue begins by correcting the autonomy freaks with the observation that persons are erotic or animated by love. That means that charity or caregiving is a higher virtue than justice, precisely because it's more personal. By neglecting—in the name of autonomy—thinking about or cherishing intentionally the social or relational dimension of being personal, we've actually made personal existence seem more contingent—or detached and ephemeral—than ever. But that's not to say that persons have, or even could, become unreal; the very good news is that who we are continues to elude our efforts at rational control.

My view is that love is a personal capability we've been given by nature. There's some ground for being a "relational" person in nature itself, perhaps because both we and it were created by a personal God. The personal *logos* of the early Church Fathers seems to be more reasonable than the impersonal *logos* that's been characteristic of most of science from its beginning. The most dense and most ambitious chapters in this book are about the great thinkers from whom I've begun to learn something, at least, about the personal *logos*—our philosopher-pope Benedict XVI (chapter 7), Alexis de Tocqueville (chapter 5), Chantal Delsol (chapter 4), and John Courtney Murray (chapter 8).

I have also written, more personally, about two profound and heroic men who show us what we seem to need to know most today—how to be very old and still very happily purpose-driven. They are Aleksandr Solzhenitsyn (chapter 9) and Socrates (chapter 10).

The final two chapters explain why being personal (or inescapably dignified) is necessarily being pro-life (and adapting virtue to unprecedented longevity and biotechnological enhancement) and being political (or being loyally responsible for securing the way of life of people in a particular part of the world). That's not to say that being a citizen, from either a modern or an American view, is the last word on who any of us dignified persons is.

This book, as a whole, examines the whole who is the dignified human person.

Versions of these chapters were published in the *Intercollegiate Review, Society, Perspectives on Political Science,* the *New Atlantis,* the *Krakow Journal of International Affairs,* the *City,* and in books published by Lexington Books and St. Augustine's Press and by the President's Council on Bioethics.

I want to thank Berry College students Mallory Owens, Will Harper, and especially Andrea Lowry for helping to get this manuscript in shape for publication. Thanks also to the perfect and endlessly patient Diane Land for rooting errors out of the proofs. The Earhart Foundation funded the leisure that made possible several of these chapters.

My greatest debts, as always, are to Rita and Catherine.

1

MODERN AND AMERICAN DIGNITY

Modern society—or at least its more sophisticated parts—is distinguished by its concern for individual dignity. Individuals demand to exist for themselves. They refuse to be reduced to useful and expendable means for ends that are not their own. Increasingly, modern government is based on the dignified principle that the individual can't be understood to exist for a community, a country, an ideology, a God, or even a family. We think it undignified to believe that earthly or real human beings exist for heavenly or imaginary ones, as we think religions once led us to believe. We also think it undignified to regard today's individuals as existing for human beings of the future, as did the millenarian ideologies that disappeared with the twentieth century. Protecting my dignity, from this view, means protecting what the moral fanatics are all too ready to sacrifice—my particular life, my particular being, myself.[1] My purpose here is to explore some of the modern dimensions of the dignified "I," and so to show how indispensable, wonderful, and strange the idea of personal dignity is for us Americans. One reason for this exploration is to show how technology and biotechnology are both reflections of and challenges to our proper understanding of our ineradicable human dignity.

The Christian Understanding of Human Freedom

Our understanding of the dignity of the individual or the person, I think, originates with Christianity, particularly with St. Augustine. We find it in Augustine's criticism of the civil and natural theologies— the respectable theologies—of the Greeks and the Romans for misunderstanding who the human being is. Civil theology—the gods of the city or political community—is based on the premise that human beings are essentially citizens or part of a city. But that's not true. Human longings point beyond one's own country and can't be satisfied by any kind of political dedication or success. It's finally undignified or untruthful for a Roman to identify himself or his fate with Rome. Augustine didn't deny there was a certain nobility or dignity of citizens who subordinated their selfish interests for their country's common good. But even or especially the best Romans were looking in the wrong place for genuine personal security and significance or immortality. They were looking in the wrong place for personal meaning, or transcendence, or perfection.[2]

The polytheism of civil theology was also undignified insofar as it was an offense against the human mind. It required that educated men degrade themselves by feigning belief in unbelievable gods and by engaging in a futile effort to fend off moral deterioration as their country became more sophisticated. Such efforts were also degrading to others. These efforts opposed the particular human being's efforts to free himself from what are finally selfish communal illusions. Civil theology, by defining us as citizens and nothing more, hides from us the dignity that all human beings share in common.

Sophisticated Greeks and Romans, Augustine adds, rejected the gods of their country for nature's God, the God of the philosophers. But that growth in theological sophistication in the direction of impersonal monotheism was only ambiguous progress. All reasonable theology is monotheistic; the orderly universe and essentially equal human beings must be governed by a single God. But Augustine still saw two problems with nature's God. First, he is too distant or too impersonal to provide any real support for the moral duties of particular human beings; dignified personal action or personal existence can't be based on a God that is finally not a "who" but a "what." Second, natural theology is based on the premise that the human being is a part of nature and nothing more. It can't account for the realities of human freedom and dignity.

The God of the philosophers is meant as a replacement for civil theology and becomes a competitor to Biblical theology. The philosopher orients himself toward the truth about God by liberating his mind from all the moral, political, and religious illusions that allow human beings to experience themselves confidently as at home in the world as whole persons. He frees himself from the illusions that give most people some sense of dignity or significance. The philosopher discovers that the human mind is at home in the world, and so God must be the perfection of our intellectual capacity to comprehend all that exists.

We grasp our true dignity—the dignity of our minds—only by seeing that the mind necessarily depends on a body that exists for a moment nowhere in particular and is gone. So my being at home as a mind depends on my radical homelessness or insignificance as a whole, embodied being. Any being that genuinely appears to us as eternal— such as a star—couldn't possibly know anything at all. Only a being who is absolutely mortal—or, better, absolutely contingent as a living being—could know both the truth about the stars and the truth about the insignificance of himself. Nature's God can establish the dignity of human minds, but only at the expense of denying the dignity of all human lives to the extent that they aren't genuinely governed by thought.[3]

Understanding ourselves as wholly natural beings means surrendering any sense of real personal dignity to impersonal natural necessity, to a God who is a principle, not a person. But according to Augustine, human beings are more than merely natural beings. They long to be seen, in their particular, distinctive, infinitely significant freedom, by a personal God who knows them as they truly are. Natural theology can't account for equally free, unique, indispensable, and irreplaceable beings under God, or for human persons who can distinguish themselves not only from the other animals and God but from each other.

Natural theology also can't account for, much less point to the satisfaction of, the longing of each particular human being really to be. Each human being longs to be and is an exception to the general, necessitarian laws that account for the rest of creation. Each of us has the freedom and dignity that comes with personal transcendence: The laws of nature can't account for our free will, for either our sinfulness or our virtue, for our love of particular persons (including the personal God), for the misery of our personal contingency and mortality without a personal, loving God, for our capacity to sense, even without revelation, that we were made for eternal life through our ineradicable alienation in this world, or for our literal transcendence of our biological existence as whole persons through God's grace.

The Dignity of the Individual

The Augustinian criticism of both natural and civil theology on behalf of the particular person's dignity retains its force in the post-Christian climate of modern thought. The individual's claim for transcendent and dignified freedom actually intensifies as faith in the Biblical God recedes. What we once faithfully trusted God to do for us, we now have to do for ourselves. Our claim is also more insistent because it can now be based in our manly pride; my infinite significance no longer depends on my feigning humble self-surrender to an omnipotent God who cares for me in particular.

The human individual described by John Locke and the other liberal philosophers regards himself as free, unique, and irreplaceable. I'm so full of dignity or inestimable worth that the whole world should center on what's best for me. The individual has the right to use his freedom to transform his natural condition, to act against the nature that's indifferent or hostile to his particular existence. And he has the right to oppose freely every effort of other human beings—even, or especially, priests and kings—to risk or even deploy his life for purposes other than his individual ones. His dignity isn't given to him by God or nature; it is found in his freedom, in his singular capability to exercise rights.[4]

We can call rights natural insofar as we acknowledge that we didn't make ourselves capable of making ourselves free. Freedom from nature is a quality mysteriously possessed by members of our species alone, and that mystery deepens, of course, when we doubt that the Bible can even begin to explain it. But that means, paradoxically, that our singular natural quality is our free or transcendent ability to transform nature to give to ourselves what nature did not give us. There is, in fact, no life according to nature that is worthy of my particular freedom and dignity. From the individual view, the natural life that the undignified species are stuck with living is nasty, brutish, and short, not to mention nontranscendent or un-free.[5]

There was an attempt to revive natural theology or "Nature's God" in the modern world, but it was disabled from the beginning by a basic contradiction: the modern view of nature, like the one of the Greeks and Romans, is of an impersonal principle that governs all that exists. But the view that we're completely or eternally governed by fixed principles of eternal natural necessity can't capture the existence of the free individual—the being who has the right to use his reason and his will to free himself from his natural limitations.

"Nature's God" returns us to the ancient thought that the world is the home of the human mind, and the Americans today who most firmly believe in such a God might be the physicists who believe that their minds have cracked the cosmic code. But can the mind really grasp as a whole a world in which the individual is distinguished in his self-consciousness and his freedom from everything else? The physicist may be able to comprehend the mind or the body of the physicist, but not the whole human person who, among other things, engages in physical inquiry. That's one reason why the more characteristically modern view is that the mind is for transforming nature to make the individual genuinely at home or secure. Insofar as Nature's God is taken seriously, it mostly undermines the individual's sense of his irreplaceable and unique dignity. If, as Tom Wolfe explains, the dignity of the individual (which we can see with our own eyes) is taken seriously, then we can't help but conclude that the integrity of the natural world—or the rule of Nature's God—came to an end with the mysterious emergence of the free and self-conscious individual.[6]

For the modern individualist, the truth remains that our dignified pretensions still point in the direction of a personal God, but only a blind sucker relies upon such an imaginary projection. For Locke, it makes some sense to speak of a Creator as the source of the visible universe and our mysterious liberty. But it's foolish to think of oneself as a

creature or fundamentally dependent on a providential God who guar-
antees us eternal life. Locke's Creator is not personal or present-tense
enough to do anything for particular individuals.

Our dignity, from this individual view, comes from facing up to the
truth about how on our own we really are. Man's existence is radically
contingent and mortal. But he has the resources to improve upon his
condition, to act intelligently and responsibly on his own behalf. The
dignity of the individual flows from his authentic self-consciousness,
from what sets him apart from his natural, political, and familial environment. All the other animals act unconsciously to perpetuate their
species. To the extent that we are dignified in our difference from
them, we consciously act on behalf of free individuals. The other particular animals aren't conscious of their temporary, utterly vulnerable,
and irreplaceable existences. They're utterly replaceable because they
don't know they're irreplaceable. I know others will come along a lot
like me, but they won't be me. The evidence of my dignity is my acting
in response to my self-consciousness, my thought about myself. It's in
my truthful and resolute efforts to continue to be me.

I feel indignation toward anyone who denies the truth about my
self-consciousness and my freedom, my being. I feel especially righ-
teous indignation toward those who would morally criticize or con-
strain me by imagining me to be other than who I really am. That's
because I'm convinced of the fundamental rightness of my free and
responsible efforts to sustain my individual existence—my existence as
a self-conscious, free, and body-dependent being—as long as possible.[7]
I'm indignant enough to endanger my life freely in order to secure my
freedom. I know enough to know that free beings can't pursue even
cowardly ends with consistently cowardly means. So I know I may be
stuck with displaying my dignity by risking my life on behalf of my
right to life.

Sometimes indignantly insisting on my rights to life and liberty
can seem undignified: I might say I have the right to sell my allegedly surplus kidney for the right price, because my body is my property, to be used as I think best. But surely it is undignified to regard
my body—part of me—as merely part of my net worth of dollars.
And surely a man or woman with a strong sense of personal worth—
and so with a strong desire to display the nobler virtues of courage or

generosity—would always want to do more than merely secure his or her biological existence. The individual responds that he's going to be courageous or generous on his own terms; such risky virtue is not to be required of him. And an obsession with the needlessly risky noble virtues is for losers who don't understand themselves. Dead people have no real dignity or significance at all.

The real evidence, the individual notices, is on the side of identifying dignity with the protection of rights. Leon Kass reminds us that "liberal polities, founded on this doctrine of equal natural rights, do vastly less violence to human dignity than do their illiberal (and often moralistic and perfection-seeking) antagonists."[8] The twentieth century's monstrous offenses against human dignity—so monstrous that they can't be described as mere violations of rights[9]—came from those who denied the real existence of individuals and their rights. Particular human beings were ideologically reduced to fodder for their race, class, or nation, for murderous and insane visions of humanity's non-individualistic future. Every attempt to restore civil theology in the modern world—from the Rousseau-inspired dimensions of the French Revolution onward—morphed into insane frenzies of unprecedented cruelty aiming to exterminate the alienation that inevitably accompanies our freedom. In a post-Christian context, we really can't defend personal dignity by neglecting individual rights.

Autonomy

A sensible understanding of "inalienable rights" might be the protections given to or required by self-conscious mortals, to beings stuck in between the other animals and God. But the modern individual characteristically isn't content with locating his dignity in his acceptance of the intractable limitations of his embodiment. The modern individual—the modern self—aims to be autonomous, to use the mind as an instrument of liberation from or transcendence of dependence on material or natural necessity. From this view, modern individualism is not that different from the twentieth century's historical or ideological projects to radically transform the human condition. The difference is that the individual never loses his focus on his own freedom, his rights; communism, fascism, and so forth were all diversions from what we really know, impossible efforts to transfer man's truthful sense of his individual significance to some impersonal or ideological cause. The Europeans regard those efforts as the last and worst vestiges of civil theology. That's why they've apparently decided to abandon both religious and political life on behalf of a humanitarian concern for individual dignity.[10]

But the modern self is even more than a humanitarian or a humanist; he's the very opposite of a materialist in his own case. My mind is free to transform my body. The modern self identifies itself with the mind ("I think, therefore I am") liberating itself through technology and enlightened education from the undignified drudgery of material necessity and the tyranny of the unconscious. The mind frees the self from both material and moral repression for self-determination.[11] Our struggle for the rational control that really would secure our dignity really does point in the direction of transhumanism.[12] We aim to use technology and biotechnology to overcome our human limitations as embodied beings. We aim at the overcoming of time, infirmity, death, and all the cruel indignities nature randomly piles upon us. Our dignity, from this view, depends on the orders we're really capable of giving to ourselves, meaning to our natures.

Our dignity is in our awareness that what we're given by nature is worthless unless we bring it under our conscious control. So the individual doesn't really aim to secure himself as a biological being, because he's fully aware that he's more or other than a biological being. His biological dependence has already been lessened by his freedom, and he recognizes no limits to how much his mind might take command over his body and bodies. Nature has been and will be increasingly shaped and limited by his free action on behalf of his individual being. Impersonal natural evolution is being supplanted by personal or conscious and volitional evolution.

Dignity vs. Anxious Contingency

The trouble, of course, is that for the foreseeable future the pursuit of transcendence of our biological being is bound to fail every particular human individual in the end. The individual now makes only quite ambiguous and radically unsatisfactory progress toward indefinitely continuing to be. So our best efforts do little to free us from the anxious sense of contingency that comes with self-consciousness—the undignified perception that we're meaningless accidents that exist for a moment between two abysses. The more secure our efforts make us, it may be, the more anxious or disoriented we feel. The more we push back the necessity of death, the more accidental death becomes. And we have to work harder and harder not to be an accident. If, despite our best efforts, all we succeed in doing is making our lives more accidental or pitiful, it's hard to say that our technological successes have made our individual existences more secure or dignified.[13]

It's because of this sense of final futility that Hobbes says people become particularly restless and troublesome—unreasonable and dignity-obsessed—in times of peace. Freed somewhat from their rather dignified struggle against natural necessity, they can't avoid reflection on the inevitability of their long-run failure. No matter what I do, I won't be important or dignified for long, because I won't be around for long, or at least long enough. As long as death remains an accidental possibility and an eventual certainty, my dignity defined as autonomy remains constantly in question. Modern individuals, as Tocqueville explains, are restlessly time- and death-haunted in the midst of prosperity, unable really to enjoy what seem to be the most fortunate circumstances in the history of their species. Just below the surface of our proud pragmatism lurks, as Solzhenitsyn writes, "the howl of existentialism." For the modern individual, "the thought of death becomes unbearable. It is the extinction of the entire universe at a stroke."[14]

Today, American restlessness doesn't usually display itself as dangerous political ambition, as Hobbes feared.[15] Our self-understanding is too individualistic for us to connect easily dignity with political recognition. Instead, we find evidence of our restless pursuit of dignity in a workaholic security-consciousness among sophisticated Americans. They're laidback or relativistic on the traditional moral issues, partly to avoid the moralism that deprives other individuals of the dignity of determining their own lives. But they are also increasingly health and safety conscious, and it's there that their paranoid, puritanical, and prohibitionist sides now show themselves.

Our drive to secure ourselves has, for example, caused us to be extremely moralistic about safe sex. Whatever you prefer to do is dignified as long as it's responsible, and being responsible means methodically disconnecting your sexual behavior from birth and death, from babies and fatal diseases. It's easy to imagine a complete separation of sex and procreation in the name of security, in the name of minimizing all the risk factors associated with having unprotected sex. But of course that separation will deprive our sexual behavior of the shared hopes, fears, and responsibilities that made it seem dignified in itself and the main antidote to individualistic self-obsession. The domination of *eros* by security consciousness may be good for the individual's effort to continue to exist, but of course he'll be more anxious than ever. Safe sex is dignified in the sense that it's a responsible choice impossible for the naturally determined animals, but it might be undignified in the sense that it's ridiculous to be that bourgeois about *eros*, to work too hard to prefer security over distinctively human enjoyment. Sex—like God—used to be a way we could get our minds off ourselves.[16]

Tocqueville feared that modern individuals would end up becoming so apathetic and withdrawn that they would surrender the details of their lives—their own futures—to a meddlesome, schoolmarmish administrative state.[17] But that undignified surrender of personal concern hasn't happened. Individuals continue to become in many ways more on their own than ever, which is why we still increasingly connect individual dignity with personal responsibility or self-ownership. Sophisticated individuals are more aware than ever that they exist contingently in hostile environments, although their lives are in some ways more secure and certainly longer than ever. Some dignity remains in their resolute efforts to be more than accidents, and their desire to be irreplaceable has intensified. That's why more of them than ever decide that it's undignified even to produce replacements—children.

Pantheism

Arguably, the modern goal is not the achievement of real security for one's being, which is impossible, but freedom from the anxiety that accompanies our true perception of the individual's contingency.

Maybe freedom from anxiety is our true goal—then we should consent to anyone or anything that would deprive us of our self-consciousness. Maybe that's why there's some evidence that natural theology is making yet another comeback as a way of connecting our dignity—even our divinity—to being at home in our natural environment. The most radically modern natural theology, as Tocqueville explains, is pantheism.[18] According to the pantheist, there are two pieces of good news. First, everything is divine. Second, our individuality—what separates each of us from the other animals and our conception of God—is an illusion. Pantheism is the true theological expression of modern natural science, of, say, sociobiology. There is, our scientists say, no evidence that one species is really qualitatively distinct from another; our species has received one scientific demotion after another until nothing of our proud individuality is left. So why shouldn't we say that our struggle against nature is a senseless illusion and surrender ourselves to the natural whole that we can call god?

Certainly pantheism is at the heart of most attempts to establish a post-Christian religion in our country—those of the New Agers, the neo-Gnostics, the Western Buddhists, and so forth. Tocqueville regarded pantheism as such a seductive, radically egalitarian lullaby that he attempted to rally all true defenders of the true dignity of human individuality against it. The brilliant French social critic Chantal Delsol adds that the pervasiveness of pantheistic speculation today is evidence that our idea of human dignity "is now hanging by a thread."[19]

But it seems to me that the self-help in the form of the self-surrender offered by pantheism is just incredible to us. I receive no solace from the fact that the matter that makes up my body continues to exist after my death as part of a tree—even a sacred tree. And it is really very, very little consolation for me to know that the genes I spread live on. I know I'm not my genes, and I also know that, even if I were, nature would soon enough disperse me into insignificance. Maybe that's why the more people become aware, through sociobiological enlightenment, that their true purpose on earth is gene spreading, the less they end up doing it. It's surely part of our dignity that we're incapable of not resisting pantheism's seduction, of not really knowing that natural theology can't account for the existence of individuals or particular

persons. All of our efforts to find a post-Christian way of reinstitut-
ing a credible natural or civil theology seem doomed to fail, despite
the efforts of some great philosophers and our human longing—one,
thank God, among many—to regress to infancy or subhumanity.

Dignity vs. Mood Control

If pantheism and other similar forms of linguistic therapy don't work,
there's still the biotechnological promise to relieve us of the burden
of our self-conscious freedom. Psychopharmacological mood control
might free us from our anxiety and make us feel happy and safe, and
it might even release reliably the serotonin that can produce feelings of
dignified self-esteem without having to do anything great. Contrary
to Hobbes, we might want to say that the chemical surrender of the
dignified, truthful assertion of personal sovereignty is what's required
to live well. Certainly the objection that we'd no longer be living in
the truth is at least very questionable. If our moods are nothing more
than the result of chemical reactions, as our scientists say, then who's
to say which reaction is truer than another? Why shouldn't we call true
whatever makes us most comfortable? Our ability to produce reliably
such a mood for ourselves might be the decisive evidence for our real
ability to free ourselves from our miserable natural condition.

But Hobbes would respond: the surrender of sovereignty is misguided. It would be unreasonable for me to trust anyone with unac-
countable control over me. My moods, after all, are part of my capacity
for self-defense and surely I shouldn't turn them over to some expert.[20]
It's bad for both my dignity and my security not to insist that I'm a
free being with rights and so not an animal to be controlled through
the introduction of alien chemicals into my body. Those who would
compassionately assume control over others to alleviate their cruel suffering always exempt themselves from their prescribed treatment. Their
compassion is always a mask for my self-destruction. Certainly the goal
of every tyrant is to free subjects, allegedly for their own good, of their
longing to be free. As Walker Percy reminds us, surely our right to our
moods is a very fundamental one; even Hobbes takes his bearings from
the moods individuals as individuals really have on their own.[21]

These concerns are worth expressing. But it's still true that the worry that individuals can or will employ psychopharmacology to embrace happiness over worry is overblown. The truth is that free individuals want both security and self-consciousness and can't imagine themselves surrendering one aspect of themselves for the other. They certainly don't want to be deprived of the truthful awareness that allows them genuinely to be. When we think of the promise of mood control, we really believe that we can be self-conscious without being anxious. We certainly don't want to surrender our individual freedom or personal productivity. We don't want to be so zoned out by technology-produced virtual experiences that we would lose interest in the real technology that can protect us from terrorists, asteroids, diseases, and so forth. We also want to remain alienated or moody enough to enjoy music and art, without, of course, being so moved that we try to lose ourselves in nontherapeutic drugs or are even habitually late for work. We want to appreciate Johnny Cash, without having to suffer through actually being Johnny Cash.

If we really took mood control seriously, we would start to recover the truth that we're both more and less than free individuals, that it's as individuals that we pursue happiness, but it's as friends, lovers, family members, creatures, neighbors, and so forth that we actually are happy. If we took it seriously, we'd start to see that it's because we too readily understand ourselves as free individuals and nothing more that life seems so hard. Only such individuals could be miserable enough to think even our natural moods need to be redesigned to be bearable. The other animals are typically content with the moods nature has given them. Lurking behind effort to design or engineer moods is the really bad mood. And, thank God, the perpetuation of that bad mood will be needed to fuel our pursuit of artificially good ones. We individuals just can't surrender the self that generates "the self."[22]

Moral Autonomy

Maybe our worst mood remains directed against nature as we understand it. Certainly if the evolutionists, or sociobiologists, or the modern scientists in general are right, there's no natural room for individual dignity. The Darwinian view is that particular animals have significance only as members of a species; their behavior is oriented, by nature, toward species preservation. The future of the species doesn't depend upon my indispensable contribution; its fate is contingent on the average behavior of large numbers of anonymous people.[23] The very existence of any particular species is a meaningless accident, and my particular existence as a random member of one species among many is infinitely more accidental.

Our most extreme or whiny moral individualists—the existentialists—may say that their personal struggle for meaning in a world governed by chance and necessity is absurd, but they don't quite believe it. For them, the dramatic personal assertion of dignity or purpose, absurd as it is in theory, produces beautiful deeds and is what makes life worth living. But for the evolutionist (including the evolutionary neuroscientist), such dramatic displays are, at this point in the development of science, inexplicable perversities that will eventually be shown to be nothing more than mechanisms for species survival. What we now think of as absurd—what we now call the behavior of the dignified human individual or person—we will eventually understand not to be absurd at all. There is, we have to admit, something Socratic (or natural theological) about evolutionism's and neuroscience's denial of individual pretensions about one's own soul or dignified personal identity, even in its denial of "the self" that distinguishes you from me, and us from all the other animals.[24]

But sophisticated people today, even sophisticated scientists, rarely talk as if evolutionism is completely true, as if particular human beings are best understood as species fodder. They speak of human dignity, and they identify dignity with autonomy. They don't understand autonomy, of course, as the literal conquest of nature or the limitations of our embodiment. Otherwise, nobody around right now would have dignity at all.

Our idea of autonomy comes from Kant: human dignity comes from neither God nor nature, but from our personal capability to transcend natural determination through our obedience to a rational, moral law we give to ourselves.[25] We aren't contained, as Hobbes might be understood to say, by mere calculation about how to survive as biological beings in this time and place. We have the abstract and idealistic capability not to be defined by our bodily existences.[26] We have the capability to act morally, or as something other than animals with instincts, and reason can show us that our true practical standard is not merely an arbitrary assertion against impersonal necessity. The capability for moral freedom is what gives each person a unique value. It makes that person priceless. Everything exists to be used—or bought and sold at some finite cost—except us.

The idea of moral autonomy finds strength in the thought that there's no support in what we know about nature—our natures—for our freedom and dignity. The Darwinian can say that evolution accounts for everything but the irreducible freedom from natural determination of the human person. But the Kantian draws the line at evolutionism, with its view that the person's perception of his dignity, or autonomy, or free, rational will is merely an illusion. We are, most fundamentally, what distinguishes us from nature. We may be chimps, but we're autonomous chimps, which means we're not really chimps at all. When I give way to natural inclination—and especially to the happiness that it might make possible—I'm not being what gives me respect. To the extent that we're natural beings, we have no dignity at all.

Kant's tough and precise distinction between subhuman natural inclination and genuine free and rational obedience to a law we make for ourselves compels us to prefer intentions to results or a freedom that we can't see with our own eyes. For the Kantian, it's unreasonable to demand evidence that any particular person is free. To connect dignity with the actual practice of moral virtue produces inequality or undermines the universality required for the rational apprehension of moral autonomy. Some people act more courageously than others, and others hardly ever do. But our dignity doesn't depend on what we actually do, but on who we are as free or moral beings. We have dignity as persons deserving of respect, and not as individuals exercising their rights.

Some of our most materialistic natural scientists tend to embrace human dignity as a sort of religious dogma. That doesn't mean that they believe in the Bible, but that they find nothing reasonable about the dignity they affirm. For them, human dignity is simply an inexplicable leftover from the cosmos they can otherwise scientifically explain. Our scientists tend to exempt themselves and others like themselves, usually without good reason, from their rational or scientific account of everything that exists. They are less rigorous, rationalist moralists than hopeless romantics when it comes to human beings, to themselves in particular. So they've seen no reason not to go along with the existentialists in detaching autonomy from reason defined as either the technological or the moral overcoming of our natures.[27]

Self-Definition

Autonomy has tended to become self-definition simply. No other animal can say who he or she is, and surely what we say transforms both who we are and what we do. Self-definition allows us to waffle on whether we really make ourselves—or merely imagine ourselves—as free and singularly dignified beings. And so it allows us to waffle on whether natural science really has room for dignity, because it certainly can make room for the imaginative qualities of the beast with speech. Self-definition leaves open the possibility associated with the freedom of the modern individual that whatever we can imagine we can make real, while not denying the viewpoint of natural theology that we are all governed by impersonal necessity in the end.

Self-definition straddles the line between realism and pragmatism. We can call true or real whatever makes us feel comfortable, free, and dignified. But self-definers differ from pantheists because they know their imaginative freedom has its limits: We can't imagine the self to be anything other than an end in itself. I can't define myself merely as an indistinguishable part of a greater whole, a means for someone else's ends, or as a part of some future tree.[28]

The Christian person or creature, the modern individual, and the Kantian person all experience themselves as unique and irreplaceable. The self-defined self must make himself that way. Because I have to make myself out of nothing without any guidance, I can be unique without being utterly contingent only if you accord me the respect I say I deserve. I can't really be so unique that I'm not recognizable by others in my infinite dignity. So I need you to recognize my dignified uniqueness. Self-definition requires a social dimension.

This view of dignity puts a greater burden on those who must acknowledge it than the Kantian one. According to Kant, I must respect you or treat you as an end only as a person capable of obeying the autonomous moral law. But I don't have to—or can't—respect anything you do that falls short of full obedience to that law. The Kantian must distinguish between moral and immoral intentions, and Kant himself was sometimes quite judgmental or morally severe. But now we believe we must respect the intention of whatever the self-defining person chooses, even if it's affirming as one's whole identity a natural inclination, such as being gay or straight.

That means we have the duty to go further than mere indifference or nonjudgmentalism. You don't accord me dignity by saying, "not that there's anything wrong with it," where "it" is whatever it is I'm doing. Your yawning, in fact, is undignified. You must respect what I do because I do it, even if—or especially—because you wouldn't do it yourself. My dignity requires that you suspend your rational faculties and moral judgment. Otherwise, your intention might intrude upon my self-definition: I'm indignant when you employ your self-definition or lifeplan not to have a respectful view of mine. That indignation, of course, is merely an intensification of that felt by the individual Hobbes describes: you must do more than merely allow me to exercise my rights for my autonomy to have its inescapably moral dimension.[29]

But the burden of autonomy defined as moral self-definition is even greater on the person who claims it. Tocqueville tells us that the characteristically modern and democratic view is that our dignity rests in our intellectual freedom. We must free our minds from the authority of parents, country, tradition, nature, God, and so forth. But that means that it's much more clear what a radically free or genuinely autonomous judgment *is not* than what one *is*. Be yourself and be unique, we're told. But the individual human mind is anxious, disoriented, and paralyzed if it has to work all by itself. The pretense of radical doubt—or pop Cartesianism—eventually leads the individual to lose confidence both in the soundness of his mind and the personal foundation of his dignity. Modern scientific skepticism makes every particular being seem puny, impotent, insignificant, and ever more readily absorbed by forces beyond his control. Surely in a globalizing, democratizing, techno-driven world, the dignified contributions of particular individuals are harder to discern than ever.[30]

The solitude of radical freedom makes effective human thought and action impossible. That's why autonomy requires a social dimension; consciousness necessarily is knowing with others. And the genuine sharing of self-knowledge requires, Kant thought, a rational standard we can genuinely have in common. But for the individual who looks up to no personal authority—even or especially the authority of reason as described by some moralistic philosopher—all that's left for orientation is impersonal public opinion and what the reigning experts are saying about what impersonal or objective scientific studies are showing.

The deepest question for dignity in our time is where is the self-defining individual supposed to get the point of view, the character or virtue, the genuinely inward life or conscience required to resist degrading social or scientistic conformity?[31] The self-defining individual characteristically can't lose the self in "the self" that he consciously constructs to be pleasing to or to have status in the eyes of others. But that doesn't mean it's possible for the self to resist the imperatives of "the self" without the help of nature or God or a stable tradition that embodies natural and divine wisdom. We increasingly libertarian sophisticates are so obsessed with the threat that the tyrannical moralism of others poses to our moral autonomy that we've neglected the necessarily social, natural, and personal sources of the moral resolution of the dignified "I."

Even human rights, as Delsol concludes, can't "guarantee the dignity of each human being unless they are grounded in an understanding of man that ensures his [personal] uniqueness." Her view is that a dignified democracy—one composed "of unique persons endowed with free minds and wills"—depends upon the "religious partner" of "a monotheism that preaches personal eternity, one in which each irreducible being survives in his irreducibility."[32] The dignified person depends upon a personal eternity to survive intact in an increasingly impersonal environment.

But Delsol's conclusion might be compromised, to say the least, by her modern suggestion that we have no reason to believe there's a personal God who grants each of us eternal life. Does human dignity really depend on each human person living beyond his biological existence? Or merely on the conscious utilitarian effort to restore a "personal theology" that does justice to human dignity in the way a natural or civil theology never could? How could that theology really survive, in our time, the modern, individualistic criticism that it leads to the undignified surrender of our real, earthly lives as particular individuals for an illusory, otherworldly one? From the radically modern view, there's nothing less dignified than the blind sacrifice of the one and only life that I will ever have.

An American Conclusion

Our view of human dignity as human freedom from impersonal natural necessity or merely political determination may well depend on the Christian view of inner, spiritual freedom. As Bob Kraynak explains, the Christians believe that each person is radically independent of the social and political order and does not depend on external recognition from other human beings, although it may depend on my genuine recognition by the personal God who sees me as I truly am. And that inner freedom, in fact, is perfectly compatible with external servitude.[33] My true understanding of my freedom comes, in fact, from coming to terms with the truth about my dependence, my limitations, my inability to achieve autonomy through either technological or rational efforts. According to St. Augustine, this truthful self-understanding is impossible without faith. Otherwise, we sinful beings are blinded by unreasonable pride or fatalistic despair about our personal or individual freedom.

Does the American understanding of dignity depend upon Christian faith, or a belief in the personal God? The view expressed in our Founding documents and our complex tradition is not that clear. Our understanding of human dignity draws from both the modern understanding of the free beings with rights and the Christian understanding of the dignity of the being made in the image and likeness of the personal Creator.[34] In our eyes, the doctrine of rights presupposes the real, infinite significance of every particular human being. For us our dignity is guaranteed not only by the individual's own assertiveness but with some natural or divine center of personal meaning. Nature's God, for us, is also a providential and judgmental God, a personal God. That means our understanding of natural theology is not the one criticized by St. Augustine or the one that was quickly displaced by morally autonomous and "historical" claims for freedom by the modern individual.

The American view on whether we're more than natural beings, or on whether there's natural support for our personal existences, is left somewhat undetermined. That means that we waffle on whether or not we're free individuals as Locke describes them, on whether being human is all about the conquest of nature or about the grateful acceptance of the goods nature and God have given us. That waffling is judicious or even truthful. Even many Christians would admit there's a lot to the Lockean criticism of Augustinian otherworldliness, if not taken too extremely. And the Americans Tocqueville describes and the American evangelicals we observe today find their dignity in both their proud individual achievement and their humble personal faith.

America is largely about the romance of the dignified citizen; all human beings, in principle, can be equal citizens of our country. The politically homeless from everywhere have found a political home here. But that's because we've regarded citizenship as more than just a convenient construction to serve free individuals. We Americans take citizenship seriously without succumbing to political theology because we can see that we're all equal citizens because we're all more than citizens. Being citizens reflects a real part, but not the deepest part, of human dignity.[35]

All human beings can, in principle, become American citizens because they are all, in another way, irreducibly homeless or alienated from political life. Human beings are free from political life because of the irreducible personal significance they all share. We regard religious freedom as for religion, for the transpolitical, personal discovery of our duties to God. Our religious liberty reflects the dignity we share as, in some sense, creatures. We seem to agree with the anti-ideological dissident Havel that each of us can be a "dignified human 'I,' responsible for ourselves" because we experience ourselves truly as "bound to something higher, and capable of sacrificing something, in the extreme cases even everything . . . for the sake of that which gives life meaning," to the foundation of our sense of transcendence of our merely biological existence.[36]

So there is, in our tradition, a personal criticism of the dominant modern understandings of nature and God. If human beings are naturally fitted to know and love particular persons, then their natural social instincts can't be reduced to mechanisms of species perpetuation. Our dignity, from this view, comes from the mixture of our social instincts with self-consciousness found in members of the species with the natural capacity for language. It comes from our ability to know and love—and to be known and loved—by other, particular persons. And, as Kass writes, "if we know where to look, we find evidence of human dignity all around us, in the valiant efforts ordinary people make to meet necessity, to combat adversity and disappointment, to provide for their children, to care for their parents, to help their neighbors, to serve their country."[37] Each of us, thank God, is given demanding responsibilities as self-conscious, loving, social, finite, and dependent beings, and so plenty of opportunity, if we think about it, to display our dignity or irreplaceable personal significance.

My personal significance doesn't depend primarily on my overcoming of an indifferent or impersonal nature or even necessarily in my hopeful faith in a personal God. The evidence of my personal dignity comes from lovingly and sometimes heroically performing my responsibilities that I've been given by nature to those I know and love, and from living well with others in love and hope with what we can't help but know about the possibilities and limits of our true situation. My dignity depends, of course, on the natural freedom that accompanies my flawed self-consciousness, my freedom to choose to deny what I really know and not to do what I know I should. I'm given a social and natural personal destiny that I can either fulfill or betray.[38]

From this view, Augustine misled us by unrealistically minimizing the personal satisfactions that come from friendship, erotic and romantic love, families, and political life. His goal was to focus our attention on our longing for the personal God and really to be, but the effect of his rhetoric in the absence of that faith was to make human individuals too focused on securing their dignified independence from their natural limitations and each other—even at the expense of the accompanying natural goods—for themselves. It's just not realistic to say, as we often do today, that each human individual exists for himself. It's not even good for the species.

The truth is that our dignified personal significance is not our own creation. It depends upon natural gifts, gifts that we can misuse or distort but not destroy. Biotechnology will in some ways make us more free and more miserable. And we will continue to display our dignity even in the futile perversity of our efforts to free ourselves completely from our misery. We will continue to fail to make ourselves more or less than human, and human happiness will elude us when we're too ungrateful for—when we fail to see the good in—what we've been given, in our selves or souls. Our dignity rightly understood will continue to come from assuming gratefully the moral responsibilities we've been given as parents, children, friends, lovers, citizens, thinkers, and creatures, and in subordinating our strange and wonderful technological freedom to these natural purposes.

The bad news is that to the extent our dignity depends on securing our freedom from nature, we will remain undignified. The good news is that our real human dignity—even in the absence of a personal God on whom we can depend—is more secure than we sometimes think. Thank God, we have no good reason to hope or fear that we have the power or freedom to create some posthuman or transhuman freedom. We're stuck with ourselves, with our souls, with being good in order to feel good.

2

THE HUMAN DIGNITY CONSPIRACY

In 2001 George W. Bush created the President's Council on Bioethics to "provide a forum for the national discussion of bioethics issues." The elusive idea of human dignity lay behind many contemporary controversies in bioethics, the Council believed, so it commissioned twenty essays by a diverse group of writers and published them in a collection, *Human Dignity and Bioethics.*[1] The book intended more to highlight controversy than to produce consensus, and it offered no particular set of policy recommendations. Council members— of which I was one—considered the volume a Socratic invitation to inquiry: nothing more, and nothing less.

The best-selling Harvard sociobiological psychologist Steven Pinker saw a lot more. In a widely noticed, long review in the *New Republic,* he described the book as an aggressive attempt, fueled by radical "religious impulses," to roll back the American experiment in ordered liberty by "imposing a Catholic agenda on American secular democracy." Dignity, in that agenda, would trump the scientific progress that enhances our pursuits of life, liberty, and happiness. Bioethics would become a weapon in opposition to innovative medical breakthroughs that aim "to maximize health and flourishing."[2]

In his *New Republic* essay, Pinker complains that the word "dignity" is simply stupid; it corresponds to no reality known by science. Pinker does not really think that the word "justice" corresponds to any "scientific" reality either, but he endorses appeals to justice as a beneficial way of deterring criminals. The "scientific" fact that we always do an injustice when we punish someone according to an objectively unrealistic standard of justice does not bother him.[3] After all, most people are better off as a result. So it is not so much that dignity is stupid; rather, it is worse than useless—it is an instrument of tyranny. "Dignity" has been mobilized as part of the conservatives' war against science and human liberty.

Pinker both outs what he sees as a Catholic conspiracy and directs most of his fire against a writer who is not even a Catholic: the Council's first chairman, Leon Kass. It is Kass's "pro-death, anti-freedom" views, which are "well outside the American mainstream," that Pinker particularly loathes. He accuses Kass of calling undignified anything that gives anyone "the creeps"—including licking an ice-cream cone. The dignity-freak Kass, Pinker goes on, is guilty of wild exaggerations. Kass calls efforts to extend the duration of particular human lives "the pursuit of immortality," efforts to improve human performance "the pursuit of perfection," and screening to protect babies from genetic defects and diseases "designing babies."[4]

Pinker wildly exaggerates Kass's propensity to exaggerate, but I do agree that Kass might be overly concerned about the possibility of a Brave New World. Only one chapter of the Council's book is by Kass, however, and most of the other writers disagree with him in a variety of ways. Still, Pinker's objection to "dignity" *in toto* is fundamentally misguided and most unscientific. It is perfectly reasonable to wonder whether our views of dignity, equality, and liberty depend on religious premises, and reasonable men—including reasonable scientists—disagree on the answer. It is just as reasonable to wonder how "scientific" some scientists really are who cannot account for the dignified human behavior we observe every day.

What Is Dignity?

The word "dignity" is not particularly Christian. It has no special significance in the Scriptures and not much history as a theological concept. Only in the twentieth century did moral theologians begin to use it when addressing issues such as abortion, religious liberty, and economic justice. Neither does the word come to us from the classical philosophers such as Plato and Aristotle, who were concerned with the phenomena of undeniable human excellence and the "manly" human need to be important or significant. Aristotle's magnanimous man, we would now say, possesses dignified self-confidence. Aristotle also writes that nobility—what we would now likely call dignity—shines forth in even the most unfortunate circumstances. My nobility or dignity is more my own than is my happiness, which depends on forces beyond my control.[5]

It was with such Greek reflections in mind that the Roman word *dignitas* took on a basically aristocratic connotation. Dignity is a worthiness or virtue that must be earned, and the dignified man is someone exceptional who attains distinction by his inner strength of character. *Dignitas* is a self-contained serenity, a kind of solid immobility that cannot be affected by worldly fortunes. For the Stoics, and especially for Cicero, dignity is democratic in the sense that it does not depend on social status; it is within reach of everyone from the slave (Epictetus) to the emperor (Marcus Aurelius). Dignity refers to the rational life possible for us all, but it is really characteristic only of the rare human being who is genuinely devoted to living according to reason.

Dignity, the contemporary Stoic novelist Tom Wolfe shows in *A Man in Full*,[6] can shine through even in the life of a maximum-security prisoner who seems to have been deprived of every human good. Wolfe's novel shows both that the Stoic way of thinking is almost completely alien to American life today and that it still has powerful explanatory power. He shows us that our sociobiologists and neuroscientists have something to learn from what we might call *Stoic science*. The Council's book would have been more comprehensive had a genuine Stoic contributed a chapter, but no critic has yet registered that complaint.

The early modern philosophers—following, in a certain way, St. Augustine's Christian critique of Stoic vanity—denied that human beings could ever achieve a rational, inward insulation from the effects of fortune. They contended instead that it is undignified to allow oneself be a plaything of fortune—of forces and people beyond your control. There is nothing genuinely dignified in Stoic self-deception about our real bodily dependence. Human beings are stuck with being concerned, most of all, with keeping their fragile bodies alive. So there is something dignified in facing up to that truth and doing something about it—acting with freedom and intelligence to make yourself more secure.

In Hobbes's view, your own life is infinitely valuable and irreplaceable to you, but it cannot seem that way to anyone else. Therefore, Hobbes reasons, your dignity is nothing more than your "public worth." And that is nothing more than the price your powers can bring: your dignity is your productivity.[7] Others recognize your worth only insofar as they can use—and are willing to pay for—what you can do. We have every right to work to become as dignified as we can be, but we do not have an equal right to dignity. Hobbes is for equal rights, but equal dignity is impossible.

There is a lot to be said for ranking people—determining their excellence or importance—according to their productivity. Vain illusions which generate the idleness that comes with inward serenity are dispelled. There is, we learn, no invisible realm of freedom, no impregnable Stoic fortress, into which we can securely retreat. It is undeniable progress to stop ranking people according to their social class, gender, race, religion, and so forth. Productivity is the most visible and surest foundation for a meritocracy—which is why Americans today are having more trouble than ever finding a higher standard than productivity to determine their dignity. Even with the economic downturn, Americans are wealthier and freer than ever, but their dignity seems to depend more than ever on being useful and pleasing to others. They increasingly lack the inward self-confidence that comes with having a personal standard higher than "success." We might want to say that Americans are both more and less free than ever—and in a way that would earn a Stoic's cold contempt.

Transhumanists, Charles Rubin explains in his contribution to the Council volume, highlight through exaggeration another reason why it might make sense to identify our dignity with productivity: namely, our powerful inventions. Our present existence is most undignified. We are, as Agent Smith says in *The Matrix,* a kind of virus or cancer plaguing nature. We are the only animal that cannot achieve equilibrium with its natural environment. We individuals cannot help but be restlessly discontent with nature's cruel and random indifference to each of our particular existences. Nature itself is an accidental, impersonal process, and we, in our freedom, are accidental exceptions to every natural rule. Surely it is undignified for us meekly to accept what nature imposes on us.[8]

We—the free, technological beings—can transform nature with our desire for individual security and significance in mind. We display our dignity by imposing our will on nature to create a world where we can live as dignified beings—or not as miserably self-conscious and utterly precarious accidents. We can free ourselves from our all-too-human or natural limitations; we can bring our bodies under our rational and willful control. Dignity is displayed in the freedom that produces the rational control allowing us to give orders to nature, including to our own bodies.

The transhumanist impulse vividly illuminates Hobbes's latent misanthropy. The point of human freedom is to devote yourself to an endless and ultimately futile effort to make yourself into something else. Kant attempted to counter that misanthropy with the other characteristically modern view of dignity. "Humanity itself," according to Kant, "is a dignity."[9] Kant agrees with the modern transhumanists that we are undignified insofar as we are determined by nature, by our embodiment. But he disagrees that our dignity depends on our technological transformation of nature. Each of us is already free and dignified, because what we think and do, insofar as we are human, is not determined by impersonal natural forces. We are free to treat other dignified persons as persons—not merely as impersonal means to achieve our personal goals. Anyone who reduces dignity to productivity turns other human beings into exploitable resources. The dignified being does not have a price, and we are all, as free and rational persons, capable of acting with our equal dignity in mind.

Leon Kass, in his own contribution to the Council volume, explains that Kant actually joins the transhumanists in opposing dignity to the way human beings actually are. For Kant, we are dignified insofar as we are free from the limitations of our embodiment. That means there is no dignity in "begetting"—what we do as devoted parents and children—and there is no dignity in "belonging"—what we do as devoted members of particular communities.[10] Kant's dignity of rational choice accords no respect to what we do out of love; to be human is to be rational and willful, but not at all erotic. This means that Kant is the source of a kind of humanitarianism that reduces dignity to personal autonomy. For Kant, the person is fundamentally distinct from the human animal—the whole biological being—whom we actually know and love.[11]

Given the inhuman premises of Hobbes's and Kant's views of dignity, as well as the inegalitarian and somewhat vain premises of the Stoics, we might conclude that prudence dictates dignity *not* guide American public policy. Americans will be free to display their dignity through productivity, but that will be their private affair. Kantians will be similarly free to display their nobility, but the law itself should not aim any higher than the protection of "natural rights." The Declaration of Independence does not say that the Creator gave men equal dignity, only equal rights. The Declaration does implicitly affirm a kind of dignity or rare excellence in the actions of men who put their lives and fortunes on the line for their "sacred honor," but it does not suggest that in a rights-based country men should be *required* to put their honor before their rights. Rights, unlike dignity, neither reduce men to their "cash value" nor require of them some supra-natural virtue. We might therefore conclude that our political community is sufficiently formed by our common devotion to equal rights, and that our necessarily unequal dignity should remain a merely private concern.

Dignity Now

Almost all the contributors to the Council's volume, including the scientist Daniel Dennett, however, share a relatively new but widespread belief that our lives will become worse if we cannot speak publicly and confidently about human dignity. This new belief arose from what was learned in the experiences of the twentieth century—and the twenty-first. What the totalitarian regimes did was much worse than violating rights. The Nazis engaged in murderous eugenics on a massive scale, intending to extinguish whole classes of human beings and to reduce us all to less than who we really are. The Communists wanted to eliminate the very possibility of experiencing the dignity of living in light of the truth. Their goal was to have the historical lie of ideology replace who we really are and what we can really know. Through their courageous and truthful thought and action, great anti-Communist dissidents such as Aleksandr Solzhenitsyn and Václav Havel displayed evidence of human dignity in the face of the ideological lie; their achievement is trivialized if one says they were merely defending their rights. Anyone who mistakenly identifies dignity with bare productivity or abstract autonomy cannot really see the natural, spiritual greatness of men and women ready to sacrifice everything to defend who we really are.

In the twenty-first century, biotechnology promises to provide us with the means of changing our nature to maximize our comfort, security, and happiness. Our dignity—as Solzhenitsyn showed us—might be a natural gift, and so we can say that historical efforts at ideological depersonalization were defeated by the indestructible greatness of who we are. Who we are *by nature* triumphed over "History." But all bets might be off if we can actually change our nature. Our spirited resistance to biotechnological assaults on human nature cannot be viewed as merely a defense of our "natural rights."

After all, Hobbes and Locke were clear enough that we should do what we can to change our natural condition with our comfort, security, and individual freedom in mind. In their view, our natural "gifts" are virtually worthless, and neither Hobbes nor Locke can really tell us why the transhumanist pursuit of freedom from all that we have been given is undignified. They cannot tell us why a professor, for example, has a right to resist taking a mood brightener to improve his teaching evaluations and enhance his research productivity, or why it is undignified to believe moods are just collections of chemicals in the brain rather than indispensable, natural clues to who we really are.

So it is little wonder that the defense of human dignity started to rise to prominence after the Second World War—in, for example, the 1945 United Nations Charter and the 1948 Universal Declaration of Human Rights. These documents do not claim to depend on any clear consensus about why we have dignity or rights, but they sprang from a new awareness that rights are insecure without some deeper notion of dignity. Human dignity also became a special concern of the Christian Democratic parties in Europe and was the foundation for religious liberty in the Second Vatican Council. We are dignified, the Vatican Council document said, because we are open to the truth about God and the human good. The Catholic emphasis came to be on the natural dignity of the whole human person—in opposition to the modern view that our dignity resides only in our autonomy.

Christian thinkers generally began to distinguish between dignity and (the illusions of) autonomy. Secular or Kantian thinkers either identified dignity with autonomy completely or else stopped speaking of dignity at all, since it had come to mean something other than autonomy. For the Kantians, anyone with an integral view of human dignity had fallen victim to "religious prejudice" incompatible with modern scientific materialism. But our scientists actually tend to say that there is no reality that corresponds to *either* autonomy or dignity. In their view, both ideas are based upon illusions about our moral freedom.

When Leon Kass wrote *Life, Liberty, and the Defense of Dignity* (2002),[12] he was dissenting, as a scientist, from the scientific denial of dignity. He was reflecting on what he could see with his own eyes about the unique place human beings have in nature. For most scientists, the discrediting of traditional religion has made all views of "human distinctiveness and special dignity" incredible, leaving us with the "scientific" conclusion that "[h]uman capabilities appear to differ in degree, not in kind, from those found in the higher animals."[13] For Kass, the inability to see the dignified difference that separates us from the chimps and the dolphins is not genuine science, but "soulless scientism."[14]

The Christian thinkers and Kass agree that we have dignity, and that dignity is more than our productivity or autonomy. But their concerns about dignity differ, at least in emphasis. The Christians' concern is for the equal dignity of all human beings against the ideological and scientific destruction of unfit or inconvenient human lives. They uphold the dignity of every human being against euthanasia, "death with dignity," denial of equal treatment to the disabled or otherwise "unfit," murderous eugenics, abortion, and the scientific destruction of human embryos. Actually, not all the writers in this category are Christian, and many of them show with considerable credibility that theirs is the genuinely scientific view.

The special concern of Kass and others like him is that modern biotechnology will destroy the social conditions and natural capabilities that make a dignified human life possible—a concern more classical than Christian. They hold that a large part of human dignity is living well in the acceptance of necessity, and not in the undignified effort to throw every resource into fending off death, eradicating every form of human suffering, and creating for oneself an absolutely secure environment. The dignified flourishing of human beings is based on using our natural gifts well—not in replacing natural meritocracy with techno-equality. We assault our dignity, for example, when we chemically alter our memories and moods to make ourselves happy and proud without any real accomplishments or enduring relationships. These classical concerns are given a new urgency in Kass's writing by the Nietzschean fear that we might actually be capable of transforming ourselves into contemptible "last men" living in a Brave New World of chemically induced contentment. In a certain way, Kass writes to defend the natural *inequality* of human dignity; he writes to fend off the degradation that would make absolute equality all too real. It is perfectly possible to be alive to the concerns of both groups, and to see that human dignity, in truth, has its egalitarian and inegalitarian dimensions. But the writers in the Council's book do mostly focus on either one concern or the other.

Why Do We Have Equal Dignity?

The thoughtful evolutionary scientist Daniel Dennett, in his very positive contribution to the Council volume, says that human beings are different enough from the other animals to need morality, and he adds, contrary to Pinker, that we even need confidence in our equal dignity. He agrees with Pinker that claims for dignity have been basically Christian, and that these claims have been refuted by the scientific discovery that everything we think and do has a material cause. Our beliefs in dignity and the soul have the same status as the discredited belief in mermaids. It is no sillier to believe in a half-woman/half-fish that no one has seen than to believe in a half-body/half-soul that no one has seen.[15]

Dennett, however, has a scientific explanation for why we need the scientifically discredited belief in dignity. We are social animals who have brains big enough to conceive of projects that will enable us to live purposeful lives, but there is no scientific basis for the freedom at the foundation of human conceptions of purpose. So we cannot live well without useful illusions—free will, love, dignity, and so forth. Even the idea that any particular human life matters at all is merely a fiction—but a fiction worth maintaining. We have seen that nihilism has all sorts of undesirable social consequences; therefore, we need to sustain these illusions in the face of what we know about our accidental, material, and evolutionary existences.

Dennett's ingenious solution to the incompatibility between scientific truth and our need for dignified belief is that we should justify our allegiance to the useful fiction of equal dignity by acknowledging the good life that it makes possible. It is indispensable for the habits and trust needed to perpetuate social and political institutions. We can stop all this pointless obsessing over whether the belief is actually true by just admitting that it is not, but science can explain why we need to believe it anyway.

Dennett's pragmatic hope that we can stop caring about whether our belief in dignity is actually true is not shared by any other author in the Council's book. In fact, the pragmatic philosopher Richard Rorty had a simpler idea: let's call true whatever belief makes us happy. Rorty, of course, never called his approach dignified. Dennett himself is too dignified to deny the truth of what he thinks he knows, and there is some dignity, too, in his humane intention to spare us the consequences of a dignity-free world. It seems he denies the reality of the dignity he himself displays only because to do otherwise would require admitting that human beings are mysteriously free from nature or materialistic causation. Yet in Dennett's well-intentioned confusion, he is stuck with acknowledging that, in some way, we are the only species that can be held responsible for perpetuating both human nature and the very conditions of life on our planet. Is there really no dignity in *that*?

The eloquent and profound Lutheran theologian Gilbert Meilaender agrees with Dennett in his contribution that any adequate defense of equal dignity would have to be Christian. For Dennett, this means that there is nothing you can really do to make yourself dignified. For Meilaender, there is nothing you can do to make yourself undignified, because your dignity comes from God.[16]

Meilaender acknowledges that the limited truth of the classical view of dignity is reflected in the ways we rank people according to their excellence in life. That is why the reconciliation of equality and dignity cannot be achieved through our relationships with each other, but only in our common relation to God. We are all loved by and equally distant from him. Christianity, Meilaender claims, "caused a great rupture in Western culture . . . that gradually reshaped the classical notion of dignity." We cannot see our equal dignity without Christian eyes—which is not quite the same as saying "without Christian belief." There is a dim perception of the truth about the mystery of our being in anyone who reflects compassionately about our common weaknesses and limitations, especially "our common subjection to mortality." Every attempt to speak of dignity or equality in a wholly secular way leaves us disoriented, angry, and sputtering.

Meilaender means to distance himself from Kass's view that dignity depends on human agency—and thus, necessarily, on unequal human accomplishments. Kass is wrong, he claims, to say that patients who lack agency lack the capacity to display their dignity. He gives the example of the patient who patiently endures his increasingly (but always) dependent condition. Such patients can be *more* dignified than Aristotle's magnanimous man—who takes pleasure in his greatness, in part, by forgetting about his natural dependence.

Kass responds that a dignified patient remains dependent on his capacity to engage in thought and action appropriate to his human situation; he is always partly patient and partly not. A pure patient—say, someone in the last stage of Alzheimer's—would be perfectly passive and so incapable of displaying his dignity. It is not so clear that, for Kass, pure patients are dignified, and that explains why he does not defend human embryos on the basis of equal dignity and equal rights. It is finally Meilaender's faith that gives him confidence that every human life has equally irreplaceable significance, and so he never has to engage in deliberation about the dignity of any particular patient. But to what extent should anyone's religious faith be the basis of public policy? Part of Meilaender's response is that even our Declaration's defense of equality depends upon a Christian premise, and I explain later in this book why that response makes sense.

The Roman Catholic, Augustinian political theorist Robert Kraynak agrees with Meilaender that in the genuinely Biblical view what we call our dignity is ultimately based not on our natural "essential attributes" but on God's "mysterious love" for each of us. Kraynak adds that "God's mysterious election" of each of us is what gives us an irreplaceable worth. Nothing is as important for understanding our dignity as "God's creation of each of us for special care," and that care is the basis of our loving duty to care equally and specially for each other.[17]

For Kraynak, neither philosophy nor science is capable of comprehending our full dignity. Science is bound to understand us impersonally or materially—as nothing more than "physio-chemical" reactions. Philosophy understands our dignity in terms of minds alone or of minds united to bodies. So philosophy, too, is incapable of seeing each of us in our irreplaceable uniqueness. The philosophic view of the world as primarily hospitable to the human mind is, in its own way, just as opposed to the mystery of personal uniqueness as is materialistic science. Both philosophy and science reduce the "who" each of us really is to some kind of "what." As dignified "whos," we know that we are mysteriously more than we can describe, and it is that elusive dignity that should temper the pride of the scientists and philosophers in any biotechnological effort to change who we are.

Dennett's response to Kraynak is that any perception of mystery is only temporary. We will, soon enough, have a wholly materialistic explanation for all we think and do. That's good news, however, because we will then be able to perfect our use of the fiction of dignity.[18] It seems to me that if dignity really is nothing more than a useful fiction, then what could protect our dignity better than a fictional theology based on a personal God who promises each unique and irreplaceable human being eternal life? Lots of people these days think that nothing matters because there is no support from God or nature for their personal experiences. Their anxious feelings of being so precariously contingent overwhelm any confidence they might have about their personal significance. The scientific hypothesis that our need for personal dignity is best served by a lie about personal theology is one that deserves more attention.

Moral philosophers Robert P. George and Patrick Lee seem to say in their contribution that Dennett makes dignity dependent on seeing ourselves as less than we really are;[19] we can see with our own eyes that our dignity is no illusion. Kraynak, meanwhile, insists on making dignity dependent on what we can see only with the eyes of faith. George and Lee, as good Catholics, surely believe in personal immortality and God's personal love for each of us, but they do not think that each person's unique dignity really depends on such beliefs. For George, human dignity is a natural human excellence we all share. It is our "rational nature" (and not, as Kant says, our denatured reason) that elevates us, making each of us a person, not a thing, with the natural capabilities for conceptual thought, deliberation, and free choice. Each of us has what it takes to shape our lives as persons. That capacity to give moral self-direction to one's own life is worthy of "intrinsic respect"—whether or not a particular person has accomplished anything along those lines. We have dignity—and with it, absolute rights—the whole duration of our existence, because we are unique beings from the moment of our conception to our biological death. So we can never be viewed as expendable or degradable with someone else's purposes in mind. The standard of nature allows George and Lee to include Aristotle, Thomas Aquinas, Locke, the Declaration of Independence, and Abraham Lincoln among those who basically share their view.

Diana Schaub, who takes her bearings from the American Founders and Lincoln and not at all from the Bible, wonders whether there is any need to speak of dignity at all to make George and Lee's case. Our free and rational awareness of our irreplaceability and precariousness—and our natural desire to preserve ourselves—is what should condition our relationships with other human beings. We refuse to be fodder for anyone else, and the contractual relationships we form are based on the reciprocal recognition of the justice of our refusals. The latest advances in science have shown that George and Lee are right to say that I am "there" from conception to natural death. Our Framers did not know enough to be able to say whether or not embryos have rights, but, Schaub reminds us, they did tell us to follow the light of science.[20]

For Schaub, it is science—and not some Stoic or Kantian or Christian conception of dignity—that has led us to a truer understanding of what is required to protect the rights of human beings. Her objection to dignity is that it introduces questionable, meritocratic, and completely unnecessary considerations into our political discourse. So Schaub sides with Pinker on dignity but with George and Lee on the reality of natural rights.

George and Lee do concede that, according to reason, there is only a very strong case for free will, while somehow remaining scientifically certain about human dignity and human rights. Schaub is less than fully scientific when she contends that, for public policy, it is better to rely on the authority of our Framers and Lincoln than on any theoretical or religious certainty about human rights. Less than fully certain is different, of course, from basically uncertain, and the preponderance of evidence about human freedom and dignity is clearly more on the side of Schaub and George and Lee than with Pinker or Dennett.

Meilaender and Kraynak still have reason to believe George and Lee cannot give an adequate account of who we are without accounting for the mystery of love or personal *logos,* for that which animates our rationality. Even Kass, in thinking about our obvious dignity as begetting and belonging animals—in thinking about how we are godlike in some ways but not in others—turns from the scientists and philosophers to the superior psychology of Genesis.

Thinking about Dignity

This sketch of only part of the argument that animates the authors in the Council's volume on human dignity has not resolved anything for certain. The defense of liberty in our time might well depend on knowing who we really are and why we are dignified beings; it is also possible that we can get by without talking truthfully about our dignity at all. Dignity, as Dennett claims, might only be a useful fiction or, as Schaub claims, a private concern. What should be obvious is that Steven Pinker is simply wrong to claim that only tyrants and fanatics believe it is time to think carefully about dignity.

3

HUMAN DIGNITY AND
HIGHER EDUCATION TODAY

The fundamental fact of our time is the gradual encroachment of principled individualism—or unregulated personal freedom—into all areas of our lives. That means that every moral and communal certainty—except those that can be justified through contract and consent—has been transformed into a question. The great human institutions that shape the character of human beings—the family, the church, the local community, and the country—are weaker than ever. So, more than ever, human selves aren't shaped into souls through the formation or habituation Aristotle says is the source of moral virtue. Young people, more than ever, don't come to colleges with characters formed by firsthand experience. They show up at college seeking—rather than bringing—selves or souls. They don't know who they are, and so they don't know what to do. They don't know what it means to live a personally significant or dignified life.

The experience of the young is, increasingly, that every human attachment is basically voluntary. Life is all about designing one-self according to an ever-expanding menu of choices provided by an increasingly free, prosperous, and globalizing society. A choice, they've been told, is nothing more or less than a preference, and nobody can tell an individual why he or she should prefer this rather than that, as long as he or she doesn't violate the rights of another free chooser. Deep down, our students don't know whether they are or will be parents, children, creatures, citizens, or friends. All they're told is that in our wonderful, enlightened, high-tech world, such commitments are up to them. They're coming to college with the sense that their options have been kept open, and with a real but weak sense that eventually some of those options will have to close.

Professors, meanwhile, used to think they were all about the shaping of souls. They used to believe their main job was to pass on the truth embedded in a religious tradition or the truths embedded in a traditional moral code—one that was often some version of classical or Stoic thought—that should thoughtfully define the lives of educated gentlemen and ladies. Or at least they thought, as Anthony Kronman explains in *Education's End,* that their job was to open students' eyes to the alternative forms of human excellence displayed in the greatest works of philosophy and literature: the saint, the philosopher, the poet, the warrior, the inventor, the entrepreneur, the scientist, and the statesman. It was obvious that these models of human excellence were more than whimsical preferences. Jesus, Socrates, Washington, Shakespeare, Newton, Lewis and Clark, and Marcus Aurelius all differed in important ways about who an excellent person must be. But appreciating the nobility or dignity of each of these men is one mark of any educated person. Professors used to think it was obvious that every human life is a dramatic display of a free and responsible human soul choosing between good and evil on the tough and risky journey to moral perfection.

Professors used to think students needed both their guidance and that of the models of human greatness they could reveal to them to discover who they are and what to do. One irony, of course, is that when professors offered such guidance, students didn't particularly need or want it. They came to college with their character already formed, already habituated to the practice of moral virtue. In those days, the real experience of professors was often a kind of blithe irresponsibility that came with moral impotence. They could say what they wanted without the fear of doing all that much harm—or all that much good. In many cases, students thought, with good reason, that their professors were basically reinforcing what they already knew from firsthand—or not merely bookish—communal experience.

Today's students, we can say, are often stuck with being searchers. They are—or might be—particularly open to the traditional claim of liberal education: We can find the answers to the questions concerning human identity through reading and talking about those books that take fundamental questions with genuine seriousness. By default, we might say, college is stuck with the job that religion—the Bible and churches—used to do. For today's colleges at their secular best—at, say, Great Books places like St. John's—education is about articulating the perennial human questions for young men and women who clearly don't know the truth about the dignified direction their lives should take. But even Great Books education has morphed into the celebration of the questions in the absence of real answers. Who can be satisfied with merely celebrating the questions or reveling in the impotent indecision of Socrates about who we are and what to do? Great Books education—detached altogether from any religious or (very broadly speaking) Stoic context—seems to present us with the alternatives of either being a self-knowing philosopher and losing oneself in either fundamentalist dogmatism or aimless relativism. But the searcher doesn't really need or want to be told that the point of life is searching. Or that, as Allan Bloom claims in *The Closing of the American Mind,* the only real point of life is being a Socratic philosopher, which means, in part, getting over illusions about personal significance.

So another irony is that at a time when students, more than ever, long for more guidance than could possibly be provided by their teachers, professors no longer believe that they have what it takes to provide any at all. Sometimes, they still think that they're charged with liberating the student from "the cave" or traditional or religious or bourgeois conformity to think for themselves. Yet, they must at least half-way know that their empty dogmas of nonconformism or self-creation or promiscuous libertarianism are a large part of the cave of any free and prosperous society.

The Americans, as Tocqueville wrote, are Cartesians without ever having read a word of Descartes; methodical doubt is the natural approach of a democrat who believes that "nobody is better than me." But there are no more conformist slaves of fashion than members of a society formed by the doctrine that nonconformity—or merely questioning authority—is the bottom line. The good news, the American democrat naturally thinks, is that nobody is better than I am, but the bad is that I'm no better than anyone else, and so he or she has no real point of view by which to resist the pressure of the anonymous public opinion. "Think for yourself" and "be creative" are, by themselves, hardly the best advice for establishing personal dignity in times like ours, in times when everyone is skeptical of claims for personal virtue.

Our professors often seem to live fairly traditional lives themselves. They have certainly become more bourgeois or careerist and a lot less bohemian or countercultural. What even the so-called tenured radicals say about liberation and nonjudgmentalism is often contradicted by their ordinary, tenured lives. But like most Americans, they don't believe they have any right to impose—meaning defend with any authority—their preferences about personal morality on others. They proclaim a principled indifference to the character of students' souls. They don't think it's the job of specialized scholars to take the place of parents. What scholars know is too narrow, provisional, and impersonal to guide the whole lives of young people.

Limitless Freedom—a Hostile Environment

So while our professors used to be stuck with moral impotence, they now embrace it as a theory that justifies their irresponsibility. Students, more than ever, are free to choose in all areas of their lives in college. They have almost limitless freedom in choosing what to study, and hardly anything moral or intellectual is required of them. What few requirements are imposed on students are so broad and flexible as to point them in no particular direction at all. In the name of freedom and diversity, little goes on in college that gives them any guidance concerning who they are or what to choose.

Students, in fact, are often taught that what they do is both completely voluntary and utterly meaningless. They're even taught that their freedom to choose is close to unlimited and completely unreal. The human person has no real existence in the wholly impersonal nature described by our scientists. Students learn from neuroscientists that "the soul" must always be put in quotes, because it doesn't correspond to any material or chemical reality. From biologists, they learn that what particular individuals or members of species do is insignificant or makes no real difference to the flourishing of our species.

Sometimes our students learn that although the self or the "I" is really an illusion, it's one we can't live without. According to the evolutionary scientist Daniel Dennett, belief in human dignity is indispensable for the flourishing of members of our species. So we should embrace that belief in view of its beneficial social consequences. But it's still the case that there's nothing real backing up any confidence we might have in personal importance, just as there's nothing real backing up our experiences of love or free will. We need to call true, our philosopher Richard Rorty explained, those illusions that make us feel free, comfortable, and secure. And one way to do that, Rorty adds, is not to believe the scientists when they compare our personal experiences to some objective truth. By saying that "truth" must always appear in quotes, we avoid disparaging what we choose to believe by comparing it with a "real" standard.

Despite the best efforts of talented professors, students, it goes without saying, never really believe that the "I"—the reality of the person each sees in the mirror—doesn't exist. They can't really reduce what they think they know about themselves as particular beings with names and personal destinies to merely useful illusions. So the main effect of higher education is to show each of them how really alone in a hostile environment he or she is. There's no better way to convince someone of his or her utter isolation than to tell him or her that you—meaning your personal experiences—don't really exist, although it's okay if you pretend that you do. That's why it's easy for profound outside observers, such as the great anti-Communist dissident Aleksandr Solzhenitsyn, to hear the howl of existentialism just beneath the surface of our happy-talk pragmatism. In part, our students are so lonely because they don't think they have the words—only howls of desperation—to describe truthfully who they are to others.

Despite all the therapeutic efforts to build inclusive and diverse communities, our colleges are often very lonely places. Because our highest educators believe they have no authority to rule the young, they've allowed our campuses, in many respects, to revert to a kind of state of nature, something like the war of all against all for the scarce resource of personal significance or dignity. There, as Tom Wolfe has described in *I Am Charlotte Simmons,* the strong and beautiful "hook up," the weak and ugly are condemned to "sexile," the clever use their cunning to master the fraudulent arts of networking and teambuilding or to become trendy, marketable intellectuals, and the timid and decent are shown the vanity of their slavish moral illusions. Meanwhile, administrators look on with politically correct nonjudgmental cluelessness about how their officially egalitarian and inclusive doctrine has liberated their charges for ruthless competition with necessarily inegalitarian results. Students are stuck with using all means available to establish who they are through their successes in manipulating and dominating others. Of course, they're also stuck with being able to distinguish between how they "dress for success" and who they really are, between the self they construct to impress themselves upon others and the self that stands behind the constructed selves. So, no matter how much a student succeeds in establishing his or her importance in the eyes of others, he or she is stuck, in some ways, with being more lonely and undignified than ever. Students are characterized, perhaps more than ever, by the inauthentic emptiness Christopher Lasch described in *The Culture of Narcissism*.

All in all, it seems that today's student gets to college more free in the sense of lost or empty or more disoriented than ever, and the effect of college, in most cases, is to make him or her more lost. It's still not true that the graduate ends up believing that freedom really is having nothing left to lose, because the personal self or soul and its longings are more exposed than ever. Students may be told that they're stuck with self-creation, but they are not God. They can't create themselves out of nothing, and so they can't help but know that they're more than nothing, although without any clear of view of who or what that might be.

So our colleges don't really deny the reality of personal freedom. They assume to be true or leave intact the two dominant understandings of freedom and dignity in our technological society—productivity and autonomy. Productivity is the standard of the techno-majors chosen by an overwhelming majority of our students—from engineering to the health sciences to marketing, public relations, and turf management. Autonomy dominates the soft social sciences—such as sociology and women's studies—and the humanities.

According to the philosopher Hobbes, our dignified freedom is displayed in our productivity, in our generation of power in opposition to nature, in what we can do that commands a price. Nature, in truth, treats each of us with a most cruel indifference. She accords persons no dignity at all. We can, however, use our freedom to change our natural environment to make our particular existences more secure, and that's the only change we should believe in. For Hobbes, the point of freedom is to generate power to not not be. Nature is out to kill me in all sorts of ways, and to secure my dignity I have to get to work and do something about that.

According to the philosopher Kant, Hobbes assumes that each human individual regards him- or herself as unique and irreplaceable. So his dignity couldn't possibly be found in his productivity or price, in being just another natural resource. Our dignity is found in our ability to act freely against natural instinct and inclination, and we do so by respecting the dignity of other free beings which are able to do the same. Our dignity is in our autonomy, in our moral freedom, in our ability to tell ourselves, in freedom, what to do.

Hobbes and Kant really aren't that opposed to each other. They both agree that our dignity can only be found in our freedom from nature, and that there's nothing dignified in living according to nature. They both say that the human being is on his or her own to acquire his freedom or dignity, and that God and nature—and even community and tradition—can provide no authoritative guidance for who we are. For Hobbes, our common political life is an invention by free beings to achieve a level of personal security which has not been given to us by nature. After we've achieved a certain level of security and prosperity, each of us is on his or her own to live as he or she pleases with no natural guidance. We are free, as Maslow says, to pursue self-actualization, to discover or invent the "real me" who is more than a mere body. Kant does say that the only way to be free from nature or selfish interest and inclination is to act rationally and morally. But today's proponent of autonomy is satisfied to say that anything a free being chooses is dignified. And so the productivity unleashed by technological progress serves autonomy by expanding the number of free choices possible in our lives.

Most sophisticated graduates of our better colleges today—those David Brooks called bourgeois bohemians—take pride in both their productivity and their autonomy. They both work hard and display their uniquely human self-fulfillment through their free personal choices. They believe there's no dignity in choosing for natural instinct, for being the species-perpetuating machine described by Mr. Darwin. There's no dignity in being merely begetting or belonging beings, in being social, gregarious animals. Being autonomous means refusing to be defined by what comes naturally, by, for example, having babies. That's why today's productive and autonomous woman is so insistent about her reproductive freedom, about resisting the tyranny of her body's baby-making equipment and her natural inclination to be a mother. That's also why our sophisticated intellectuals are so insistent about affirming the right to same-sex marriage: No free human institution can be constrained by natural or biological imperatives. Two or more autonomous beings can come together for any purpose they choose, and marriage should be nothing but the public affirmation of the dignity of that personal choice.

There's no dignity in living well with any of our natural limitations, in, for example, living well with death or being grateful for the human goods that depend upon our mortality or finite existence in this world. Productivity is about fending death off as long as possible. Nature's victory over each of us may be inevitable, but its timing is indefinite enough that there's no need for me to relax and accept the inevitability of my not being. The idea of autonomy points in the direction of implacable hatred of our bodies and the control they have over us. Our autonomy freaks are in rebellion against all those institutions that our bodily limitations seem to make necessary and good—such as the family, the nation, and the church. The autonomous being aims to live in cosmopolitan detachment from all those particular constraints, to live a free or sort of ghostly existence nowhere in particular.

Productivity and autonomy both point in the direction of "transhumanism" or toward a free existence unlimited by bodily constraints. The experience of incompleteness that animates the various forms of love is undignified. The modern techno-view of freedom is to be disembodied, and disembodied *eros* is surely an oxymoron. Even God had to become man to display his personal love for each of us. And even Socrates said philosophy is learning how to die, which is just about impossible to do if you don't have a body.

The imperatives of productivity and autonomy both suggest that there's dignity in separating sex from birth or death and so making it an absolutely free expression of who I am. The productive view—the one put forward by our college administrators—is that the only limitations to sexual behavior should be *safety* and *consent*. A free being does what he or she pleases so long as he or she doesn't bring a free being into existence, cause a free being's demise, or tyrannize over another free being. Of course, a productive being also doesn't allow love to get in the way of work. An autonomous being refuses to allow love—the result of mere biological instinct run amok—to produce undignified or unfree behavior. So it's no wonder that we seem to live in a particularly *unerotic* time. Neither the productive nor the autonomous being can extend his or her autonomous imagination to include families, children, countries, or maybe even real friends and lovers.

Maybe that's why food has become more exciting—more a dangerous liaison and risky business—than sex. We're increasingly paranoid, puritanical, and prohibitionist when it comes to food from a health and safety perspective. Gluttony is a vice that can kill you, or at least make you fat and so less pretty, pleasing, and productive. Sex can kill you only if it gets mixed up with too much love—like in the case of Romeo and Juliet—or if it is unprotected. The bourgeois bohemian says the truth is that you can't get too much safe, recreational sex, and it's puritanical and prohibitionist to think otherwise. How bohemian could it be to make sex that unerotic and food that scary? "Safe sex" is the bourgeois view of sex, and obsessive calorie and carb counting is the bourgeois view of food.

To see how fundamentally unbohemian our alleged bourgeois bohemians are, you have to look no further than the trendy TV show, *Mad Men* (about Manhattan advertising executives around 1960): These "mad men" smoked, drank lots of martinis day and night, only exercised when they thought it was fun, and had all sorts of reckless extramarital liaisons. We can see they were "mad" because they lacked caution in their pursuit of personal self-fulfillment. Today's sophisticates are so unbohemian that the advertising executives of the recent past look like bohemians in comparison with us. In the lives of our students and teachers, the conflict between being bourgeois and being bohemian has withered away only because productivity trumps autonomy at every turn.

The Origin of the Bourgeois Bohemian

The conflict between being bourgeois and being bohemian was previously displayed as evidence of the limits of the American idea of freedom. For a while, college professors and students seemed to be divided between those who aimed to be productive and those who aimed to be artistically self-fulfilled. We learn from books and movies such as *Revolutionary Road* that our 1950s suburbs were full of people who were boring and desperately conformist, people incapable of living interesting lives. We used to think that the people who earned the money didn't know how to live, and those who chose la vie bohème couldn't even pay the rent. And the bohemians criticized our multiversities for producing corporate techno-cloned, other-directed organization men, while often dropping out of college themselves to soar higher than their professors. Even bohemian Tories with a genuine concern for living well, such as the conservative Russell Kirk, sometimes dropped out of an increasingly bureaucratized and standardized university system.

The bohemian critics of the 1950s were already making the criticisms of technocratic education for productivity we make today. The American university was lacking a unifying vision of a whole human life, and it was incapable of preparing young people for the art of life. The bohemians noticed that only scientific and technical courses were taken seriously as conveying real knowledge. They were the classes all about "facts," where the humanities were all about emoting mere "values." Autonomy or self-actualization was presented as nothing more than whimsical self-indulgence, as nothing real.

The theorists of the 1960s claimed that education for productivity had become obsolete. The techno-conquest of scarcity now allows the surrender of bourgeois discipline for unprecedented liberation of huge numbers of people to "Do your own thing." The "how" or the acquisition of the material means for living a good life had become easy. So we had become free not to be guided by the necessity of obsessing over productivity in choosing how to live. The Sixties' theorists agreed with the proponents of productivity that there was no returning to the repression and prejudice of the past. Capitalism, they assumed whether they knew it or not, had discredited all past standards and ways of life. So they thought of themselves as both freed by and from productivity for imagining a wholly unprecedented vision of free or unconstrained self-fulfillment.

The view of the bourgeois 1950s establishment suggested that all virtue that doesn't contribute to productivity is repressive or "surplus," and the indispensable families and religion were reconfigured in a sort of utilitarian direction by the social scientific brigade of our organization men. The bohemian claim of the Sixties' theorists was that even virtue that served productivity is "surplus," and so reason, freedom, creativity, and love could be liberated, for the first time, from alienating distortions. The true meaning of bourgeois success is that many people are now free to be bohemian without experiencing the downsides of judgmental marginalization and material deprivation.

The Sixties' theorists miss the irony of what's most true in Marx: Capitalism makes human beings miserably anxious by turning every human purpose, except those that serve productivity, into a meaningless whim. The Sixties' theorists, we can say, made us more miserably anxious or disoriented still by reducing even bourgeois virtue to meaninglessness. Despite their best efforts at being creative, their thinking really did culminate in the anarchist or nihilist conclusion that freedom really is "just another word for nothing left to lose." They certainly gave us no new support for our longings for personal significance or dignity. Their view of freedom was really the same as that found in Marx's description of the communism to come: Life is nothing but a series of disconnected, unobsessive pursuits that have no meaning beyond immediate enjoyment.

The 1960s intellectual rebellion rightly began against the technocratic view that factual statements always begin not with "I think," but rather with "studies show." Real knowledge is always to be expressed impersonally, and so has nothing to do with who real people are and what they're supposed to do. But by the end of the 1960s, "studies show" courses in the social sciences were replaced by aggressively personal and merely subjective "studies" courses—black studies, women's studies, and so forth. These courses were based on the premise that human identity is nothing more or less than an assertion of power because, as Hobbes claims, there's no truth, only power. So "studies" courses, unwittingly, reinforced Hobbes's bourgeois lesson: My dignity depends upon my power and nothing more. And taking "studies" courses is no way to prepare oneself to live a genuinely powerful or productive and so dignified life. Anyone who really believes what's taught in a "studies" course would switch over to a technical major, and surely that's what many blacks and women did who genuinely craved dignified liberation.

The scientists and technocrats are usually aware enough that the clarity of their studies comes from abstraction from all perceptions of personal reality. And they were certainly right in concluding that "studies" courses are nothing more than emotional outbursts of "value" that correspond to nothing real. So the progress of science and technology was never really challenged by the know-nothing propaganda coming from the social sciences and humanities in the late 1960s. The effectual truth of the 1960s was to empty the humanities of much of their real content—which came from taking virtue seriously as more than a way to productivity or autonomy.

That meant humanities courses became, on balance, less challenging and even less interesting to students as real alternatives to the domination of productivity (or "quantitative assessment") in higher education. Autonomy, to say the least, failed to liberate itself from productivity. Nor did autonomy in the form of Sixties' liberationism really discredit the virtues connected with productivity. One contradiction of Sixties' radicalism was that its new "art of living" both depended upon and rejected the disciplined habits and social institutions that make possible techno-prosperity. Those radicals embraced, naively, a key error of Marx, who believed, for no clear reason, that the conquest of nature can occur once and for all, allowing the alienation associated with the division of labor responsible for the conquest to wither away.

The conquest of past scarcity, as the libertarian Brink Lindsey patiently explains in *The Age of Abundance,* continues to depend on people doing what's required to be productive. To be productive, people continue to have to be calculating, inventive, flexible, industrious, pleasing, capable of abstract or impersonal loyalty, thoughtful and disciplined enough to defer gratification today for an even better tomorrow, stuck with anxious stress of competition, and genuinely willing to accept the alienation that comes with the division of labor. The dignity that comes with practicing these bourgeois virtues is more real, of course, than any associated with merely unobsessively doing one's own thing.

The Real Lesson of the Sixties

The real lesson of the Sixties is that we can't dispense with the virtues that empower us to be free from nature for doing what we please when we're not working. Our neocons and New Democrats of the seventies, eighties, and nineties taught us that deviance, dysfunction, and the pseudo-profundity of romantic bohemian sentimentalism are all self-indulgent and self-destructive vices, at least if they flourish at the expense of personal productivity. But, from our sophisticated bourgeois bohemian view, there's still much to appreciate about Sixties' transformations in the direction of autonomy. The moral repression that had nothing to do with and, in fact, inhibited productivity was overcome. The freedom of individuals from the arbitrary categories of race, class, gender, and even sexual orientation was undeniably progress. So too was the liberation of sexual appetites from pointless guilt, shame, and ignorant frustration, as was even their desublimation in the direction of commodification. From a bourgeois bohemian view, Sixties' progress included luring women out of the home and into the workplace in the name of both autonomy and productivity, heightened skepticism about traditional religious dogmas, and a new openness—even through the use of soft and safe recreational drugs—to demystified, Aquarian, New Agey forms of spirituality. So, for our colleges today, it's clear what was good about the Sixties. That decade's new forms of autonomous self-fulfillment have been safely reconfigured to be perfectly compatible with health, safety, and productivity.

Our libertarian thinkers, like Tyler Cowen in *Creative Destruction: How Globalization is Changing the World's Cultures,* are best at explaining what the bohemian side of bourgeois bohemian means now. Our techno-globalizing world makes it possible for prosperous people to be appreciative and tasteful consumers of the products of a diverse array of cultures. It's easier than ever to enjoy the food, music, literature, and art of other cultures without having to be actually dragged into the repressive morality and limited, unindividualistic horizon of any particular culture. It's surely wonderful to be able to consume French food without having to be saddled with all the emotional baggage that comes with actually being French, just as it's amazingly convenient to admire the art of Papua New Guinea without having to engage in the sweaty, risky business of hunting and gathering and fighting and being haunted by the imaginary presence of evil spirits.

Today's bohemian is a multiculturalist, finding self-fulfillment from the relatively unobsessive but still meaningful perspective of the tourist or hobbyist exploring the huge and diverse menu of good things the world has to offer. That's why the study of world religions has become so popular; it's basically unthreatening fun to learn about all the sundry gods and goddesses without being stuck with all the love, cruelty, fear, and tough personal discipline that comes with actually believing in any of them. Such enjoyment is perfectly compatible with the individualistic view that every human endeavor is to be voluntary or freely chosen, and it's evidence of the individual's freedom from defining one's whole life according to productivity or the necessity of alienating work. The free individual, in fact, is free from the puritanical moral obsessiveness that would make a life a "whole." His personal life is characterized by diverse self-fulfilling enjoyments that don't need to be ranked, as long as he or she remembers that his autonomy depends on his productivity. He claims not to have to know who he or she is—beyond being a productive being—to know how to live.

Cowen retains some of the Sixties' confidence that a free society will not only consume—but produce—high culture, because of all the liberated reason, freedom, creativity, and love. But mostly he seems to acknowledge the irony that the globalizing conditions that produce the unfettered consumption of culture by more and more will also undermine the real diversity of cultures in the world. The growth of diversity on the individual level tends to level diversity on the social or cultural level. Eventually, of course, the effects will even be bad for diversity on the individual level. We can't withhold individualistic enlightenment from various cultures for that reason—that would be holding some in "cultural slavery" for the enjoyment of freer individuals. We can hope, the libertarian can perversely add, that some people will remain irrational or tribal enough to keep real cultural diversity alive against the forces of enlightenment. We can appreciate as consumers—but not imitate or even condone as free beings—people who choose an understanding of dignity or significance that's something other than autonomy or productivity.

The old bohemians, of course, meant to be genuinely countercultural, to define themselves authentically as whole artistic or poetic or even religious beings against bourgeois productivity or an empty view of autonomy that's indistinguishable from productivity. They claimed to know who they are and what they are supposed to do with their lives. And they willingly and even irresponsibly sacrificed careerist productivity for personal, self-fulfilled, purposeful happiness. That meant, of course, they seemed, like Socrates, to live like parasites off of the productive. But we still looked to them for some alternative guidance for what human life is for, because we sometimes believed them when they said they had a clue about human meaning or purpose.

The End of the Humanities? The End of Humanity?

Today's "postmodern" humanities professors don't even claim to some "holistic" view of the art of human life, although they still enjoy the perks of professors who thought they could offer people real guidance. Stanley Fish, one of our most notable practitioners and defenders of liberal education, sees in his ironic way that privileges without responsibility can't last long. Fish, in "The Last Professor" (*New York Times*, January 19, 2009), acknowledges that our universities are, more than ever, defined by the "ethic" of measurable productivity and efficiency. Increasingly, the humanities seem impractical and unaffordable. Higher education, it would seem, need not waste time and money on teaching students how to enjoy the products of other cultures tastefully. They can pursue their hobbies on their own.

The faculty member, Fish also observes, who "delivers insight and inspiration" is obsolete, because neither he nor his bosses really believe he has the warrant to tell students how to live. The postmodern Fish doesn't spend enough time blaming himself for this state of affairs: He admits he doesn't believe he teaches anything real, and yet he still wants what he does to be given noninstrumental value, to be cherished in its "inutility." Despite himself, Fish accepts the "business model" of the university administrators. He really doesn't defend the traditional proposition that what we most need to know in order to live well can't be measured. In his view, it would seem that professors like himself can and should disappear because they do not know a true standard of human significance or dignity that trumps productivity. Professors of humanities, Fish concludes, have about put themselves out of business.

It's easy to criticize the bourgeois bohemian product of our colleges and universities for his or her superficiality. Some critics, such as Allan Bloom, say we're producing a generation of emotional solitaries—people unable to be moved to thought or action by love or death. By raising and teaching the young as if they didn't have souls, we're producing souls that are flat or one-dimensional. They're not lost or homeless, but all too at home in a world made for emotional tourists, for being at home everywhere because they're not at home anywhere in particular. But there's actually more truth to what Solzhenitsyn says about our pragmatism barely concealing the howl of existentialism: People experience themselves as more alone than ever. We really do, more than ever, have a meritocracy based on productivity, which means the pressure is on like never before to be productive. These are the best times ever to be young, smart, pretty, flexible, and industrious, but the pressure is on to display those qualities to avoid loneliness and possess dignified significance. Not only that, people are full of moral anxiety. They know, for example, that they've been given the responsibility to raise their kids to be more than survivalists or slackers. But, unless they've turned to very personal religion, it's very hard for them to figure out how or why.

Dignity and Higher Education

It's no secret that most of our colleges that give lip service to "liberal education" don't deliver it, and what they do teach exaggerates—not moderates—the undignified confusion of our time. They certainly don't give students the impression that there's much—if any—moral or humanistic "content" (versus "method"—such as critical thinking or analytical reasoning) that they need to know. And so they don't give students the impression that their education is about who they are or what they're supposed to do. Not only that, but the permissive and indulgent atmosphere of our colleges extends adolescence far more than it serves as a bridge between being a playful child and assuming the serious responsibilities of an adult. Everyone knows that our colleges are positively antagonistic to the formation of moral virtue and often undermine the good habits and confident beliefs students sometimes actually bring with them to college.

So Charles Murray, in *Real Education,* seems on strong ground when he argues that we should declare the brick-and-mortar college obsolete for most purposes it now claims to serve. The students who go to college in pursuit of a technical career—the overwhelming majority of them—might be better served by a more focused and condensed education that would take much less than four years and wouldn't require "the residential experience." Maybe we should abandon the pretense that the B.A. is the admission ticket to the world of most white-collar work. Students might actually be less confused if they were free from the fantasy that anything about college can give them a standard of freedom and dignity higher than productivity, and they might be better off and closer to the truth by sticking with what they've picked up from their family, their church, and their community, even if all that isn't what it once was. Liberal education—in a society that has abdicated on most fronts the project of sound "cultural transmission"—couldn't possibly function as the cure for what most ails us. Murray is surely right that the project of civic and cultural literacy belongs in grade and high school, and it's the fault of our colleges—particularly, but not only, our schools of education—that it's not there. We can't expect the institutions that have eviscerated our high schools to make up for what they haven't done.

Murray concludes that "liberal education"—including real precision in the use of language and real knowledge of what's required for moral choices—might be preserved for those most likely to assume positions of political, intellectual, and economic leadership in our country. Tocqueville, we remember, said something not so different: Those with literary careers—or those charged with perpetuating key distinctions in our language—should study the Greek and Roman authors in their original language. That way our language will retain some contact with the metaphysical, theological, and moral distinctions that correspond to the multilayered truth about the human soul. Otherwise, the trend will continue to be for our language to become exclusively impersonal, vague in crucial respects, and too technical for us to say anything true about our freedom and dignity. For Tocqueville and Murray, we need a few excellent universities far more than many mediocre colleges.

This sort of conclusion is unsatisfying if we believe that every human being has a soul worthy of being educated. Everyone, of course, has to live well with the responsibilities given to begetting and belonging beings open to the truth, including the personal truths of love and death. In a time when every claim about truth and morality invites skepticism, religious training and moral habituation, by themselves, won't be enough to inspire the self-confidence and good judgment required for lives of genuine personal significance.

The traditional claim of liberal education that every person needs more than a technical education remains true. Tocqueville reminds us that the first impetus for universal education in our country was the puritanical insistence that everyone should read the Bible for him- or herself. From the middle-class conditions of modern, democratic life came the need for universal literacy for every free being to make his or her own living; from our religion came our view that every person has a soul and so spiritual needs. Modern, democratic education is first of all practical or technical, but we puritancial Americans add that each person was made for more than mere survival. We Americans have always been dissatisfied with the classical view that liberal education was only for the leisurely few who ruled the productive many. Our view is that everyone has a duty to work, but nobody was made only to work.

Liberal education does exist here and there within our country, and it exists particularly in the smaller liberal arts colleges. In fact, many of those colleges are inspired to aim high through their vibrant religious missions, through their concern for the personal destiny of particular souls. We are most likely to find liberal education geared towards a wide variety of students in our religious colleges. Some of it is little more than apologetics to support pious indoctrination, but St. Thomas Aquinas in California, for example, is thought by many to be the best Great Books college in the country. Students who choose religious colleges are usually clearer about who they are than many of our lost souls when they get to college, but that doesn't mean that they don't need—really need—the kind of intellectual challenge and depth that can only come through higher education. It seems unlikely that in our time—a time without a secular moral code (or without any confidence in the reality of ladies and gentlemen) or any real moral consensus—secular colleges and universities can be up to the task of dignified liberal education in any big way. If not, the future of human dignity—or at least dignified higher education—may depend more than ever on our religious institutions.

4

DELSOL ON HUMAN RIGHTS
AND PERSONAL DIGNITY

This is a commentary on a prominent theme found in Chantal Delsol's trilogy—*Icarus Fallen: The Search for Meaning in an Uncertain World*; *The Unlearned Lessons of the Twentieth Century: An Essay on Late Modernity*; and *Unjust Justice: Against the Tyranny of International Law* (all published in excellent translation by ISI Books).[1] Everything I say is based on something I learned from this contemporary French political philosopher's three great books, but I've done some focusing, clarifying, and reconciling of her argument—not to mention adding to it here and there. So I'm not sure I've been entirely faithful to the letter or even the spirit of these books, and even the attempt to provide specific citations for everything I say would clog up my text without being all that illuminating. Almost every point I make, I will say, she's made more than once. My goal is to employ Delsol to make a distinctive contribution to understanding who we are.

Today's world is distinguished by its devotion to human rights. The idea that each and every human being has rights, according to Delsol, is an unavoidably ontological statement—a statement about what or, better, who particular human beings are. It is a statement about what dignifies each of us—our irreplaceable, immeasurable uniqueness. It depends upon human beings really being persons or subjects or, as Delsol occasionally says, person/subjects. The future of human rights is intertwined with the future of our true understanding of dignity. We can't just decide to accord each other dignity; there's no stability and, in fact, no dignity in a merely social and readily changeable decision.

We acknowledge our true dignity through our true belief in our personal greatness. Rights only belong to beings who aren't anonymous, who have names, who are aware of and claim their undeniable exceptionality. The world, the rights claim must be, is full of billions and billions of exceptions to the impersonal laws that govern the rest of the natural or visible world. Those exceptions, the claim must also be, are far more mysterious and wonderful and lovable than the billions and billions of stars that the physicists claim to find so fascinating. The philosophy of rights must be based on the intrinsic dignity of the beings who mysteriously transcend the rest of nature. The idea of rights is incompatible with too much scientific skepticism about whether we're really different in any personally significant way from the other animals.

Our dignity must be rooted in what's most undeniably different about each of us—knowing about and being moved to thought and action by the precariousness and finitude of one's own being. Knowing that I die raises me above the rest of the animal world and separates *me* fundamentally from every other self-conscious mortal. An animal can be identified completely with his species. He can't die as a unique being, and he's unable to experience or make a claim for his uniqueness. Because I (the person) am open to the truth about *my* being, I can't truthfully live as merely part of some whole.

My point of distinction, my greatness, is, from a purely natural view, a wound. I can't share completely in the healthy contentment enjoyed by the other animals. I'm also stuck with being somewhat miserably dissatisfied with who I know I really am. Each of us makes a claim for dignity to the extent that we're proud of living well with our insecurity and uncertainty. Nothing great can come without noble risk or some dramatic moral adventure; that's why no other animal is capable of greatness. It's not easy for me to live well with what I really know. I can't help but experience myself as merely a passenger in this world. I can't lose myself in some whole or cosmos or group, so I'm never fully at home. My truthful goal is to seek harmony—not identity—with the reality—including the persons—outside of myself. My search for a comprehensive and truthful reality outside myself—a certain standard of personal responsibility—is never completed, although I can't deny that I know enough to act or choose responsibly. As a dignified being, I can't lose myself in any reality outside myself; I can't help but live in some distance—both ironic and caring—from who and what I think I know.

My personal experience will always be, to some extent, one of maladjustment. I want to be good, but often do evil. The moral conflict between good and evil reaches through every person and is never fully resolved. I long for immortality—or to be much more secure and durable than my biological being allows me to be, but I know I'm bound to die. I have to admit that I don't really know whether I will continue to exist after my biological death. We self-conscious mortals can't help but want more than nature gives us, but each of us can't know for certain how and in what sense he gets more. Nothing we know is great or dignified but the meaningful, moral adventures of particular persons. Nothing a dignified being does can completely reflect the unique and irreducible being he is. A person confident of his dignity always knows that there's more to him than he can ever display, and that he is somewhat obscure even to himself. That means he can't reduce what he knows and doesn't know to some doctrine or dogma. He also avoids dogma because he knows that his dignity doesn't depend on moral or intellectual impositions on others. His place is somewhere between the nihilistic extremes of relativism and fanaticism. A man confident of his dignity doesn't feign indifference to the questions he can't help but ask, but neither does he aggressively assert to be true what he knows to be, at best, uncertain or partially true.

The person/subject pursues personal perfection. All human perfection—and finally all human meaning—is personal, not collective. When the person identifies himself entirely with some group or collectivity, it's always by seeing himself as less than he really is. Delsol, for that reason, is hard on every conceivable form of identity politics. Nobody is merely black or white, man or woman, hetero- or homosexual, Christian or Jew, citizen or alien, husband or daughter, or a member of some species. Destiny is always personal, not collective. "The good" always applies to and is found in real human beings. It is never conceptual, abstract or impersonal. Only particular flesh-and-blood human beings are lovable. The mysterious, irreducible, irreplaceable uniqueness of human beings is the source of both dignity and love, and there's no adequate conception of justice or rights that abstracts from either dignity or love.

Our finitude and precariousness at the foundation of both dignity and love can also make us repulsive to ourselves. So a perennial personal temptation is to care more for theological or theoretical visions of human perfection than who we actually are. It is tough to care for what and especially who really exists, but that, according to Delsol, is most properly human. We dignified beings are much more caregivers than producers. Our products or inventions aren't lovable and dignified at all, and that goes, of course, for our abstract or idealistic and always reductionistic distortions of who we are. Loving, solicitous, generous caregiving corresponds to the immeasurable, irreplaceable being each of us is better than production does—which is about measurable, standardized, anonymous results.

Caregiving and production are indispensable and incommensurable human activities; we can't do without either. But the one that attends more to invisible mystery and less to visible display is actually more dignified. Caregiving is directed not only to particular persons but also to our cultural and institutional inheritances on which every finite human subject depends for the shaping of his personhood. Only abstract beings—reductionistic products of our imaginations—can exist outside a particular, problematic cultural context in the pure domain of unmediated truth. Unquestionable certainty—or the wholesale replacement of "convention" by "nature"—is never a characteristic of a particular human being or a particular culture, and the interdependence of personal dignity and cultural inheritance is an inevitable mark of the finitude of both.

The Person as a Modern Invention

The person/subject, Delsol seems to claim, didn't always exist. He is both the creation and the point of the modern world. In the past, men spoke of honor, but now they speak of dignity. In both cases, they mean to speak of their greatness. Honor was achieved through an exhausting effort to live up to some externally defined standard—the reigning code of honor. Honor had to be earned, and it wasn't up to the particular human being to decide what honor was or what to do to earn it. In those days, men thought they knew how to live, what they were supposed to do. The premodern world was composed of "holistic" or organic societies, where a man found his meaning by finding his place in a whole outside himself. He knew his place, and so he felt the maladjustment or alienation that's characteristic of being open to the truth much less than we do. In the premodern world, meaning was imposed on particular people, and so personal opinion, strictly speaking, was unimaginable. The unity that formed opinion was not the person, and the person found purposeful opinions as part of that greater unity.

The Christians, strictly speaking, discovered the person. The Christian could, from the beginning, differentiate himself from all impersonal or collective wholes with a belief in a personal conscience, a personal immortality, and a personal relationship with God. The premodern Christian, however, still understood himself to work out his unique destiny in a communitarian context and with numerous cultural certitudes. He didn't doubt what came after death or achieve any distance from what he believed to be the true source of cultural authority. Modern European culture is distinguished by the conscious intention to make the personal insight of the Christians more consistent and real. The modern invention of the person or subject was based, Delsol contends, on the ambitious intuition that each human being could flourish as a coherent entity. That meant that particular persons were to be far more completely liberated from the virtual cloning of selves characteristic of holistic societies for real personal responsibility. He would much more consciously and consistently come to terms with what he can't help but know about his personal contingency and mortality. His self-understanding would become less anonymous; he would see himself more clearly as a unique, irreplaceable being with a name.

Personal dignity is most clearly displayed, Delsol says, only in societies where the subject comes first. The modern subject seems somehow both a novel invention and a more truthful reflection of what beings like us have always known, quite imperfectly, about ourselves. Personal dignity is based on a true ontological intuition about who we are. Acting on an ontological intuition is not self-creation. Delsol's opinion is clearly not that human ontology is a tale of man making himself over time.

When we live in light of the truth, it seems, we see ourselves as persons, and we discover our dignity. But human beings haven't always or even usually done that, and so they were somewhat blind to what they had the capability to know. Honor, we know, was a distorted if somewhat reasonable view of dignity, and so even when honorable men didn't understand themselves correctly—as persons—they still displayed much of the greatness of who they are. Delsol shows us in various ways that her presentation of premodern man as merely a part of some collectivity is an exaggeration. She also seems to say, however, that only the modern person or subject fully sees his own dignity for what it is.

The modern intention was that each man become more dignified. He would assume the responsibility of a person, which is not freedom from being human, from our precariousness and finiteness. The thought was that we would become more aware than ever of our personal limits, and each of us would display the dignity of facing up to them. Modern liberation was not meant to be the pursuit of an illusory emotional and intellectual freedom from other people. It was for a more conscious coming to terms with finiteness through a more deliberate involving of oneself in the world. That involvement would be based on our limited but real ability to share moral truths in common and to love and care for each other and the world we share.

The modern person would even affirm his need for some limited identification with specific places and institutions. The person can't dispense with being a citizen, a parent, and a devoted participant in various local communities. He doesn't aim to detach himself wholly from his territorial roots. Delsol says the person is aware of his incarnation, and so his beneficial dependence on various institutional forms of embodiment. He certainly doesn't want to detach himself from the conditions that allow him to know and love particular persons. The truth is we can't exist without all kinds of determinations, and so the person situates himself in a precarious position between under- and over-determination. He doesn't lose his personal identity in any external whole while understanding his identity as personal, not abstract or disembodied. The place here between abstract universalism and unselfconscious communitarianism is as precarious, it seems, as personal existence itself. Because there's no single, certain, or perfect way of finding that place, efforts to achieve it in freedom are the highest cause of the diversity that characterizes cultural and political life.

Dissident Responsibility

Delsol sometimes suggests that the modern intention was that every human being live a heroic life of personal responsibility. She sometimes takes her bearings from those extraordinary dissidents (such as the Czech Jan Patočka) who displayed their dignity in neon letters by living in courageous resistance to communist totalitarianism. The dignified person is always resisting, it seems, the dominant forms of depersonalization—the various forms of flight from the truth—in his time. The dissident's resistance to the depersonalizing lie of ideology was illuminated, Delsol says, by a source of meaning outside of himself, but he never forgot that his comprehension of that source was incomplete and uncertain. Patočka called that life of a searcher "negative Platonism," a refusal ever to replace the dialectical pursuit with dogma.[2] Patočka's amazing courage—his giving of his life—was in the service of saving the subject—the being responsible and animated enough to engage in meaningful search—from being absorbed in an impersonal, ideological lie. The dissident didn't act blindly or absurdly; his dignity was evident enough to himself to be able to act with truthful responsibility.

The fall of communism may have reminded us of the limits of the dissidents and Delsol's sometimes high idea of personal dignity or greatness. The experience of heroically resisting depersonalization has not yet been routinized or become the foundation for most ordinary lives. It hasn't become the foundation of the various postcommunist regimes in Europe. How could most people ordinarily be dissidents? In *Democracy in America*, Alexis de Tocqueville thought that Americans could preserve their political liberty only because they quite consciously subordinated themselves to religious dogma. Living well in freedom seems to depend on affirming answers to certain fundamental questions without discussion. Some reliance on dogma, according to Tocqueville, is in accord with the truth about our precarious and limited condition.[3] The view of American students of Leo Strauss—who often think of themselves as negative or zetetic Platonists—is similar; the Socratic way of life can't be for most people most of the time.[4]

Most people most of the time, Platonists think, can't live well in light of the truth and nothing but. They need to limit their doubt and affirm some cultural certitudes with their hearts and minds in order to find what personal integrity they can. Patočka, I have to add, might have been extreme among the dissidents in his identification of meaning with uncertainty. Aleksandr Solzhenitsyn and Václav Havel, for example, seem more certain that there is a clear ontological foundation—a foundation in a reality higher and greater than ourselves—for dignified, personal responsibility. Havel and Solzhenitsyn were often less than clear about what or who that higher reality is, and to what or to whom the person is conscientiously responsible. But they seemed to have no doubt about the reality of a dignified, personal "I" who can and should resist absorption into the anonymous crowd.[5]

The American philosopher/novelist Walker Percy provides a defense of the view that the person is always, to some extent, a dissident. We can say that the being who wonders seems to necessarily wander. He can't really locate himself completely in the natural world that scientists can truthfully describe. Nor can he locate himself securely in the political community or "cave" that the best citizens can fully describe. The wandering personal dissident is in constant, caring search for loving harmony, but not identity, with other persons, including, perhaps, the personal God. The being who knows he wonders and wanders can't help but know that the only beings deeply worthy of his wonder, his care, and his love are other persons.[6] Human searchers can care truthfully for the culture they inhabit without being certain of the truth of any cultural or even personal answer to any fundamental human questions. Maybe it's still the case, however, that the dissident or, we might say, the person who fully displays his dignity must be the exception to the rule among human beings. The anti-Communist dissidents, we remember, also dissented from the banality of ordinary life in the West, and even Tocqueville knew he was too hard on the comparatively unmemorable way most people live.[7]

Delsol actually shows us that all the evidence we have so far is that the personal responsibility required of the modern subject has been too hard. That's why she goes as far as to say that the modern subject or person, strictly speaking, has not yet been born. We still can't say that the person or subject can even be a realistic model of human excellence for guiding a particular culture or society. Most modern men have fallen prey to depersonalization, to thinking and experiencing themselves as less than who they really are. The two forms of modern society of the twentieth century—ideological totalitarianism and the individualism prevalent today—have not even had the intention of forming persons or subjects ready to think and act for themselves.

The Modern Individual

Men today mourn the fact that they both seem to lack what it takes to become subjects and are stuck with an impotent and very selectively nostalgic longing to regress to organic society. Their real complaint is that they're stuck in a place where it's so hard to know who they are or what to do. They're especially displaced and disoriented, because they can neither form themselves into coherent, dignified entities nor lose themselves in wholes greater than themselves.

Ideological societies were based on fanatical imposition of definite answers on individuals miserably worn out by the seemingly unlimited freedom and perpetual questioning of modern life. Individuals today aim at passive serenity by feigning indifference to the answers of fundamental questions. Ideological fanaticism was cruelly, monstrously, and pointlessly destructive of lots of persons. For individuals and individualistic societies, the antidote is relativism. Relativism may be equally opposed to the truth about the question-laden, risk-taking person, but the relativistic alternative has the advantage that nobody gets hurt.

The free individual surrenders the subject's adventure of the uncertain pursuit of the truth and caring harmony with other people. It's not worth the risk; it's more trouble than it's worth. Out of fear of perpetuating useless conflict, he rejects the civilizing inheritance of his culture. His pride is to be so self-sufficient as to have absolutely transcended the need for culture. He retains the right to have any opinion he pleases about his soul, and he accords that right easily to others. Anything anyone knows about the soul, he adds, is both incommunicable and dangerous to communicate. For the contemporary individual, to have rights is to have the freedom to be securely imprisoned in one's own private fantasies. The soul is no longer a subject for human conversation. Anger at the destruction of particular human beings, Delsol acknowledges, caused by religious and ideological human ideals is legitimate. Destruction ran amok like never before in the twentieth century.

Today's defenders of human rights devote themselves to protecting what past idealism destroyed—the bare existence of human beings. We have to stop sacrificing present existence for some imaginary future, degrading this life for illusions about eternity or immortality. We have to stop thinking or doing anything that would cause us to sacrifice the security and enjoyment we can have now. The ontological question of who we are threatens the very fact that each of us *is* right now. We can't and don't have to know *why* each of us is irreplaceable and irreducible to do what we can to continue *to be* as material beings. The question of being, we now know, annihilates being.

So the free individual—allegedly certain of his rights—is supposedly free from cultural prejudices and dangerous conflicts over necessarily elusive meaning. He is perfectly free from the past to define himself for himself, to have his own, unique frame of reference, which he knows he can't impose on or even communicate deeply to others. He certainly doesn't bind himself through shared meaning or caring responsibility for a common world. He works to be connected with others only through voluntary contracts that secure his interests in order that truth, love, or duty don't cause him to surrender his own judgment. He aims to achieve completeness not by living in harmony with others in the world, but through emotional withdrawal. Because, he claims, his judgment is undistorted by social emotions or longings, he thinks clearly about what's best for him as an isolated, material being.

The individual's self-sufficiency means to free him from all dependency—social, familial, sexual, political, and cultural. Our perception of a need for common worlds comes from our awareness of our finitude; Socrates questioned others because he needed to know the answers to questions we share. The individual aims to experience no such needs. He even refuses to acknowledge his dependence on the institutions of the welfare state for the exercise of his freedom; those institutions exist, he thinks, as a matter of right, and he is free not to think about that to which he is entitled. Thinking of others exclusively in terms of rights spares the individual the tyranny of gratitude.

Delsol shows us in many ways that the individual's judgment that he can do it alone is mistaken. He is certainly wrong to believe that he could maintain even his sanity without a huge number of acts of caregiving from others for which he has not and could not have contracted and can't be understood according to the logic of consent. He is certainly wrong to believe that he doesn't owe others lots of the same sort of solicitous and generous treatment. He has deluded himself when he believes that human beings have evolved beyond the need—as finite, precarious beings—for collective ventures. The dependencies and duties connected with citizenship and war and churches and families have not really withered away. Political life, for example, is still with us, and it still involves the uncertain clash of different understandings of human meaning and the human good. Our irreducibly political world remains a dangerous place, and that danger is a price we pay for our freedom. It's just not true that we can replace political communities with an abstract or reductionistic humanitarian moralism that will allow each of us to focus on enjoyment or private fantasies in security. That could only happen if death or self-conscious mortality withered away, but then we wouldn't even need to be talking about rights.

Evidence of the individual's greatness is his inability, despite his best efforts, to identify himself and so be satisfied with his merely biological being. He thinks he knows for certain that the death of his body is the end of his being, but he still can't reduce his being to his body. By being discontent with his material being, he shows he is more than a material being. If he were a merely biological being like the other animals, he would be immersed in the social, gregarious life we see among the dolphins and chimps. He wouldn't be repulsed by his contingency and inevitable bodily demise.

The individual's solitary utopianism is, in fact, contrary to nature and potentially a threat to the future of the human species. He can choose to devote himself to losing himself in private fantasies rather than do his social and reproductive duties to his species. Chimps do nothing to try to make themselves eternal or immortal, and contemporary individuals may be the first members of our species to be chimp-like in that sense. In another sense, however, they're less chimp-like than ever: The birth dearth that plagues Europe is evidence that they're choosing for themselves and against their replacements and so their species, and chimps are incapable of doing that. Contemporary individuals aren't, in fact, free of the human longings that produced eternalizing delusions. The individual, unlike the chimp, has freed himself from some delusions only to fall prey to others.

All the individual really claims to know is that his being (which depends on but is not only his biological being) is the opposite of nonbeing. He thinks he can free himself from every form of dependence but dependence on his body. So he can't help but hate his body and everything that reminds him of the limitations it imposes on him, and he can't see anything good or wonderful in his experiences of limitation. He lacks the resources to give himself any meaning or positive content beyond avoiding personal extinction.

The individual's mirror, as Delsol says, reflects no image. His emptiness is the foundation of the kind of subjection most characteristic of our world. The empty self is really a kind of lobotomized subject who fantastically refuses to be moved by what he really knows. Being lobotomized means being and not being diverted. In one sense, the individual never takes his eyes off the terrible truth he knows about himself. In doing everything he can not to be moved by it, he remains moved by it. The lobotomy never really quite takes.

Recent experience suggests, Delsol observes, that without some conception of eternity or immortality or measureless time human beings can't think of themselves as the irreplaceable and immeasurable wholes they really are. The individual has shown us that as soon as the categories of immortality or eternity disappear human existence becomes fragmented. Individuals abandon the idea of a lifework that is a testimony to their integrity. People used to think that some image of them remained in the mirror, so to speak, even after their bodies disappeared from view. But the individual lacks the resources to generate an image to leave behind. Because he refuses to think of his life as a whole, the individual lives, in a way, through a succession of disconnected deaths. Each of his successive, disconnected projects or "lives" is much more fleeting than the life of a person or subject.

It's the individual's terrified inability to believe in anything beyond himself that's the cause of his increasingly ephemeral existence. He's increasingly defined in some ways by his materialism—by health, safety, comfort, and material productivity, although he finds no enduring satisfaction in material pursuits. He certainly has the right to but lacks what it really takes to engage in independent thought. When all alone with his thoughts, he experiences paralyzing vertigo, and so he's all too ready to work to lose himself in a fashionable crowd. He swings incoherently between his proclaimed relativistic indifference to truth and craven submission to public opinion. His relativism—a reflection of his fragmented inability to find himself or a personal point of view—affords him no protection from either enervating materialism or the reigning moralistic dogmatism. Whether in a relativistic or a moralistic mode, he, Delsol observes, suffers from a deteriorated relationship with the truth.

Productivity vs. Caregiving

All the individual has to escape dogmatic relativism is the solid ground of measurable productivity as described by economists. Because his self-content is a meaningless private fantasy, the individual can't resist the impersonal and anonymous conclusion that everything real about him can be measured. There's nothing more to him that really deserves to be honored or recognized by others. Our dignity or "public worth," as the individualist Hobbes says, is in our productivity, our ability to be of use to other individuals.[8]

Not so long ago, the activities connected with production were pretty much confined to men, and caregiving was for women and priests. Once medicine, for example, became an intellectual and obviously productive activity—about the real business of saving lots of lives—it became the province of men who got paid for their work. Providing for the basic needs of vigilance, care, friendship and patience—what we all need—seemed to require no official knowledge or special competency. The results of their work were characteristically neither visible nor measurable—or not, strictly speaking, results at all. What caregiving requires and provides can't be captured by the categories of time and profit. Its solicitude and generosity is expressed in an infinite number of simple, personal gestures.

It used to be understood that the seemingly boring and easy work of the caregiver goes unpaid because it's priceless. The sphere of giving and gratitude can't be reduced to the sphere of contractual exchange. It was possible for women and priests (and nuns) to live well enough without wages or even much personal recognition because of the irreducible importance accorded to the activity of caregiving.

Caregiving, finally, is in its way infinitely more important than mere production, because it is more personal. Delsol explains that the seeming banality of the world of caregiving readily connected with the profound wisdom of religious spirituality. The middle-class man achieved his productive accomplishments at the expense of some disconnection from both the mystery of the personal goodness of ordinary life and the mystery of God. Because there's little mysterious about what works in business and politics, it's easy for those occupied there to forget the mystery of human being.

Surely Delsol's eloquent praise of the personal caregiving of the past must qualify what she generally says about the premodern world. The caregiver didn't regard herself as primarily part of some group or external whole. She was a person who served particular persons. The activity of caregiving is evidence that there's always been personal reality, and spiritual life has always had a personal dimension. That caregiving and spirituality became more personal with the coming of Christianity is surely true, as is the fact that their deterioration is an understandable consequence of modern depersonalization. The unique and irreplaceable activity of the ordinary caregiver must at least qualify the thought that the person or subject must be a dissident. The devoted caregiver is evidence that total immersion in the details of ordinary life might, in fact, be more personal in certain ways than dissident heroism in the face of uncertainty. The ordinary caregiver and the dissident are different manifestations of the complexity of being a person, different ways of caring for the human beings we actually know and love.

Delsol doesn't deny for a moment the advantages of women having the opportunity to enter the productive worlds of business and politics. Excluding them from productive activities was an unjust denial of some their real personal capabilities, but the price of that progress has been the effort to turn caregiving into paid work and redefine human value in terms of measurable results. The new distinction is between being paid and being idle, and there's no dignity in merely being idle. More and more people who aren't productive and can't pay are left out in the cold—delinquent children, the lonely elderly, and all who are poor and vulnerable. The truth is that people—mistakenly thinking of themselves as solitary individuals more and more of the time—are in many ways more lonely and so more in need of the solicitude of caregiving than ever. What they most need is held in more contempt than ever.

It makes no sense, of course, to speak of a human right to caregiving. Our undeniable crisis of caregiving is a key piece of evidence of the impossibility of orienting ourselves around human rights with no thought about who we are. The individual mistakenly believes that it's undignified to devote one's life to caring for persons or the institutions on which persons depend. Without that devotion, of course, depersonalization extends even to the raising of children, who go unformed or uncivilized as anything more than productive beings.

Dignity and Original Sin

Thinking about the crisis in caregiving—the crisis in confidence that we really are more than productive beings—causes us to wonder to what extent the modern effort to detach the person from any specifically Biblical teaching is doomed to failure. Is it possible to become a person without some cultural determination by certainties presented by the Bible? The dignified person, to understand himself, must believe that good and evil are real and personal, and that the dramatic moral adventure of every human life is the inward struggle between good and evil. The Bible recognizes this through the myth of original sin. That sin was the result of the freedom given to each of us, and the possibility of sinning is part of what dignifies each of us.

Aristotle also thought, Delsol goes on, that human strife was rooted in human nature, and not caused by the absence of an institutional remedy such as communism. The mystery of freedom for believers was a source of philosophical astonishment for Aristotle. For Aristotle, the enigma of human freedom was the source of the inevitable conflict between partisans, and it was the source of the West's discovery or invention of political life. Political liberty—which is the exception in human history, as despotism or uniform imposition is the rule—has its foundation, for Aristotle, in the natural diversity of opinion and the uncertainty of any solutions. When writing about Aristotle and politics, Delsol makes it clear that the premodern world was not only about the imposition of opinion on people as parts of wholes. A lot—if not everything—about the free and responsible person was discovered with the philosophic articulation of man's political or partisan nature. Aristotelian political life, like the myth of original sin, aims to both protect and display true human diversity and liberty.

Modern thought quickly dismissed the idea of original sin as mere myth and the diversity of political life as a mere social construction. Evil itself was our historical creation and so could have a historical solution. Rousseau, among others, said that our original or pure natures were innocence perfected. So the idea of original sin is a slander against who we really are. We can reasonably work to eliminate evil from this world; the cause of evil can be located and scapegoated. We will be perfect—we will redeem ourselves—through our destruction of the bourgeoisie or the Jews. That Manichean, regressive distinction between historical guilt and perfect innocence is based on denial of the real complexity of every human person. The Rousseaueans and the Marxists divided us into angels and demons. That means they reduced everyone to less than he or she is.

The dignity of the personal moral struggle—the fact that it's an irreducible and irreplaceable part of each of our beings—is dissipated by unrealistic historical hopes of bringing it to an end. Under communism, finitude and precariousness will not distort human experience, just as they didn't distort the experience of Rousseau's unconscious or perfectly undignified natural man. Under communism, the life of every human being will be as pointless or weightless as those of the other animals. Actually, human lives will be more meaningless still; they won't even be social beings instinctually doing our duty to the species and serving a natural end.

The genuinely self-aware person/subject thinks that he is the author of what he does. He is capable of being both good and evil, and so he can't reasonably blame society or some collective conception of responsibility for what ails him. Only the facts that we're never entirely innocent nor entirely dependent on forces beyond our control allow us to claim the high status of subject. We're all given the dignified capability to approach personal perfection but we can never actually attain it.

Overcoming Manicheanism, Delsol concludes, requires the recovery of the postulate of an original evil that's part of our dignified condition as free—and so self-consciously finite and precarious—beings. It requires certainty concerning the ubiquity of good and evil. That postulation or certainty, it seems, would require something like Christian belief in the reality of the person—including, of course, personal conscience. Can we say the anti-Communist dissidents had at least that much certainty, even without belief in Christian revelation? For them, the myth of original sin was a reflection of who we really are, whether or not the Biblical account of creation is actually true.

Personal vs. Impersonal Theology

Delsol says that persons make a claim for uniqueness because they die as unique beings. But she also doubts that self-conscious mortality is really enough to sustain the person's truthful self-understanding. Delsol claims that the Biblical religion—the religion of personal transcendence—really saved the unique person by extending his unique existence eternally. That belief supported the emergence of the idea of personal conscience and personal responsibility, and the emergence of the modern subject.

The personal religion of the Bible, she explains, was an indispensable contribution to progress toward a true understanding of who each of us is. Personal theology showed us and gave us confidence in the reality of a conscious and responsible person as a whole or integrated being. Even Aristotle's God was a principle, not a person. Aristotle's impersonal theological suggestion is that, finally, each of us is an anonymous part of some natural whole. His astonishment at the moral phenomena of good and evil was subordinated to an impersonal idea of eternity that had no place for our moral pretensions.

The Biblical personal relationship between man and God preserves the real integrity of both persons. God and each man know and love each other as persons; neither surrenders his personal identity or judgment to the other. The real question for Delsol is whether our faith in the reality of the human person can survive our skepticism or denial of the reality of the divine person. Can our faith in the human person—and so our confidence in the inalienability of human rights and human dignity—survive without anyone to guarantee what we can't provide for ourselves—continued personal existence after biological death?

Delsol says that the abandonment of personal theology was a key error of the Enlightenment. The human person was left all on his own, without any support from natural or divine reality. With the eighteenth-century advent of Deism, God, once again, became an impersonal principle. The eternal, mechanical laws of nature replaced the providential, personal God. Nature's God, unlike the Biblical God, doesn't care for or even recognize the reality of persons.

We might want to say that the Enlightened return to Aristotle's impersonal science of nature was on behalf of the truth about the subject as questioner. Certainly any belief in a personal God is, at best, uncertain and faith-based, and the modern subject takes no certainty on faith. Delsol herself says in one place that belief in personal eternity devalues the real existence of persons in this world. We should care for persons as we actually know them, and not think of them as more or less than who they really are. We shouldn't sacrifice the precarious beings who live in time to any illusory conception of their immortality or eternity. Thinking of them as more than who they really are keeps us from caring properly for them as they are, from living as well as we can in the only world we really know.

So it might be possible to say that the Enlightenment skepticism concerning the personal God was in the service of real persons. The premise of the personal, providential God is one way among many we express the fact that we can't help but find our precariousness repulsive, that we can't help but long to be more than who we really are. The person or subject surely aims to overcome that aversion in the name of living in light of the truth. Like Socrates, the modern subject, it would appear, should affirm the truth that, despite our best efforts, we don't yet know whether or not particular persons survive biological death. Our view of personal dignity can't depend on aggressively asserting with certainty what we don't really know. Surely our unique, irreducible irreplaceability can't depend on personal immortality. Doesn't it depend, as Delsol sometimes says, on our knowledge of personal death, which is actually compromised in those who don't believe that biological death is real?

Delsol can readily respond that the Enlightenment return to impersonal theology doesn't really serve what we can't help but know. As a theological view, it is a dogmatic assertion about death ending the reality of the person and about God and nature being intransigently indifferent to the person's very existence. The theology of "Nature's God" returns us to the pre-Biblical or Aristotelian thought that the person is unreal; from the perspective of the truth about human dignity, it is regression. The (we Americans say) Lockean individualism of the Enlightenment seems to make the person or individual responsible for creating himself out of nothing—for literally doing what the Creator allegedly did. Scientific (for example, Darwinian) doubt about the very reality of the person came from the complete disconnection between the alleged experience of personal freedom and what we know through science and even theology.

The Enlightenment theology, from this view, seems to be a spin on the Aristotelian observation that particular human beings want to be important or dignified, with an implicit denial that they really are who they want to be. It's no wonder that the Enlightenment so readily morphed into a full-scale rebellion against human finitude. The relentless impersonality of Nature's God is the cause of fanatical historical and technological efforts to defeat death or achieve immortality through our own efforts. And those efforts, of course, were undignified denials of the real foundation of our dignity. Impersonal theology is one cause of the individual's inability to find personal content.

The effect of the death of the personal God wasn't to free the human person to be who he is. It turned modernity in the direction of depersonalization. The subject, freed to be wholly on his own, was free for his individualistic dilution and even pantheistic disappearance. The post-Christian modern theology, Delsol explains, is pantheism, the perfectly egalitarian version of impersonal theology. Personal claims for uniqueness or distinctiveness are abolished through dissolving the person's existence into a whole that is somehow both homogeneous and divine. We are all indistinguishable parts of the One which is all of being. Pantheism completes the victory of modern equality over modern liberty by revealing that we are nothing more than parts of an undifferentiated whole. Our New Agey, sort of Asian pantheism is the logical culmination of the victory of modern impersonal science over the pretensions of free persons to be able to sustain themselves all alone in a hostile environment.

The self-effacing oneness of pantheism, of course, is really one display among many of the fearful flight from the truth about the self or the person. Pantheism gives meaning to death as the decisive abolition of the illusions that produced the misery of personal alienation. I am absorbed into the sacralized or divinized whole of which, in truth, I was always nothing more than a part. Pantheism actually claims to abolish the reality of personal death. Because the divine matter of which I am composed can be neither created nor destroyed, what I really am is really immortal. I can become a dolphin or tree as soon as I surrender the illusion that the "I" that I am now will not really be the dolphin or the tree. The only thing that stands in the way of affirming pantheism's truth is the illusion that the self or subject is real, that I am different from and greater than a dolphin or a tree. The emergence of pantheism, deep ecologists say, is a natural antidote to the individual's unsustainable effort to free himself from his natural dependence.

Pantheism, it seems to me, is pretty much a failed lullaby for modern individuals. The individual lacks the resources to be his own whole or have personal integrity. But the individual also can't think of himself as a part of a larger or greater whole. He depends on the dogma that his own death is the extinction of being itself. He can't lose himself in the private fantasy of a pantheistic reverie, even with the help of mood-enhancing drugs. He never doesn't know that the tree his matter becomes isn't really him. Modern science and, increasingly, modern theology denies the existence of the individual or person, but they can't eradicate the experience of the individual, which is based on what he knows about his precariousness and his finitude.

The pantheistic or even the Darwinian denial of his alienation from nature can't help but be incredible to the individual. He may be induced to pray to the One, but he still knows all too well that he himself is or at least aspires to be the One. His failed attempts at self-denial are the products of his inability to achieve either successful self-creation or self-destruction. Pantheism reflects both his longing for regression and his longing for immortality, both of which appear to be natural results of what we really know about ourselves. It goes without saying that neither the Deistic God nor the pantheistic One can save anyone in particular. The individual also, of course, does not have the cultural resources to generate the personal self-discipline to experience the complete self-negation that might be the real experience of a true Buddhist.

Because individuals still exist, Delsol says, they still demand human rights, and the real problem with pantheism is that it makes no sense of such claims. Delsol says that any claim for human rights has to be based on some understanding of the human being that persuasively defends his claim for irreducible uniqueness and irreplaceability. No theology denies that claim more radically than pantheism. Delsol follows Tocqueville in holding that a society full of undifferentiated beings who surrender their liberty—especially their intellectual liberty—to the impersonal, schoolmarmish authority of a meddlesome bureaucracy and/or the anonymous authorities of either public opinion or popularized science would be well served by pantheism.[9] So pantheism would appear to be the theology of the abstract universalism of the empty cosmopolitanism or the "humanitarian" or apolitical version of human rights. But if our goal is a society animated by free and self-confident persons or subjects, "the more appropriate partner would be a monotheism that preaches personal eternity, one in which each irreducible being survives in its irreducibility."[10]

What Delsol seems to mean is that those who want to encourage the emergence of the modern person or subject should choose what is preached about what occurs after death. Persons should be preached a certainty that's not, of course, self-evident. Religious and social/political/cultural choices are characteristically interdependent. Delsol doesn't want to say the religious choice is prior to the social or political or vice versa. She doesn't even want to say that religion should be judged only by its utility in preserving our devotion to inalienable human dignity. Social or cultural arrangements can be a product of human choice, but religion—the truth about God and all that—is surely beyond our determination.

Delsol might say that all cultures have been based on some preaching about man's transcendence of his merely biological or temporal existence. The person/subject knows that such transcendence is real; he can see that the self-consciously finite and precarious being exhibits a dignity or greatness that can't be reduced to the impersonal laws of science. Impersonal science can't account for the mystery of the reality of the human person. Whenever we deny the real existence of that person, we always speak unempirically or abstractly. Those who have said that human beings are merely one part of nature among many or merely part of some social or political whole have always been wrong, although the full understanding of that truth was only made possible by the coming of the personal God of Biblical religion.

The literal belief in personal survival of death is uncertain; anything we say about what happens after death is, for the Socratic questioner, speculative. But that belief reflects what each person in a genuinely personal or dignified culture should think, with plenty of evidence in this world, about his or her unique and immeasurable irreplaceability. Our own experience suggests in many ways that it's more credible than the impersonal theology of "Nature's God." Some persons will always live a somewhat dissident distance from any particular cultural certainty, but they can still affirm it as a more adequate representation of who we are than the theological alternatives. It's inhuman and undignified to feign indifference to the answers to the theological questions we can't help but raise.

The ontological issue, it turns out, that would have to be resolved for human rights to be rooted securely in a truthful account of human dignity is whether there's a foundation for the human person in the structure of being itself. The contradiction between personal experience and impersonal theology or science may be the deepest source of modern instability, of why the person—or a culture devoted to personal flourishing—has not yet been born. Maybe both the dissidents and the most thoughtful of the Christians have shown us that the experience of personal dignity, thought through, makes personal theology the most credible of the uncertain possibilities.[11]

5

TOCQUEVILLE ON
GREATNESS AND JUSTICE

Two of the most fundamental tensions in human life seem to be between magnanimity and democracy and magnanimity and justice. Our vague but real awareness of these tensions is the reason that we democrats distrust claims for the greatness of particular individuals. We are repulsed by the inegalitarian or unjust tendency of the great-souled or magnanimous person to privilege him- or herself over others. And we notice that historical circumstances that seem to make great men happy—such as wars and revolution—make most people miserable. In a just society, maybe we would neither need nor want displays of individual greatness, and the great modern effort in pursuit of justice seemed to depend upon giving men especially concerned with displaying their political excellence less and less to do. That means, of course, the more spirited or manly a human being is—the more concerned he or she is with asserting his or her outstanding personal significance or greatness—the more the modern regime of egalitarian justice is going to frustrate him or her. And in fact, great human aspirations and great human deeds have not disappeared, although each may have become both rarer and more misunderstood. As the novelist Tom Wolfe has often portrayed, it's the nature of human beings to be concerned—with widely varying levels of intensity—with their status as individuals and to act in all sorts of ways to establish their personal significance even or especially in our officially egalitarian time.[1]

Nobody has considered with more relentless self-examination and political astuteness the place of greatness of soul in the modern, progressively more egalitarian world than Alexis de Tocqueville. Tocqueville discovered in himself many of the qualities and longings that Aristotle described in his classic description of the magnanimous man, and most of the personal shortcomings Tocqueville discovered in himself brought to the surface limitations or tensions in any understanding of human greatness, even Aristotle's. Despite what amounts to a claim for divine self-sufficiency, magnanimity is the quality of a human being, not God or even a god. Greatness is based on specifically human accomplishment judged by specifically human standards and even dependent on specifically human limitations. Tocqueville's self-criticism—which led to his choice for God's standard of justice over his own merely human standard of greatness—is already largely present in tensions and contradictions that Aristotle allows us to discover in the character he portrays. My purpose is to highlight certain of Tocqueville's democratic, Christian, and Socratic corrections of Aristotle's presentation of the magnanimous man's self-understanding. I can't do that without saying something about Aristotle first.

Aristotle's Magnanimous Man[2]

Human greatness, according to Aristotle, is the rational perfection of the spirited part of the human soul—the part of the soul concerned with one's own significance or excellence. Greatness or outstanding virtue is necessarily a point of personal distinction or pride; it's more than ordinary or commonplace or average or everyday. Greatness, first of all, distinguishes our species from all the others; even the chimps and the dolphins don't have our capacity to live rationally and excellently, and not even the chimps and the dolphins are that concerned with displaying and discovering their personal significance. Particular members of our species can be ranked according to their greatness, according to the magnificence of their personal accomplishments.

Aristotle describes the great-souled or magnanimous man as rising above the petty concerns of most human beings. He appears to be confidently conscious of his superiority, of his proud detachment from the inordinate pursuit of money, power, and security that characterizes most human lives. He takes pleasure in thinking about what he knows about his own greatness. It pleases him to think that *who* he *is* depends on himself alone. He does accept the honor or praise of others as the least he deserves, but he prides himself in not being overly concerned with it. He doesn't regard any external good—even honor or glory—as *the* point of *his* particularly noble life. This self-confidence is the foundation of what anyone can see is his noble demeanor. He scorns flattery and gossip; he is kind or not haughty to those beneath him, and he only defers to the opinions of others out of friendship.

Because he is in the decisive respect the most secure of men, the great-souled man gives remarkably little attention to his material security. Although he must be aware of the place of luck in human affairs, it pleases him to free his thoughts about his own excellence from any sense of contingency. His stable self-certainty is the cause of what might be his most admirable characteristic—his extraordinary ability to be unaffected by the inevitable vicissitudes of life. Because he doesn't think of himself as defined by his material existence, he readily risks his life. That's not to say his life is defined by risk-taking. There's no point to such courage except to display one's greatness, and such a display wouldn't be virtuous unless it were really needed. So the great-souled man wouldn't go into battle for light and transient causes, and he wouldn't wander in search of adventure like some soldier of fortune. He only engages in activities that will provide evidence of his *lasting* greatness. Because *he* in some sense endures, only such deeds are worthy of *him*. Because such deeds also need to be performed on a scale that corresponds to his greatness, it would seem that he would only act to somehow save the whole community or even the whole world from ruin. His great deeds might have to even be indispensable for the community's salvation—the greatness of Lincoln or Churchill.

The great-souled man regards himself—always with evidence—as the greatest of benefactors. The greatness of the good that he does can in some measure be comprehended and so honored by others, if not so much the experience of greatness of soul that is at the foundation of his activity. But the great-souled man refuses to acknowledge that his greatness actually depends upon this or that deed. It certainly doesn't depend on his success, even if some failure deprives him of the honor which is his due. He's not tyrannically enslaved to some desire for recognition. So his self-conception and his judgment aren't distorted—or at least he doesn't become blindly angry—when insulted or slighted or otherwise misjudged. His true knowledge of his own greatness keeps him from either the anger or the overconfidence that would produce rash action. Because his virtue is real, reason remains in command.

For Aristotle, greatness of soul is a real human pleasure that corresponds in some way to real human accomplishment. Reason is able to confirm that the spirited assertion of one's own transcendent significance is more than mere vanity. Only a very few *names* correspond to beings worthy of being known and remembered for the splendor of who they *are* and what they've done. The experience of greatness of soul is real when it is enjoyed by a really great man—and such men really exist.

Because this experience reaches its height through the perfect cooperation of the rational and spirited parts of the human soul, it depends on neglecting or abstracting from anything that would disturb that cooperation. The experience of greatness of soul suppresses or ignores the erotic part of the soul, the part that reveals to us our dependence on and gratitude to others, our need for love and friendship, our incompleteness as solitary or self-sufficient beings, the perverse futility of all our striving for self-sufficiency, and our wondrous openness to the truth about all things, including other strange and wonderful human beings such as ourselves. An erotic being *is* one who is born and will die, and the great-souled man does what he can not to understand himself that way. He is, his critic might say, in willful rebellion against what he really knows about the necessarily ephemeral, contingent, and socially embedded and indebted character of his merely human existence. He may not exaggerate his greatness, but he likes to forget much of its source. By exaggerating the self-sufficiency of *his being,* he downplays the reality and the goodness of his natural sociality.

The magnanimous man finds it impossible to take pleasure in or even to acknowledge the goods in life that don't have their source or their cause in him, and he hates to think of himself as having received anything good from anyone else. It pains him to acknowledge who and what has contributed to his greatness, and he would, in fact, prefer to perform great deeds alone, or not with others, perhaps not even with friends. By neglecting what he owes and is owed by others, he is blind or indifferent to the demands of justice. He knows far too well he is owed much more than anyone can give him, but he doesn't even really think he owes his community the great deeds he performs on its behalf. He acts out of magnificent generosity—his greatness can't be required or commanded by others—and not out of justice. It's likely that he acts unjustly by ignoring or slighting the mundane duties that all citizens—including those who have benefited him greatly—share. Aristotle does say that the magnanimous man does to some extent live for his friends, but it's still hard to see why he would have friends and especially why he would enjoy them for who they are.

Despite all these unjust pretensions in the direction of self-sufficiency, the truth is that the great-souled man's standard of greatness is rather social. He assumes the truth of the political opinion that the most divine human activity—the one most worthy of prayer and praise—is benefiting others. He tends to think of himself as a civil theological god, while averting his eyes from the obvious conventionality and falsity of all civil theology. According to Aristotle, an utterly self-sufficient god would be completely indifferent to the affairs of men. He would be unerotic and uncaring, and without any reason to act. Divine perfection, from Aristotle's view, is pure thought; it is the characteristic of a disembodied being that exists apart from the social and moral world of action.

So the great-souled man imagines himself free from the constraints of his social and political world, while remaining stuck with being concerned about honor that he can't help but think he shouldn't need and is unworthy of him. Insofar as he must act, he's stuck with judging himself in some measure by the moral standards of others. He's stuck with some care for *who* other men are and *what* they think, although it doesn't seem that he really cares for, admires, or loves them. He both rises above and depends upon the judgment of ordinary men.

If he had any erotic openness at all, the magnanimous man would have some sense of the neediness that comes with this care. Aristotle reports three times that for the great-souled man "nothing is great." And, Aristotle adds, he's not given to wonder. Wonder, according to Aristotle, is the foundation of philosophy. It points the human being in the direction of something greater than himself, toward a perfection which he lacks and toward which he can both look up and is drawn. He doesn't share in the closest thing to humility in Aristotle's thought—the perception that human beings are not the greatest or most wonderful beings in the world. He's blind to both the wondrous greatness of heavenly order and how strange and wonderful most people are. He doesn't even wonder about himself; he takes his greatness as a given.

The great-souled man neglects the erotic dimension of his nature, in part, to avoid confrontation with the contradiction between his claim that nothing is great and the extreme—even if justified—claims he makes for his own greatness. Nothing is great, it pleases him to think, in comparison to his own greatness. So he lacks the crucial Socratic perception of the gap between his love of the truth and the actual wisdom that eludes him. Loving the truth—not to mention loving other people—ought to be a pleasure, but apparently it's overwhelmed, in the magnanimous man, by what it reveals to him about his own pretensions. Socrates, by contrast, is both erotic enough and courageous enough to think beyond the "who" or concerns about personal significance that animate the great-souled man to the "what" or the impersonal causes of all that exists. The drama of Socrates, in large part, is the anonymous truth being known by a particular person.[3] For the magnanimous man, it's far more important that the truth not be anonymous than that it be completely known.

So most of all the magnanimous man may not be given to wonder because he's not completely open to the truth about himself. He's unafraid to speak truthfully to others, but he dislikes completely truthful speech about himself. He's unlikely to be glad to get the gift of well-meaning criticism, even from those who love him. According to Thomas Aquinas, gratitude is the virtue that comes through acknowledging a debt of love, and no man should desire to be free from that debt—that is, unloved.[4] The great-souled man believes he would rather be free from what seems to make human life most worth living for most men and women. By confusing a part of virtue with the whole of virtue—because he is confusing a part of himself with the whole of himself—he is more aristocratic or conscious of his superiority and less democratic or conscious of his duties to and similarities to others than is reasonable. And although he clearly takes pleasure in thinking and hearing about his own greatness, it is very unclear that he's actually happy—or at least anywhere near as happy as a human being might be. By connecting his happiness with virtuous and honorable action, he implicitly acknowledges his mere humanity or some connection with others. By connecting his happiness with a kind of trans-social and trans-erotic self-sufficiency, he must to some extent experience the misery that comes with confusing oneself with a god.

In Aristotle's hands, all the criticisms that should flow from recognizing these human contradictions are ambiguous. They can't be resolved completely on the level of moral or spirited human action, and human beings are stuck with being spirited and with the need for great deeds. Human happiness necessarily includes some consciousness of one's own greatness or personal significance. Although it may not please him, Aristotle makes it reasonable to assume that the magnanimous man's self-consciousness inevitably includes some nagging recognition of his dependence on others. It is impossible, of course, to perform great deeds by or for oneself. Opportunities are needed for such action, and the magnanimous man can't really create them for himself and remain virtuous.

His dependence on political circumstances beyond his control is surely the source of his greatest frustration. What can he do if he's stuck living in a time when there's nothing worthy of him to do, a time in which human beings have no need of great, community-saving action? Nothing might pain him more—although he could never say it—than living in a time blessed with too much real justice—a time when it's best that he remain unemployed. Is it really possible for him proudly to sustain *himself* if nobody notices his excellence because he never has a chance to display it? Even the greatest men are surely unable to free themselves from all knowledge of the contingency of their excellence, and so from all anxious self-doubt. The magnanimous man may be able to bear bad luck better than most men, but Aristotle admits that it's unreasonable to believe that the virtuous man will be happy no matter what his circumstances might be. Aristotle acknowledges—even if he whispers for the sake of virtue—the fact that chance and contingency are characteristic of every human life.

The magnanimous man can, at best, be very imperfectly free from the need to act to establish his self-sufficient personal significance.

The inability to escape completely from something of that restless self-awareness is one reason why Aristotle attempted to show that his longing to be free from dependence points beyond itself to the way of life of the philosopher. Aristotle finally acknowledges that lives defined by moral virtue—even magnanimity—are merely human, whereas the way of life devoted to contemplation is the one that actually imitates the divine. God is characterized by a thoughtful self-sufficiency that produces a serene indifference to the affairs of men, of mixed beings composed of both bodies and souls. Insofar as we can genuinely imitate such a god through our transcendence of noble action in the direction of contemplative leisure, we achieve an unmixed form of happiness not available to merely moral and political men.

So Aristotle finally acknowledges that magnanimity is a characteristic of mixed beings aiming at a greatness that will remain somewhat beyond them, while adding that the pure pleasure of detached thought can also be experienced quite imperfectly by mere men. He causes us to see, of course, that the imperfect pleasure that comes with contemplation of one's own real greatness depends on our mixed existence. Genuine self-sufficiency would free us, no doubt, from the need to act but also from the real pleasure or pride that comes with the real performance of great deeds for beings who really need help. It would also free us from love. Aristotle certainly leaves us with the thought that thinking about the strange and wonderful magnanimous man—and spirited displays of moral virtue generally—are more a proper and pleasurable subject for human contemplation than the stars. In his view, it even seems that the best men are better and worse—and certainly more wonderful—than the impersonal god.

Tocqueville's Self-Examined Greatness

The human tensions and contradictions in the self-understanding of the great man are one of Tocqueville's explicit themes. He is less concerned about portraying some great-souled character than with *being* one, with understanding his own great but still merely human longings and accomplishments. Tocqueville's reflections on his own magnanimity are much more conscious and even ironic about the disproportion between his aspirations and his human reality than those of the character Aristotle described. He says he wrote to overcome the inevitable partisanship that comes with his concern for his own greatness through a relentless self-examination. He achieved enough self-knowledge to be able to choose justice over greatness, by being able to distinguish between his human perspective and that of the Creator.

Tocqueville's literary experiment for the primary purpose of candid self-examination was his *Souvenirs,* or his recollections of his political participation during the revolution of 1848. He employed a leisurely "solitude" he did not choose—he'd rather be in public life—to turn "my thoughts to myself." He discovered he enjoyed the "solitary pleasure of remembering great events," and so he was able to reflect and write only to please himself. That pleasure, more precisely, didn't depend on the opinions of others, but it did depend on who he was and what he did in the social context of political life. He discovered that his desire for pleasure caused his memory to be selective. It naturally gravitated to people and events that "have something of greatness about them" (3–4).[5] He had an "invincible curiosity," but not about everything, only about greatness (122–23, 257). It's not true for him, as it is for Aristotle's character, that he's not given to wonder and that nothing is great. He wonders about what is truly great, about manifestations of great human individuality.

Ordinary human beings and routine or "bourgeois" times, Tocqueville admitted, were too boring for him to remember. He admits that he can't remember most names and faces; in his eyes, most people don't really have names or personal significance (82–83). His theoretical curiosity for what people do, he admits, has a profoundly aristocratic bias. But that bias has its theoretical justification. It's only in great or revolutionary times that the full range of human virtue and vice displays itself (4). Greatness is rare but real, and it's impossible to really know human beings without seeing it for what it is. But Tocqueville is candid enough to add that the pleasure he takes in greatness requires his suspension of doubt. To distrust completely his selective perspective would make thought about human greatness—and so perhaps distinctively human happiness—impossible (62, 82).

Unlike the American democrats he describes in *Democracy in America* (2, 1, 1),[6] Tocqueville was no Cartesian—at least most of the time—when it comes to the pleasure of privileging manifestations of greatness of soul. He could even acknowledge that the only contemplation that gave him pleasure was of greatness; metaphysical and theological inquiry filled him with the misery of anxious, disorienting uncertainty about the nature and destiny of man. He could see, with Pascal, that political thought might, in part, be a passionate diversion from his misery in the absence of faith in God. But he would never acknowledge that it was only a diversion; he thought great men, virtuous liberty, and great political accomplishment were real. Great men exaggerate the effects and the goodness of their deeds, but exaggerations aren't to be confused with lies or complete self-deceptions.

We can say, at least on the level of self-presentation, that Tocqueville was much more Socratic than the Aristotelian character in the many ways he acknowledged that his obsession with greatness corresponded, in large measure, to his many human weaknesses, and in the way he really both wondered and was anxious about his own greatness. The reason that he wrote the *Souvenirs* for himself alone was that he knew that it was impossible for him to tell the truth and nothing but about himself or others in speech or writing meant for others. Great men find it impossible to display their shortcomings to others, and they aren't about to share their doubts even with their friends (80–81). Tocqueville is only able to tell himself that by nature he's both excessively proud and full of self-distrust. His passion for greatness corresponds to his "innate" weakness of extreme anxiety about his status or significance as a particular man (230), and he acknowledged that even his solitary judgments are suspect, given his self-partisanship (80–81). His primary fear, he admits, is that he might, in truth, be lacking in distinctiveness or greatness, that his life is merely petty or insignificant (231). Nothing disturbs his "peace of mind" more than threats to his pride. His "pride," he acknowledges, "is as nervous and restless as the mind itself" (84). He claims to be less afraid of danger than of doubt—doubts about *who* he is and *what* he should do. A shortage of self-confidence more than a "weak heart" is what immobilizes him in political life most of the time (84–85).

A revolution that reduced society to a "wretched state" and made most people miserable made Tocqueville happy. It gave him what he most desired—self-confidence. There was, in his mind, "no room for moral hesitation," and his great virtue was suddenly clearly indispensable (84–85). A great man of thoroughgoing excellence and integrity was needed to help save the political community and maybe civilization itself! The opportunity to "rescue society," Tocqueville remembers, "touched both my integrity and my pride" (193). He remembers himself being called to near the center of the political stage for "the great personal consideration he enjoyed outside of politics," a greatness that transcended the doubtful partisanship of political controversy (187). And "consciousness of the importance of what I was doing" elevated his pride still more, making him more "calm and tranquil" in the midst of revolutionary chaos than he was during a middle-class time of calm and tranquility (231). He was calmer because he was both more self-confident and no longer morally and politically isolated (46, 47, 222).

But even about his opportunities for great deeds Tocqueville was capable of irony. He admitted he enjoyed a touch of danger, but not too much—and certainly not actually fighting (106, 157). And he himself was never overwhelmed by the seething "chaotic anger" that produces revolutionary brutality (145). We can say that mere courage was far from the whole of virtue for him; he needed a political stage on which to display all his immaterial or moral and intellectual greatness.

The revolution gave Tocqueville an opportunity to prove his indispensable personal significance both to himself and others. He admitted that his self-esteem depended on the esteem of others, or that at least he benefited greatly from their recognition. So he cared about it more than is reasonable and sulked when it was not forthcoming (83–84). He acknowledged that he didn't get or even deserve such recognition in the middle-class or bourgeois, parliamentary regime that was toppled by the revolution. There he was both very isolated and very ineffective. To succeed he would have had to make nuanced calculations and detailed compromises among a variety of morally dubious interests, as well as take a genuine interest in the men who advanced those interests. He thought both the men and the choices to be made were unworthy of him, and he couldn't focus his attention well enough to be confident he really knew what he was doing. And in his unappreciated isolation, of course, he even doubted who he was (81–83).

So Tocqueville was not confident enough to withdraw from a political world where his greatness was unemployed. Because his passion for greatness couldn't be detached from his passion for recognition, he always took advantage of any political role—however petty—that came his way. He was always plagued by anxious misery—personal and "metaphysical"—with nothing political to do. When he was completely denied a place on the political stage—and only then—he wrote books about political life in the service of a future with a worthy place for great men like him. His books are always thought in the service of greatness, and that mixture of theory and practice always limited and directed his curiosity.[7] He, with good reason, tended to think of them as singular contributions to the perpetuation of human liberty—displays of a rare form of redemptive excellence characteristic of magnanimity.

Tocqueville admitted that his contempt for ordinary or middle-class political life was unjustly exaggerated; he couldn't view it from the perspective of the happiness it provided for most men. There is much to be said for a society that was only "corrupt," but not "cruel" and "bloodthirsty" (36). Although he couldn't remember them, the truth is that just about all men have names and a personal significance slighted by his selective vision. He could only acknowledge in passing that there might be something good natured even, or especially, in some of the most dull-witted of them. The simplicity of natural goodness rarely—if ever—impressed Tocqueville. The name he gives to the one person he describes with such a character—"Eugene"—is all too clearly a generic reference or not a particular person's real name (157).

Tocqueville's partisanship on behalf of greatness was both somewhat unrealistic and somewhat unjust, but it also had the theoretical merit of revealing the indispensability of greatness even for securing justice. The bourgeois rulers, he showed, were wrong in believing that government could be reduced to an amoral, impersonal mechanism, and the socialists were probably even more wrong to believe that political life could, in justice, just wither away. The coming of revolution was evidence that probably every effort to dispense altogether with greatness and great men is bound to fail, although the unprecedented nature of events in his time was enough for Tocqueville to lack confidence about the human future. There's enough truth in his magnanimous perspective for him to have spoken boldly and truly that "the real cause, the effective one, that makes men lose power is that they have become unworthy of it" (14). Tocqueville remembers that the bourgeois King Louis-Philippe's "profound disbelief in virtue . . . clouded his vision," keeping him from seeing both virtue's beauty and its utility (6).

Still, Tocqueville's most important contribution to our understanding of greatness of soul is his clear recognition that it depends on human weakness. From Pascal, he learned that our greatness is intertwined with our misery. Tocqueville's passionate immersion in political life rescued him, only in part, from the anxious uncertainty that plagued him when his thought was detached from great action. His solitary pleasure that comes with thoughts of greatness is not the complacent, trans-erotic solitude of a self-sufficient or self-absorbed being. Certainly Tocqueville experienced none of the serenity of those who can connect divinity with pure thought.

Greatness of soul is characteristic of the being who is neither pure mind nor pure body, and our greatness can't be detached from—it is in many ways rooted in—our miserable awareness of our contingency. It is full of the contradictions and paradoxes constantly displayed by the being who, as Tocqueville says (again following Pascal), is the beast with the angel in him (2, 2, 16). For him, greatness is the ambiguously self-confident assertion of the spirited part of the soul allied imperfectly with reason in pursuit of evidence that one's existence is not merely insignificant, dispensable, momentary, and material. The magnanimous man needs to act and be recognized to quell the doubt that comes with the thought that one's own pride might be vanity—a thought shared by neither the beasts nor the angels, not to mention God. God doesn't doubt his own greatness; nor is he particularly concerned with it. But that doesn't mean, as Aristotle thought, that God couldn't be just or providentially concerned with the affairs of men.

Justice and Greatness in *Democracy*

Although it was written about a decade later, Tocqueville's candid account of merely human greatness in his *Souvenirs* actually explains his qualified and reluctant judgment in favor of democratic justice over aristocratic greatness at the end of *Democracy in America*. There he impresses us with the difficulty of judging what his book describes—

the movement of the world of men toward equality. He reports that his vision blurs—it is neither clear nor selective enough—and his thoughts vacillate—because they're shaped by more than one perspective. He is confronting the choice between judging by his own human standard and by that of the just and providential Creator (4, 2, 8).

Tocqueville's own standard is greatness or, more precisely, the delight he experiences in observing very great men. There seems to be little place for men such as himself in the emerging egalitarian world. There "particular persons" only do "small things," and general causes or impersonal forces explain far more of historical change and human behavior. That's partly because there are only a very few men with "vast ambitions," and because "[g]enius becomes rarer." More generally, life seems unelevated and unadorned; nothing seems great. The particular greatness of extraordinary individuals gets lost in the "universal uniformity" of the emerging world (4, 2, 8).

The near-disappearance of great men both "saddens and chills" Tocqueville. It's chilling to consider that men like him might have no future (4, 2, 8). That possibility might even call into question the claim that they ever existed at all, that human greatness ever explained what people are and do (2, 1, 19). The fate of men might always have been best explained by impersonal forces beyond anyone's real control. For Tocqueville, the unadorned or unmagnanimous life is worthy of neither his thought nor his action. He's both saddened and chilled by the prospect of a life not worth living by him.

Still, Tocqueville truthfully compels himself to think beyond his own partisanship. He admits, as he did in the *Souvenirs,* that the pleasure he receives from the spectacle of greatness is "born of his weakness," and so too is the anxious chill he experiences in its absence (4, 2, 8). It's impossible for a mere man to see everything, but he can admit that his passion for greatness determines what it pleases him to see. So the aristocratic partisan of greatness unjustly diverts his eyes from the poverty, cruelty, and ignorance that characterize most lives in aristocratic times. The choice of greatness over justice comes from attributing too much significance to his particular needs or longings, to his own particular existence, and to the importance of what men like him think and do.

Tocqueville explained that the aristocratic perspective that unjustly privileges great men even limited what "the most profound and vast geniuses of Greece and Rome could see." Their thought was too intensely particular "to arrive at the idea, so general but at the same time so simple, of the similarity of men and the equal right to freedom from birth." So they complacently concluded that it was natural that human greatness would always depend on slavery, that the many, out of necessity, would always live for the few. They readily diverted their eyes from the remedial injustice of slavery; even the philosophers who were born slaves were far from abolitionists (2, 1, 3).

"Jesus Christ," Tocqueville claims, "had to come down to earth to make it understood that all members of the human species are naturally alike and equal" (2, 1, 3). Jesus made us understand what was already and remains true by nature. God becoming man—showing his personal concern for every particular human being—was necessary to correct effectively the merely human preference for greatness over justice. All human beings are equally more than slaves to nature or their country or other human beings, and they are all equal under and equally not God. Tocqueville is not necessarily affirming his personal faith in the divinity of Jesus. The confidence that faith would give him would counter more effectively, it would seem, the greatness of his anxious doubt about his personal significance. But he does refuse to doubt either that man is great or God is just.

Tocqueville chooses the unlimited, undistorted perspective of the Creator-God of the Bible over that of the Greek and Roman philosophers. He explains that only that God can see all in both our similarities and differences (2, 1, 3); only an "all-powerful and eternal Being . . . see[s] distinctly, though at once, the whole race and each man." God so understood—as opposed to the indifferent, self-sufficient, and amoral god of the philosophers—is "the *creator* and *preserver* of men." Being a creature is the deepest source of "each man's" personal significance. Because he is the source of the being of each man, God's concern must not be "the singular prosperity of some, but the greatest well-being of all." From his view, the justice of democracy is its greatness, because all men have some greatness about them that deserves to be preserved. That doesn't mean, of course, that all men are equal in their actual displays of greatness. The partial truth of both aristocracy and democracy is preserved in the unlimited vision of the Creator. And only by "enter[ing] into the point of view of God" can Tocqueville see, in justice, the greatness of each particular man, what distinguishes or elevates him above the rest of creation (2, 4, 8; italics added).

We can say that the perspective of the Creator elevated Tocqueville above the partisanship of magnanimity in the direction of the true practical wisdom described by Thomas Aquinas. According to Thomas, there's a sort of virtue that allows the magnanimous man to know when he should employ his magnanimity, and when he should contain his impulse toward greatness in the name of reason and justice—"and so ultimately for true human virtue as well."[8] Tocqueville at his best wrote and acted to preserve the creature who could distinguish between himself and the Creator, as well as between himself and merely material existence. He employed his singular greatness to preserve the greatness that all human beings—or more clearly all human beings in democratic ages—share in common.

In God's eyes, Tocqueville concludes, what seems like decadence that wounds his pride is actually progress. But he still reserves judgment about the superiority of democracy to aristocracy. That's because God, in some measure, left our future in our own hands, or at least prevents us from knowing our future with any certainty. We're always drawn in one way or another to the errors of either exaggerating or denying our liberty, of regarding ourselves as angels or brutes. The truth is that "Providence has not created the human race either entirely dependent or entirely free," and there's still room for human greatness—for properly chastened magnanimous men—in preserving both greatness and justice. God certainly has given us no reason to think that we have no role in preserving ourselves as beings who know themselves as creatures. It's true enough that we can't turn ourselves into gods, but what distinguishes us as human beings from the other animals may or may not have a future. We actually can't be sure that the Creator, without our help, will preserve our greatness—which includes our need for justice—forever (2, 4, 8). By giving us the capability of being both great and just (and so not the necessity of being so), the Creator, for our own good, introduced all sorts of contingency both into our personal lives and into our collective future.

There's reason to doubt Tocqueville's real belief in the Creator-God of the Bible, and we might want to conclude that his references to him are ironic or instrumental in the pursuit of his real goal of perpetuating liberty understood as human greatness in democratic times. "In politics," he explains, "men unite for great undertakings," and the purpose of political life for him seems less the pursuit of justice or the common good than displays of great individuality. And he certainly distinguishes, quite undemocratically, between the "true friends of freedom and greatness" and most human beings, who would, if pushed, choose equality over liberty, choose, if even futilely, against their own greatness. Only a few men "adore" freedom and regard its defense as a "holy enterprise," and that love of greatness, by its nature, transcends every effort to understand human action as predictable and uniform. Tocqueville makes it clear that magnanimity remains a rare, beautiful, and indispensable human quality, and that even genuine devotion to justice isn't possible without it (2, 4, 7).

But great men have to acknowledge, in truth, that "there is no question of reconstructing an aristocratic society," although their "circle of independence" can be larger there. Their task has become "making freedom issue from the bosom of the democratic society in which God makes us live." God, it seems for the moment, is less just than willful, and he has imposed unprecedented limitations and challenges on the great. From that view, "those of our contemporaries who want to create or secure the independence and dignity of those like themselves," the great who want to preserve some room for the dignity of greatness, have no choice but to "show themselves to be friends of equality." So Tocqueville's seemingly rather selfless choice for God over himself might be a way of "showing" that friendship, although his guiding thought is not about God's justice but human greatness (2, 4, 7).

Even if that were true, his conclusion is still based on accurate observations about the superior comprehensiveness and truthfulness of divine justice to his merely human selective perception and privileging of greatness. Tocqueville never claims to love the Creator he describes, but reflection on his existence is indispensable for explaining why the great man's existence is not so different from that of most human beings that he can justly or reasonably claim that most human beings live for his benefit. Tocqueville concludes that a return to aristocracy is not even to be "wished," because it's unreasonable or unjust to sacrifice "the prosperity of the greatest number to the greatness of the few" (2, 4, 7). The greatness of the few is only legitimately employed to preserve the greatness—the human distinctiveness of partly free creatures under God—that the many and the few share. Because Tocqueville never makes the error of confusing greatness or any manifestation of political life with some perfection of the human soul, he never sunders the connection that unites all human beings under God.[9]

Greatness and Democracy

Tocqueville has to teach the magnanimous man in democratic times to be attentive to the greatness he shares with all his fellow human beings—the experiences they all have in common that elevate each of them above all else that exists. This education that reconciles greatness—in some measure at least—to justice is far from easy; it requires, as Tocqueville admits, a sensitivity for the strange and wonderful details in the lives of the seemingly ordinary that he himself, as a political leader, often lacked. The movement toward democracy, he explains, actually dispels the illusions that obscure the true, egalitarian foundation of human greatness.

Tocqueville describes the human effort to idealize existence or portray greatness in his discussion of poetry. Aristocratic poetry idealizes human beings by exaggerating their freedom from material existence for proud transcendence of nobility and contemplation. In a certain sense, Aristotle's *Ethics* is a form of aristocratic poetry. But egalitarian progress discredits aristocratic illusions—such as the ones that supported the serene self-sufficiency of the magnanimous man—and seems, at first, to empty life of all material for poetic adornment. The unadorned democratic human experience of the truth about himself is as someone "wandering" for a moment between "two abysses"; "man comes from nothing, traverses time, and is going to disappear forever in the bosom of God." Man, in truth, is the most "marvelous" being in the universe, full "of infinite greatness and pettiness" and all sorts of contradictions (2, 1, 17). The most poetic being who *really exists* is the unadorned human being. He's the one first described by Pascal, the purest of seekers whom Tocqueville presents as free from both aristocratic and democratic illusions (2, 1, 10).

Our always obscured but never completely absent awareness of the strange, wonderful, and somewhat incomprehensible truth about ourselves is really the foundation of human greatness, and our curiosity really is best directed toward the lives of those particular souls. Our existence is always between ignorance and knowledge, especially about ourselves. We know enough to be proud and anxious and poetic, but not enough to be condemned to wallow in fatalistic despair or ascend to divine wisdom and self-sufficiency. The truthful experience that constitutes our humanity is neither shared with the other animals nor with God. And it produces all sorts of human thought and action that, in truth, can't be incorporated into some materialistic system. All human longing for greatness—and all great deeds—are rooted in some way in our truthful and singular experience of contingency or particularity. Our greatness comes from the fact that we know that we are neither God nor merely one of the unconscious and species-oriented animals; we can't help but experience ourselves as individuals concerned with our less than self-evident personal significance.

The anxious, restless, and miserable concern self-conscious mortals have for their particular being is, by itself, a sign of human greatness. That concern is the source of our immaterial and even immortal longings and hopes, and it leads us to perform great deeds, deeds which are evidence, in fact, of our enduring significance. The characteristic democratic error is to pity excessively contingent beings between abysses by giving insufficient attention to the greatness of what such beings have done with what they know (3, 1, 1). Great human accomplishments and great human thought withstand the test of time far more impressively than particular human bodies do, and our proud and anxious desire not to be merely contingent and insignificant beings need not go completely unsatisfied (2, 2, 15).

If we really believe everything human is as ephemeral as particular bodies, then great thought and action may become impossible. The truth that nothing human endures is a self-fulfilling prophecy. People who believe that their existence is in some sense immortal or transcendent really do produce monuments of their greatness in both thought and action. The dogmatic opinion that nothing human is of particular significance really immerses a man in the present—or obliterates his singular concern with his own past and future that distinguishes him from the other animals—and keeps him from being moved by what he really knows (2, 2, 15–17). Perhaps the only thing of any real significance is the liberty—for great thought and action—given to members of our species alone. The only thing of real significance, arguably, is the drama of the human being moved to great thought and action by what he really knows about himself.

Tocqueville defends democratic greatness against the untrue doctrine of materialism—a perennial human temptation that is especially pernicious in democratic ages. Materialism, its defenders say, is useful because it gives people an appropriately modest conception of themselves. They say it dispels haughty illusions that make ourselves as more than we really are. But the truth is that the materialists see us as less than we really are—as indistinguishable from the other animals. And so materialism denies what we can see with our own eyes about our distinctively human behavior. The doctrine of materialism—preached by the materialistic scientist—can't incorporate the real existence of the being who knows, unlike any other animal, the truth about the way things really are. He proudly concludes that by capturing every other human being in his materialistic system he stands above other members of his species like a god. His pride is more unrealistic and more revolting than that of the aristocrats, who usually maintain some paternalistic human connections between themselves and those they rule and who in some ways acknowledge the distinction between themselves and God (2, 2, 15).

The doctrine of materialism suggests that members of our species are as readily controlled as those of the other species. It suggests the theory of what Harvey Mansfield calls "rational control" that would characterize the soft despotism Tocqueville describes,[10] a society in which human beings have docilely surrendered everything great about themselves—any thought or action with the future in view—in favor of an easygoing security or contentment engineered for them by schoolmarmish despots armed with materialistic expertise (2, 4, 6). Partly because they aim to replace greatness with subhuman despotism, Tocqueville calls the materialists the "natural enemies" of any democratic people (2, 2, 15).

Tocqueville's other fear about the pernicious consequences of materialism, the one confirmed by American experience, is that belief in the doctrine of materialism will cause Americans to pursue material well-being with an "insane ardor" (2, 2, 15). That insanity of such diversion, of course, is not characteristic of any other animal and is actually proof that members of our species are more than material beings. The Americans are often miserable because they can distort but not eradicate the needs of their souls (2, 2, 12): They often make the mistake of believing that those needs can be satisfied through material success, partly because they half-consciously believe much of the time that their real longing is for a greatness beyond material determination that can't be satisfied (2, 2, 13).

To Tocqueville, the Americans display their greatness as beings full of contradictions through their obviously incoherent thought and action. The particularly ambitious among them readily risk their lives to better their material self-preservation (2, 2, 18). They proudly display their contempt for the life they work to preserve. They both do and do not identify their beings with their bodies. They, with some justice, lack the serene self-confidence of the magnanimous man who knows that he *is* more than a material being. The magnanimous man neglects the fact that his longing for transcendence has its roots in his perception of his contingency, and the American neglects that fact that his singular perception of contingency can be the source of real transcendence.

Tocqueville certainly shows us the incoherent greatness in the Americans' moral doctrine of self-interest rightly understood. The Americans brag about their self-sufficiency—about their freedom from natural instinct and each other. Their pride in their enlightened liberty is displayed in their explanations that what appears to be self-sacrifice on their part is not really self-sacrifice at all. They both transcend the natural world of animals and proudly refuse to be pawns in the hand of others by turning every moment of their lives over to calculation about their own interests (2, 2, 8). But they calculate about material enjoyment, about a purpose all the animals share!

Their incoherent doctrine—if it really governed their whole lives, as they brag—would turn those lives into hell. They would always be thinking about how to enjoy, but never take time to enjoy. It is impossible to have a doctrine that both does justice to the human longing for free or transcendent self-sufficiency and identifies human happiness with material enjoyment. The secure reduction of happiness to such enjoyment (as Rousseau explains) is given only to the animals unaware of their contingency and so unconcerned with their personal significance (2, 2, 16).

Why does Tocqueville seemingly strongly affirm and only gently criticize the incoherence of the *moral* doctrine of self-interest rightly understood? It's because he notices that the Americans *are* better than they *say*. The American boasting about his freedom hides the offense against freedom or self-sufficiency that is the human happiness he really does enjoy. Americans often give way to their natural impulses to love and be of service to others (2, 2, 8). Despite their individualistic talk, they often act and think like parents, spouses, children, neighbors, citizens, and creatures. They explain away the fact of their social involvement in the institutions of local government, a wide variety of voluntary associations, the family, and the church with their doctrine. It's in their self-interest, they say, to build alliances through marriage (2, 3, 11), citizenship (2, 2, 4), and going to church, and it's possible, they claim, to even play let's make a deal with God (2, 2, 9). But the truth is that, despite their perverse pride in their self-interested liberty, they come to know and love each other (2, 2, 4) and God (2, 2, 9).

Tocqueville presents the Americans as far more successfully combating than succumbing to the democratic "heart disease" of individualism or indifference to the lives of others. Like the character Aristotle describes, the American tends to describe himself as an extremely self-involved and unerotic being, but what he says is far from true either about his real personal experiences or what he actually does. A danger Tocqueville shows us, of course, is that what they *say* may gradually transform who they *are,* and that's why he reminds us that Americans unrealistically disparage their capacities for both greatness and justice—for all "great devotions"—by really believing their doctrine is true (2, 2, 8).

Middle-Class Magnanimity?

There's a more elementary way of expressing the Americans' contradiction: All the Americans attach themselves to worldly goods as if they'll never die, as if they know that their existence in this world is secure. But they pursue them in such a rush—and with such a feverish ardor—that they also seem convinced that they'll be around only a moment more. With fortunate circumstances that should be the foundation of unprecedented contentment and enjoyment, they're more restless and even sad than people ever have been. The good news is that they certainly remain too serious—and too lacking in playfulness or spontaneity—to be mere animals. The bad news is that their lives can appear to be evidence that there's no such thing as *human* happiness, and so Tocqueville reports that they sustain their liberty more as a matter of will than of reason (2, 2, 13).

Their pursuit of enjoyment is, most of all, really pursuit of self-sufficiency through the imposition of rational control on their material being. It is a confused display of materialistic magnanimity made possible by the illusion that they can look at their bodies and their needs from some undisclosed location apart from them and figure out how to satisfy them from there. They are less beings with material needs than beings with the freedom to work. Middle-class Americans define themselves as free beings who work (1, 1, 3), and as beings with interests (2, 2, 8). They see themselves as standing in a truthful location between aristocratic and materialistic illusions; they are different from all the other beings who exist because they are and know they are middle class. Their pursuit, they think, is more realistic or more effective than that of the aristocrats, while still being a proud manifestation of human liberty. It's hard to deny that the middle-class American does achieve more real security or freedom from contingency than Aristotle's character, although his confusion about who he is causes him to experience himself as progressively less secure. Arguably today's middle-class Americans are the most secure, anxious, and death- or contingency-haunted people ever.

Part of the justice of democracy is its elevation of work. Aristocrats said and to some large extent thought that, because of their greatness, work was not for them; they were fundamentally better than beings with interests (2, 2, 8). They inconsiderately believed they had no responsibility to make their lives productive. Their lives were mostly for leisure, and even their few great and glorious deeds weren't to be confused with what was required to meet ordinary human need. They proudly thought that their thoughts soared above any concern for increasing human prosperity or reducing human misery (2, 1, 10), and it didn't please them to admit that even they had to secretly give some attention to their material advantage (2, 2, 8). In general, aristocrats had an excessively proud or magnanimous understanding of their freedom from the ordinary work that must be done, because they had a very high opinion of their personal significance. It didn't strike them as unjust that most people were stuck with working for them.

America's middle-class democracy extends both freedom and the duty to work to everyone. Everyone, in justice, is free to work to sustain himself. No man is enslaved to another man's imaginary view of the nobility of freedom or leisure, and both not working for oneself (or not working for money) and not working at all become ignoble. The result, Tocqueville explains, is that "[i]n democracies nothing is greater or more brilliant than commerce." So it's in such productive activity that great ambition and talent usually display themselves, and Tocqueville remarks that the "greatness and audacity"—even the heroism—of American men of commerce is evidence of the contempt such ambitious men would have shown to chosen activities in aristocratic times (2, 2, 18). Magnanimity is displaced from politics and even philosophy into trade, industry, and invention, and the thought behind that democratic change is that nothing is more vital to particular people and the community as a whole than material prosperity.

The magnanimous man has always been stuck, to some extent, with serving some communal standard of excellence, with living for the perpetuation of the way of life of some people or another. In that sense, the magnanimous man has always been a being who works, and the magnanimous democrat who is honored for satisfying the people's vulgar and so real needs is less deluded than his aristocratic counterpart both about the claim justice makes upon him and the real source of his honor. People are surely happier if he is clever enough to satisfy their needs with "the arts of peace," as opposed to the arts of war, even if they are more disposed to honor warriors than entrepreneurs. As Tocqueville himself reflected, his preference for revolutionary over bourgeois life could only be completely coherent if revolution could be affirmed as an end in itself. His fear—from the perspective of greatness—that great revolutions will become rare in democratic ages actually expresses the intention of every modern revolution—to be the revolution that will bring revolution to an end (2, 3, 21).

The men of the twentieth century who affirmed permanent revolution were really in the thrall of "manliness run amok"; they believed that only the cruel, bloody frenzy of ideological war could save them from the modern abolition of personal significance in the names of equality, efficiency, and justice.[11] Fortunately for magnanimous men like Churchill, de Gaulle, Solzhenitsyn, Havel, and even Patton, the battles made necessary by the inhuman or antihuman ambition of those fanatics provided a basically unexpected but quite wonderful opportunity to display something like classical magnanimity, to defend a world where reason in some sense is comparatively in command. But nobody in his right mind would thank Lenin, Hitler, and Stalin for giving magnanimous men something great or even redemptive to do.

Maybe we can say that in *Democracy* Tocqueville underestimated—but didn't completely neglect (2, 3, 19)—the monstrous forms the longing of particular men for greatness would take against a world in which they believed they had no place. But we do see better than ever that "commercial greatness" deserves to be praised as having done infinitely more than Marxian revolutionary greatness in satisfying the real needs of people, and commerce really does give men "a high idea of their individual worth" in a way that "disposes them to freedom but moves them away from revolution" (2, 3, 21). The contempt of the great for middle-class life in the modern world too easily becomes contempt for the real conditions of human life itself. And we admire more than ever Tocqueville's manly and largely successful combat against that temptation in his own case.

That's not to deny that the aristocrat's contempt for the vulgar, material standard of productivity has plenty of advantages when it comes to greatness. Some people, in aristocracies, have the leisure to engage in political life for its own sake and others to pursue artistic, theological, literary, and philosophical greatness for their own sakes. And a weakness of democracy, Tocqueville explains, is that there's no way it can recapture fully the appreciation for greatness of the aristocratic ruling class (2, 1, 3). But, in justice, he can't really object to the democratic injunction that everyone work and find some honor and greatness in personal productivity. The middle-class error—or deficient self-understanding—is to view people as for work and *nothing more.* Our wealth, power, and economic and political freedom can't really either address or satisfy our deepest longings (2, 2, 12; 1, 2, 9). The middle-class way of looking at the world can neither comprehend nor allow us to live well with the true greatness of the being who is stuck self-consciously and even incoherently between the other animals and God. So democratic leaders should "attach less value to the work and more to the worker," thinking even of them as "great men" (2, 4, 7). American religion, Tocqueville explains, is in some measure an authentically middle-class antidote to the American middle-class mistake of seeing people as merely beings with interests.

Religion, Pride, and Greatness

Religion, Tocqueville says, is a natural response to the interrelated human experiences of contingency and greatness. That's because "alone among all the beings, man shows a natural disgust for existence and an immense desire to exist: he scorns life and fears annihilation" (1, 2, 9). Man, alone among the animals, desires to *be*. So he's disgusted with his merely momentary existence. His disgust causes him both to long to be and actually be more than a merely biological being; he can display his singular greatness, his freedom from material determination. But he can't free himself altogether from his body; great individuals, like the rest of us, die. This combination of both self-disgust and self-elevation *is* pride.[12] This anxious concern for one's personal significance, more than anything else, is the enduring foundation of religion. Religion, Tocqueville shows us, is the natural human response to the multiple dimensions of the human fear of *not being*. Americans, in Tocqueville's eyes, see it as providing help that human beings can't possibly provide for themselves in both chastening and supporting their magnanimous pretensions—the "manliness" they all possess in some measure or another.

Religion inspires in Americans the confidence that they're more than bodies, and it does so as a supplement to—not a replacement for—the middle-class view of the world. Six days of the week, Tocqueville observes, the American is immersed in the commercial and industrial life of his country. But on Sunday, he "is torn away for a moment from the small passions that agitate his life and the passing interests that fill it, he at once enters into an ideal world in which all is great, pure, eternal." On Sunday, he learns of the "lofty destiny" the God of "infinite magnificence" has given him; he has been made for virtue and immortality. And Christian sermons that rail against his pride actually sustain that pride against the secular, skeptical view that God, immortality, and disinterested virtue aren't really for a being with interests like himself (2, 2, 15).

Tocqueville explains that religion so understood is not to be praised for its political or even moral utility, but for what it does for the individual in opening him to the truth about his greatness that democracy on its own would deny or neglect. It would be very unrealistic and unjust for the Americans to turn every day into Sunday—into a day of rest and contemplation. Nothing would ever get done. But without a day of rest they might become so restless, disoriented, and perhaps finally deranged, that they would willingly end up surrendering their miserable and unreasonable liberty (2, 2, 12–16).

Tocqueville praises Christianity, as we have seen, for its egalitarianism. That praise, more precisely, is for its teaching concerning the immaterial greatness that all human beings share. It is the firmest foundation of the democratic concern with equality without the enervating democratic skepticism concerning the soul and its needs. It combines, properly understood, justice and greatness. So Tocqueville praises Christianity for preserving the partial but real truth about aristocratic pride in democratic times (2, 2, 15).

He is virtually silent about the Christian teaching concerning humility, because, in his opinion, a key threat to the future of greatness of soul is that particular democrats already think too little of themselves. The democrat, it's true, is proud enough to believe that his neighbor is no better than him. But the problem is his tendency to add that both he and his neighbor were made for no more than "vulgar pleasures," that they both are incapable of greatness of soul (2, 3, 20). In a sense their attraction to materialistic doctrine chains them, despite themselves, to an aristocratic prejudice about the way most people *are*.

Democracy tends to drag the great down to the level of the vulgar, despite its noble intention of universalizing greatness. Christianity, in truth, humbles men by showing them all that they're all equally not God, that even their greatest deeds are merely human and so finally unable to free them from all doubt concerning who they are. But it also raises them up by showing them that they are all creatures with souls or an immaterial dimension of existence oriented in the direction of the Creator. Christianity teaches that much of what the aristocrats inconsiderately regarded as merely vulgar, when viewed more attentively, actually is great (like Jesus and the virtues he extols). And Christianity serves justice while not obliterating greatness by connecting the greatness of the few to the greatness of many through experiences of limitation and elevation that all human beings do or ought to share in common.

The true Christian teaching is about the equal greatness or personal significance of every particular human being. But even if equal greatness is not quite an oxymoron, it does describe two qualities in tension. Even if Christianity is as egalitarian as a religion that distinguishes between creatures and the Creator can be—as a religion that sees the significance of particular individuals can be—it still is based on an inegalitarian privileging of human beings over the rest of the creation. It depends on an uncritical suspension of the democrat's habitual doubt about all immaterial privileging as a claim to rule (2, 1, 2). The rule of a personal God over all men, the democrat constantly suspects, is about to morph into the claim to rule by particular men over others on the basis of qualities of soul. A consistent democrat can't help but object to the residual magnanimity or aristocratic premises in the Christian view of the soul.

So the idea of a Creator or a just, personal God is endangered by the general trend toward impersonality or the tyranny of no one in particular of democracy. Christianity, the danger is, may well give way to pantheism. Pantheism is the perfectly egalitarian theology; everything and everyone become indistinguishably divine. So the human perception of the contingency of one's particular being turns out to be an illusion. The charm of pantheism, Tocqueville explains, is that it "destroys human individuality," or the experience at the foundation of human greatness. It both "nourishes the haughtiness and flatters the laziness of the democratic mind" (2, 1, 7). That combination of haughtiness and laziness flows from the virtually effortless comprehension of one's own divinity. There is no longer the need to think or do anything great, because everything and everyone is already as great as they could conceivably *be*. The purpose of the pantheistic lullaby is to extinguish the human longings that cause the human individual to resist being incorporated into some whole. The tyranny of the majority or public opinion or impersonal material forces is further generalized into the tyranny of the homogenous divine being.

Tocqueville concludes about pantheism that "all who remain enamored of the genuine greatness of man should unite and do combat against it" (2, 1, 7). Aristocratic lies encourage greatness; the extremely egalitarian or pantheistic lie aims utterly to negate it. Pantheism, as much or more than materialism, is a denial of the significance of the drama of the particular human life. Insofar as our religion today is moving away from the focus on the personal Creator and his particular creatures, it is no longer a real support for human pride or genuine experiences of magnanimity. According to Chantal Delsol,

> I would not hesitate to describe the climate that gives rise to pantheism as a wrong turn in the Enlightenment. . . . Human rights will not guarantee the dignity of each human being unless they are grounded in an understanding . . . that ensures his uniqueness. . . . If . . . one wants and hopes for democracy to be a society of unique persons endowed with free wills and minds, then the more appropriate religious partner would be a monotheism that preaches personal eternity, one in which each irreducible being survives in his irreducibility.[13]

Tocqueville writes of pantheism seducing democratic "minds," but not as successfully orienting the lives of whole human beings in democratic times. The linguistic therapy of an untrue and even ridiculous theology—even one that claims to satisfy the mind's real desire for unity—surely can't overcome in particular human beings the truthful experience of their contingent existence between two abysses. There is, of course, an irreducible human tension between the mind's pure desire to know and the particular being's concern for his or her own fate or significance. Pantheism, it seems, is really a failed form of self-help that can only intensify the reality of democratic disorientation or insane materialistic ardor through its futile denial of what we really experience of our particular souls. Pantheism seems, at first, the perfect antidote to the human fear of *not being,* but only if an individual can swallow the tale that he will continue to *be* after he's dead as part of some tree.

Pantheism is no real solution to the individual's anxious concern about his status or significance in a world where he experiences his contingency so intensely. Not many individuals (despite the generous and insistent efforts of many of our leading celebrities) are losing themselves with any great success in pantheistic or New Agey reveries, and people in general continue to be more restless or death-haunted than ever. The mind's love of unity or coherence, our materialistic scientist thinks, seems to be best satisfied through unrealistic denial of what anyone can see about human distinctiveness, but if we were simply minds (or for that matter bodies) we wouldn't truthfully experience our momentary existence. And without such experience—and our ability to love the strange and only partly comprehensible beings who share it, it seems to me we wouldn't be open to the truth about anything at all. The human mind, the magnanimous man rightly asserts with his "manly" view concerning the indispensability of *his* great deeds, isn't really self-sufficient at all.

In the final analysis, magnanimity is a far more realistic characteristic of the being open to the truth about all things—including himself—than either pantheism or materialism are. The Christians are right to inspire skepticism about magnanimity as a quality that makes the few fundamentally more significant than the many; all human beings are equally not God and are equally under God. But the democratic danger is that indiscriminate skepticism about all immaterial or transcendent human qualities will cause us not to be able to appreciate merely but really human greatness for what it is.

6

1968 in American Context

The year 1968 is pregnant with genuinely *political* meaning for both the French and the Czechs. But for the Americans, 1968 seems, in retrospect, much more simply strange and accidental. The year was full of televised violence—the Tet Offensive in Vietnam, the assassinations of Martin Luther King Jr. and Robert Kennedy, riots in the cities and outside the Democratic Convention—that seemed to discredit the various causes of the 1960s: the civil rights movement, the Vietnam War and the antiwar movement, and the movement of the young called the New Left. The year culminated with the election of a president, Richard Nixon, who in effect promised to bring all the violence, and the causes that inspired it, to an end. And Nixon did so, mainly by ending the military draft. Soon after 1968, the "revolution" in America was safely contained to college campuses.

In Europe, they speak not of "the Sixties" but of "Sixty-Eight," the year of the May events in Paris. In the American context, however, looking at 1968 in isolation makes the American 1960s seem nothing but a pageant of absurdity and destruction. But that is hardly a fair perspective. I have no choice, then, but to turn from an analysis of the year to an analysis of the decade to give a fair and balanced account of what was going on in our country forty years ago. Whit Stillman's insightful character Jimmy Steinway (in his novel, *The Last Days of Disco, with Cocktails at Petrossian Afterwards* [2000]) reminds us that reviewing human life in terms of decades results in "trashing" certain decades "for no very good reason." Those who wax nostalgic about the 1960s almost always trash the 1950s and the 1980s. There is, Jimmy notices, "actually a bit of *decade scarcity* in life, and so it's better to find something good in each of the few decades that make up your life." The 1980s, for example, might have been somewhat greedy, but Jimmy prefers to remember them "as years of hard work and maximum productivity." From the 1980s perspective, the 1960s were actually greedier, because people wanted to live well without working hard.

Before we praise or blame the 1960s too much, we have to remember that its liberationist excesses were an understandable episode of democracy in America. The 1960s actually seemed to prove Marx wrong; we capitalists were not, after all, sowing the seeds of our own destruction. The 1960s may, instead, have sowed the seeds of the destruction of communist totalitarianism. The Prague Spring, the attempt to construct "socialism with a human face"—which took place in 1968, and was inspired in part by the American 1960s—was violently crushed by a Soviet invasion. That was the end of the illusion that socialism within the Soviet empire could ever be reformed in accord with the spirit of liberty. Nothing that happened in America, or even France, came close to matching the genuinely revolutionary moment of 1968, which belongs to the Czechs.

Civil Rights and True Liberalism

I certainly have good memories of the beginning of the Sixties (when I was *very* young). The first was the election of JFK. It seemed as if American political life had been liberated from conservatism in the stereotypical sense—from its utter domination by white Protestants and business leaders with a tendency toward crabbed isolationism. To be a Democrat (and it seemed to me that all Catholics were Democrats) was to be all for unions, the family wage, and the pursuit of social justice through a quite minimalist welfare state. (In those days, the Republicans were the party of the Equal Rights Amendment; it was not a liberal, but a businessman's, idea.)

To be a Democrat was also to be fervently anti-Communist through a deep belief in the nobility of American purpose. Remember that Kennedy's inaugural address was civic republicanism run amok: doing for one's country took priority over everything else; government's point isn't to be merely ministerial to individual rights. The change Kennedy's New Frontier had in mind was emphatically not liberation for "Do you own thing," but liberation for the old-fashioned virtue of liberality—for being generous and dignified. (I'm obviously not talking about the ambiguous and even somewhat unremarkable reality of Kennedy's actual administration.)

If memory serves, the only genuinely political issue that inspired passion in the early 1960s was civil rights—meaning desegregation. The first and only political event I remember attending in that time (with my parents) was a very classy picnic at the Alexandria, Virginia, estate of a devout Episcopalian gentleman-lawyer from an old southern family. This man, Armistead Boothe, was widely admired as the heroic leader of those who opposed "massive resistance" to desegregation in the Virginia legislature. He was running for lieutenant governor and was narrowly defeated by the candidate of the "Byrd Machine." To us, the Byrd Machine seemed to be a corrupt alliance of business interests and segregationist fanatics. Opposition to it seemed noble, even aristocratic, a cause worthy of a dignified Christian gentleman. If Virginia didn't slowly desegregate on its own, Boothe warned, the national government would eventually make them do it in a ham-fisted way. The 1960s' "second Reconstruction" of the South was, in fact, caused by a southern failure of self-government. It could have been avoided had astute gentlemen like Boothe prevailed over demagogic populists like George Wallace.

This was also pretty much the message of what I remember to be the most edifying film of the early Sixties—*To Kill a Mockingbird*. Atticus Finch, who seemed to be a perfectly admirable Stoic southern gentleman-lawyer, used every rhetorical trick in the classical book but still failed to get a white jury to follow the law and acquit a humble and loyal black man. The cultivated aristocracy of the old South was no reliable check on the sometimes violently racist democracy of the newer South. Even Atticus, we can now see, was just too Stoic to devote himself to the pursuit of racial justice, to political equality for blacks (and women).

Maybe the worst feature of the decade as a whole was the pointless violence. One persistent piece of evidence for the basic health of American society, even during the 1960s, is that violence always aroused the politically effective anger of a silent majority. That was true of what happened on our campuses, in our cities, and at the 1968 Democratic National Convention. But it was first true about the segregationist violence in the South, especially in 1963. Until that year, the nonviolent "direct action" of the civil rights movement had not had much effect. But by mid-1964, tutored by the television nightly news, Americans were convinced that something had to be done to end southern lawlessness. That was the year that Congress finally passed civil rights legislation with real teeth, and the Democratic president who pushed the Civil Rights Act through won a huge victory over the Republican candidate who opposed it. One original intention of our Constitution and Declaration was fully achieved politically in our country in 1964 and 1965. All Americans were finally recognized as free, equal, dignified, and politically participating citizens.

The second Reconstruction was not only good for justice in the South but also good for prosperity. Air-conditioning and integration combined to produce the Sunbelt—the most "livable," entrepreneurial, and Republican part of our country. The 1960s transformation of the South was, like almost all social change, both good and bad. What was left of agrarianism and localism and the distinctively southern or aristocratic criticism of the excesses of American commercialism atrophied, and men like Boothe are now virtually extinct. Justice and prosperity took priority over personal love, communal tradition, and enduring personal significance. There are certainly good reasons to be repulsed by the wasteland of McMansions, megachurches, and big box stores that flourish better in southern suburbs than anywhere else. But there are also good reasons to appreciate the ways God (meaning churches), patriotism, honor, and manners persist, despite it all, in the newest form of the New South. We're moved by the interracial evangelical charity we see displayed in the film *The Blind Side*, and when ordinary southerners in their exurbs stand up in response to Lee Greenwood's classic country song about American pride and freedom under God. Those who say that America has become a wasteland of the displaced haven't been to the South lately.

Sexual Liberation

The civil rights movement seemed to set the precedent for subsequent forms of 1960s liberation. People, it seemed, needed to be liberated from all repressive classes and categories. Both sexual liberation and women's liberation proved more controversial and less effective than desegregation. Women, I hope, cannot help but notice that the movement for sexual liberation came first, and it was mostly led by men, allegedly on behalf of love. The Summer of Love (1967) was surely distinguished by a lot of casual sex, with bourgeois hang-ups like jealousy put on hold. But the cost of disconnecting sex from love was the trivializing of both. "All you need is love" might even be true, but love isn't much if it has nothing to do with what free beings do with their bodies.

Separating sex, or *eros*, from all repression means separating it from birth, death, and especially procreation. So the theorists of the 1960s celebrated polymorphous perversity. The real-world result was neither polymorphous nor perverse, however, but rather one-dimensional sexual commodification. Sexual preferences find their place on the liberated person's ever-expanding menu of choice. As Flannery O'Connor wrote in the 1960s, sex sentimentally or imaginatively detached from all its hard purposes *is* pornography. That is why the 1960s weren't so good for prostitutes or "sex workers"; their business depends on society *not* normalizing their distinctive purpose. The 1960s mainstreamed the big business of sex, and the result was that Americans seemed less erotic than ever. American men became capable of yawning at virtually unclad, perfectly sculpted young women on MTV.

Sex that is no more than recreation or diversion becomes progressively more disappointing. We really are polymorphously erotic, social, relational, generative, and transcendent beings who cannot help but long for a lot more than enjoyable ways to pass the time. The detachment of sex from love, birth, and death tends to isolate each of us so much that we believe that the bare act of copulation is the only way of making a human connection. But that connection, it turns out, is not particularly real: it promises much more than it, alone, can deliver.

The turn to soft drugs in the 1960s was, in part, both to facilitate and to ease the disappointment that comes with the effort to separate love from sex. There was some very erotic, blues-driven music in the late 1960s; its purpose was to restore the depth or at least the intensity of human longing in a very unpromising time. The hard drugs and alcohol those musicians abused and made appealing were associated with the genuinely marginalized and oppressed, as well as with facilitating the genuinely erotic liberation of rare geniuses in blues, jazz, and literature. Psychedelic music, however, was curiously unerotic. It reflected and supported the effort to desexualize or depersonalize love. It was about friends helping friends become less genuinely emotionally dependent on one another through getting high alone together.

Casual Sex and Civilization

The 1960s failed to routinize the orgy in America, and even wife-swapping was common nowhere but in the imagination. According to Gerard DeGroot in *The Sixties Unplugged* (2008), the lurid dimension of the sexual revolution "was often seen by those who participated in it as something fun at the time, but in retrospect embarrassing, bewildering, and sordid." The 1960s institutional alternative to the nuclear family's obsessive exclusivity was the anti-authoritarian commune. Children would flourish there in freedom and love. But it turns out that an anti-authoritarian commune is an oxymoron. Parents remain stuck with the alienating and loving reality of their own children. The 1960s damaged, but hardly abolished, the foundations of both *eros* and civilization.

In *Achieving Our Country* (1998), Richard Rorty argues that the sexual liberation of the 1960s was highly civilized. The 1960s, by reducing the amount of sexual repression in the country, also reduced the amount of cruel "socially acceptable sadism" which is its consequence. So decent men and women, such as, Rorty tells us, Walt Whitman, can't help but delight in "the kind of casual, friendly copulation that is indifferent to the homosexual-heterosexual distinction." The cruelty of sexual repression, Rorty provocatively contends, is caused by "the inability to love." That's why, in Rorty's mind, the theorists of the 1960s were able to connect sexual casualness with the liberation of love.

Rorty, we have to admit, is not completely wrong, as decent men have never approved of the cruel treatment homosexuals have received in the past. But he doesn't really explain why *indifference* is good for love. "Don't be cruel!" and "Don't hate!" are imperatives of justice for free individuals. Love, meanwhile, is a source of privilege and exclusivity; it leads people to be easily suckered or aroused. Casual, friendly copulation occurs between people who neither love nor hate each other. It is undistorted by the intense personal and social connections that are at the foundation of both hate and love. Emotional isolation is, in Rorty's eyes, the true antidote to cruelty. But if that's the case, then love, not "repression," must be the true cause of cruelty. Certainly Rorty's antidote requires an unerotic indifference to biological imperatives, to the hard purposes of bodies that generate shared human responsibilities and devotions.

To avoid the possibility of cruelty, love has to be replaced by a kind of benign fellow-feeling that falls short of both obsession and personal obligation. The 1960s' version of love really was more easygoing, nonjudgmental, and nonbinding. It made love seem more compatible with the individual's perception that the pursuit of happiness trumps one's duties to those one can't help but love. People rather quickly became far less judgmental about abortion and divorce, for example. Sexual repression experienced as guilt or sin didn't fade away but it certainly did fade, and real insouciance about sexual expression became much more common. If we believe that the right to put one's happiness first is at the core of the American view of justice, we have to conclude that what is good for justice is bad for love.

The truth, of course, is less that marital sex was replaced by casual sex than that enduring monogamy was replaced by serial monogamy. And that change was certainly countered—if not exactly weakened— by the enduring reality of parental and filial love. That change gives us more evidence than ever of the cruel loneliness that is the downside of personal indifference. The truth is also that we probably have more sexual sadism than ever before, because we have freed, to some extent, *eros* from inhibition and personal love.

Women's Liberation

Because women could see—even if they couldn't often say—that sexual liberation is bad for love, they began to demand more from justice. The core assertion of feminism is that "the personal is the political." That means that the American principles of justice are to be applied to every personal—i.e., every intimate—feature of life. Women need protection from uninhibited men, men with no authoritative guidance about how to treat women: the Summer of Love too easily morphed into the Summer of Rape. If sex is separated from love, familial duty, and communal responsibility, then it surely needs to be strictly governed by contract and consent. Consent seems both more reliable and more just than personal love, especially in a time when love had become more unreliable than ever.

The good news is that the transformations of the 1960s caused women to be treated as free individuals—just like men. Even we conservatives must admit that there is a real—if rough and incomplete—correspondence between women's gains in the direction of justice and those achieved in the 1960s by blacks. The true dignity of women as free and equal citizens has been better recognized than before. Even conservative women today would not surrender the opportunities they have as individuals, even if they choose not to exercise many of them.

The bad news is that women have found it increasingly difficult not to become wage slaves—just like men. As Marx predicted, the "halo" was stripped from women, who out of dutiful love had chosen to be simply or primarily wives and mothers. They were therefore less and less exempt from the bourgeois standard of productivity—from making money. The family wage became a distant ideal. Families increasingly were stuck working more hours than any one individual could work, just to maintain a satisfactory standard of living.

The productivity of the nation soared because women entered the workforce, but wages fell in relation to productivity. The traditional American division of labor described by Tocqueville, in which men are primarily responsible for business and politics and women for family and the household, became completely discredited. That division of labor surely did put unjust constraints on women as individuals, and in the high-tech suburbs being a wife and mom often did become boring and lonely—especially for women with college educations.

The theorists of the 1960s didn't focus on women as countercultural agents of change; to them, it seemed unjust to think of women, in particular, at all. During much of the 1960s wives and moms—often burdened or blessed with considerable wealth and leisure—flourished as never before as voluntary leaders of civic, educational, and charitable associations. But the liberationist spirit of the 1960s as a whole eventually brought to an end the abundance of feminine social capital that was the public-spirited fruit of the early 1960s. Liberation, justice, and productivity turned out to be more characteristic of the decade than love, generosity, and caregiving.

Liberation as Conquest of Scarcity

The deepest thoughts of the 1960s were all based on genuine efforts to think about who human beings are and what they are for. And the inability to focus particularly on who women are and what they are for was one example among many of the impossibility of making even quite authentic concerns about purpose compatible with radical or unprecedented visions of liberation. The most erudite New Left theorist, Herbert Marcuse, began with the Marxist premise that modern technology and the capitalist economy had conquered scarcity; people could now easily meet their material needs with very little work. The real cause of erotic repression, he explained in *Eros and Civilization* (1955), was the discipline required by scarcity. From the standpoint of our technological civilization that had conquered scarcity, we could see that Freud is wrong (although he used to be right) that the "free gratification of man's instinctual needs is incompatible with civilization."

The "pleasure principle," Marcuse proclaimed, no longer needed to be controlled by the "reality principle." The time had come when human *eros* could be liberated to be what it is according to its own uninhibited nature. As Abraham Maslow had explained to Americans, when our basic needs are met, we are free for the highest forms of self-actualization. The human greatness that used to be rare could now become common. The most enthusiastic man of the 1960s, Abbie

Hoffman, began his bizarre radical journey with the revelation that Marcuse is the right mixture of Maslow and Marx for our times.

The function of reason, Marcuse explained in *One-Dimensional Man* (1964), was now to direct technology in the service of "the art of life." The more we can reduce our physical and mental work, the more we can reduce anxiety and fear, and the more joyful self-determination becomes possible. We have freed ourselves for "trans-utilitarian ends." All of life can become the leisure celebrated by the philosophers, and as a result there will be new births of freedom, creativity, and love. Marcuse and even Maslow, both very cultivated men, thought of this erotic flourishing as genuinely polymorphous—sex, the imagination, art, music, culture, spiritual life, and even philosophy will finally be experienced as they truly are. Because there is finally no scarcity of the good things of life, nothing we think or feel or do will have to be distorted by self-denial.

Marcuse and Marx were not, to say the least, environmentalists. Many thinkers of the 1960s tended to differ from them not in rejecting technology, but by thinking about technological means in a "humane" way. The conquest of scarcity means that it is possible to imagine "alternative technologies" that reconcile living in comfort and security with the aesthetic enjoyment of our natural surroundings. Because "small is beautiful," technologies themselves might be reconfigured to reconcile abundance with beauty.

There was little in the 1960s that pointed with more than a very selective nostalgia to a genuinely "organic" life that would dispense with the benefits of techno-liberation. There was certainly no desire to return to what couldn't help but seem to be the drudgery and unjust rural idiocy of the low-tech environments of the past. The 1960s inaugurated postmaterialism in the sense that human beings, having definitively defeated nature, could now be friendlier toward their former foe. Although the poetry of the 1960s often flirted with pantheism and Buddhist self-negation, the 1960s were nothing if not humanistic, even if their tendency was to empty the human of any definitive content. Environmentalism in the 1960s was not nearly as green as today's greens, nor as apocalyptic as Al Gore's *Inconvenient Truth*.

Old and New Left

The American Old Left aimed to free the poor from poverty and for security. Its appeal was to working men and women who wanted to share in the good life that capitalism had made possible for a few. The Great Society programs of Lyndon Johnson, inspired by both the generous spirit of the early 1960s and the ambitions of the early New Left, went much further. Johnson explained in his 1964 commencement address at the University of Michigan that most of American history had been devoted to "subduing the continent," and the result of our "unbounded invention and untiring industry" had been "an order of plenty for our people." So our new goal would be to discover and employ the "wisdom . . . to enrich and elevate our national life, and to advance the quality of American civilization." Our rich and powerful society could now become great.

That Great Society would rest, of course, on "abundance and liberty for all" and therefore on a complete end to "poverty and racial injustice." Once those goals were achieved, it would be possible to create "a place where leisure is a welcome place to build and reflect, and not a feared cause of boredom and restlessness," as well as one "where the city of man serves not only the needs of the body and the demands of commerce but the desire for beauty and the hunger for community." Johnson urged us to prove that we have the power and the wisdom to shape a civilization that meets all—even the highest—of our human needs or desires.

LBJ displayed his greatness by claiming, in effect, to be the mixture of Marx and Maslow appropriate for the times. As much as the New Leftists, he thought that human or political will would be required to liberate unfulfilled human capabilities. But Johnson agreed with the Old Left that the defeat of poverty still required our unreserved commitment and the programmatic power of the national government. His somewhat noble but quite ridiculous thought was that our national government—designed for limited ends and leaving happiness to the individual—could both take on and resolve the issues of human purpose and human happiness. Johnson was a man of the 1960s, most of all, in having no realistic sense of limits.

The War on Poverty, not surprisingly, inspired the Old but not the New Left. In the privileged lives of the members of the New Left, poverty or scarcity had already been defeated. Their focus was on their *own* boredom, restlessness, and loneliness, and they didn't focus their search for meaning on government programs or on being antipoverty warriors. They thought of themselves as the idealistic children of soulless oligarchs, and they imagined themselves, as did LBJ, as occupying a privileged moment in history. Thinking of themselves primarily as intellectuals or students, they, most of all, demanded an education appropriate to their situation.

They criticized their education for being merely oligarchic or technocratic, for not preparing them for the "art of life." The "elective" system of the "multiversity" was evidence that Americans lacked a unifying vision of a whole human life. What's more, they noticed that only the scientific and technical courses were taken seriously as conveying real knowledge. They were the courses concerning "facts," whereas the humanities were concerned with emoting about arbitrary and weightless "values."

Our universities, the New Left claimed, were teaching nothing about how to live well after scarcity's conquest; the schools did nothing to direct liberated reason, love, or imagination. Nothing, of course, was an exaggeration. But even 1950s' intellectuals with a genuinely bohemian concern for living well, such as Russell Kirk, had often dropped out in disgust from an increasingly bureaucratic and standardized university system. The charges the New Left leveled in the Port Huron Statement about the University of Michigan echoed, in many ways, what Kirk had already said about Michigan State in the 1950s.

Kirk, of course, was too informed about permanent features of human nature to think for a moment that scarcity had really been overcome. But only in a high-tech time could he, lacking hereditary wealth or noble birth, devote himself so successfully to living as he pleased. He knew well enough that one good point of bourgeois success is in the alternative way of life of the bohemian. He also knew that even a Beatnik couldn't really have the imagination to become truly countercultural without some knowledge of the aristocratic and spiritual truths embodied in the high culture under bourgeois assault in the modern world. Kirk's diagnosis was that the students in the 1960s, living in abundance and freedom and without cultivated imaginations, were causing trouble because they were *bored.*

The members of the early New Left shared Kirk's spiritual, aristocratic conviction that they were made for more than merely technological knowledge. The "how" or the *means* of living well were too easy for them to seem important; they could be taken for granted. It turns out to be very hard to know what to do if you really believe that necessity gives us no guidance at all. And the members of the New Left were too attached to the liberating impersonalities of good government and high technology to embrace freely the tough constraints or personal subordination required for genuine democratic community.

Like us all, the students of the 1960s longed for the personal significance of communal life without its accompanying personal duties. They wanted both radical liberation and true purpose; they wanted to do their own thing without being lonely. The illusions of liberation caused them to be too hard on—and to not learn from—the past, and too vaguely or thoughtlessly hopeful for the future. They didn't have what it takes to really take advantage of their freedom to achieve the soaring, self-actualized excellence praised by Maslow or the leisurely cultivation of Marcuse's art of life (lived, in his own way, by Kirk).

Intellectual Anarchism

Failing to discover a purposeful standard to direct technological rationality, the New Leftists lurched toward the view that the only way to control technology is to deny the truth and goodness of all claims to knowledge. All claims to truth are equally empty, because all of life is nothing but a struggle for power and identity. The New Left's early, somewhat reasonable rebellion against technocracy on behalf of the humane use of technology culminated in deconstruction by all means available. All there is, the claim was, are assertions of significance or identity in a moral vacuum. This 1960s rebellion began against the technocratic view that true or factual statements always begin with "studies show." Real knowledge, the technocrat thinks, is nothing but impersonal and scientific. But by the end of the 1960s, courses based on "studies show" were displaced in the social sciences and humanities by aggressively personal and subjective "studies" courses—black studies, women's studies, and so forth. The deconstruction of the late 1960s trivialized the real achievements on behalf of justice of the early 1960s. Certainly no "studies" professor could explain why powerful white Americans could have been genuinely convinced or at least shamed into allowing relatively powerless black Americans to exercise their rights as free and equal citizens.

The truth is that technocratic studies are typically rational and factual, although the clarity of what the studies show usually comes through abstraction from personal reality. And "studies" courses really are mostly emotional outbursts of "value" that correspond to nothing real. So it is not surprising that progress in the natural sciences was relatively untouched by the Know-Nothing propaganda that exploded after the late 1960s. Our best scientists never lost confidence that they know what they're doing, even that they know much more than they really do. The effectual truth of the 1960s was to make American education more technological and more nihilistic than ever. The thinkers of the 1960s saw the need for—but failed to come up with—a real, personal antidote to "scientism."

The privileged young leaders of the New Left got stupider, angrier, and more violent as the 1960s approached their end. The most anti-intellectual, amoral, and blindly destructive year of that decade was the academic year of 1969–70. There were few sights more disgusting to ordinary Americans than intelligent, middle-class kids terrorizing our universities into craven submission. The result of this partial but real success of the youthful rebellion was that a college education—at least for those majoring in the social sciences and humanities—became more than ever a boring, demoralizing waste of time.

The burgeoning anarchism of the New Left was closer to what Marx actually would have predicted than the early hopes for egalitarian excellence and love. According to Marx, capitalism destroys every human illusion about morality, spirituality, and personal significance—except those that can be measured through money. The whole achievement of capitalism appears permanent—both its high-tech material productivity and its moral/emotional destructiveness. Nothing discredited can be restored—not God or love or nature or honor.

History, for the Marxist, always moves in the direction of the truth, and the end of history would be the total eradication of the repressive illusions that limit freedom.

Under communism, Marx explains, people live liberated or completely unconstrained or unalienated lives. "Do your own thing" without any guidance at all about your thing really becomes the only rule. So communism—which is only communal in the sense that the community as opposed to any particular person takes care of the necessary work—really is radical democracy or radical anarchism or radical liberation. It is not at all compatible with the love- and death-obsessed civilizations of the past, the cultural achievements of which had already been commodified into insignificance by capitalism. The laidback communes of the 1960s semi-consciously aimed to imitate what Marx had imagined. Their success would depend on leaving all the baggage of the past at the door. Freedom would mean completely shedding oneself of the obsessions that plagued the repressed, scarcity-driven, stressed-out past. It would mean that there is *nothing* you feel you really *have* to do.

Communism or democracy, so understood, has to be, as Socrates first explained, a rebellion of the young against the old. The old can't help but be distorted by experiences of scarcity; they are much more likely to be burdened by a scarcity of *time*. "Don't trust anyone over thirty" means "don't be brought down by the experiences of old folks." Due to the 1960s, the old, to avoid ostracism, increasingly have no choice but to think, talk, and look young; they have to fake the insouciant forgetfulness of necessity that is so easy for the young. The 1960s accelerated an American, democratic, and even capitalist tendency to celebrate the indefinite perfectibility of the forever young.

But there are few things more repulsive—or more ridiculous—than the tyranny of the young and privileged who believe they are entitled to live without limits, without binding social and personal responsibilities. The demand to live as if there were no scarcity offended those Americans responsible enough—usually old and/or poor enough—to know how much their lives are defined by scarcity and its attendant responsibilities. Most Americans knew well enough that to imagine a world without countries, law, family, God, tradition, and the rest was to imagine hell, and only the most self-indulgent among us could imagine otherwise.

The Enduring Legacy (as They Say)

The truth is that Marx and Marcuse and even Maslow were wrong to believe that the conquest of scarcity could be accomplished for all. The need for bourgeois virtues—the virtues useful for productivity and managing time—had not in fact withered away. Even the liberation of a few from that need always depended on most people practicing those virtues. The 1960s ended with most people still trapped in the alienating division of labor, anxiously in pursuit of seemingly endlessly deferred gratification, stuck in the midst of bureaucratic hierarchies, and thinking of themselves as abstract or unerotic individuals with impersonal loyalties to corporate processes well beyond their comprehension and control. Technological progress has in many ways made work in some sense more humane; more of it is mental, less of it is physical. The demand for intellectual and imaginative productivity, however, is much more stressful than merely manual labor—you can't help but take your work with you everywhere you go.

Marx was also wrong in thinking that the conquest of scarcity would cause the withering away of pre-bourgeois political, noble, religious, and personal longings. But he would have rightly laughed at the New Leftists who placed their faith in an unprecedented future for the satisfaction of those longings. The real human alternatives are not technocratic domination and radical liberation. If the longings remain, scarcity does too. So, too, does the credibility of pre-bourgeois accounts of what it means to live well, responsibly and in love, in light of the truth.

The 1960s were, most of all, very destructive of what remains in America of pre-bourgeois sources of truth and virtue. Community, loyalty, religion, the family, every institutional form of nobility and love were damaged by the increasingly aggressive insistence on justice and freedom. But the nihilist's inability to articulate a standard more compelling than technological success and individual liberation was probably, on balance, good for American productivity. All sorts of moral and political objections to putting productivity first eroded—both those based on higher forms of human excellence and those based on various forms of prejudice.

It is also easy to exaggerate how destructive the 1960s were. A free and productive society does depend on preexisting social capital, but the 1960s provided no real alternative to people having to raise their children. The preferential option for the young, it now seems, turns out to have been only for the most energetic, techno-savvy, and productive among us. Most features of the 1960s have become compatible with being bourgeois. The most educated and productive Americans today often have cultivated bohemian and "crunchy" tastes, for which they can thank the 1960s. And the "organic" aesthetics of the late 1960s have made our country in some ways a healthier, prettier, and cleaner place. But being bohemian or being crunchy rarely now means a whole, alternative art of life.

We cannot forget that, because of the 1960s, America is more just and in some ways less cruel than it once was. That decade's objections to "soulless wealth" and technocracy in the name of personal significance and personal love also still retain some force. They do so most powerfully in the genuinely countercultural *religious* movements that have emerged since the 1960s—both evangelical and orthodox. These movements were inspired by and opposed to the 1960s. A genuinely anti-bourgeois communitarian rebellion on behalf of personal love seems in the end to depend on the real authority of a personal God.

7

AMERICAN NOMINALISM
AND OUR NEED FOR
THE SCIENCE OF THEOLOGY

My purpose here is to show how Pope Benedict XVI's defense of a true science of theology applies to the United States of America. That defense is, finally, of the reasonableness of belief in a personal God who is rational, creative, and erotic. It requires going beyond the Regensburg lecture to the pope's path-breaking encyclical on love and to places in his writings where he makes clear that the fundamental human choice is not so much between reason and revelation as between the impersonal *logos*, or God of the classical philosophers, and the personal *logos*, or God described by the early Christians. The argument concerning which of those reasonable choices is more reasonable was what animated the study of the science of theology in the time of Hellenic Christianity. For us Americans, the greatness and the relevance of this philosopher-theologian-pope are in his articulation of a theory or science commensurate with the great practical achievement of our Founders, who, as the American Catholic political thinker John Courtney Murray claimed, built better than they knew. I'm dispensing with formality here, hoping not to rely on authority as much as to speak the truth. In my effort to do so, I gratefully acknowledge a debt to Joseph Ratzinger, Pope Benedict XVI, that couldn't be captured by any number of footnotes.*

* Here's what I read by Ratzinger/Benedict to prepare for writing this essay: the Regensburg Lecture; the encyclical on love; *Introduction to Christianity* (Ignatius Press, 1994); *In the*

Even though the modern world has been characterized by de-Christianization and de-Hellenization, that doesn't mean it's fundamentally anti-Christian or anti-Greek. We speak more of the dignity or autonomy of the human person than ever. And we certainly have more confidence in and are more dependent on the science we've inherited from the Greeks than ever. Modern de-Hellenization has been largely animated by the desire to free the willful God and willful human person made in his image from being distorted by or annihilated in the impersonal metaphysical system of Aristotle or some other philosopher or scientist. Modern de-Christianization has been largely animated by the desire to free science from all anthropomorphic or personal distortion in order to fuel real progress toward a certain understanding of the genuinely universal structure of reality, the goal of science first articulated, quite imperfectly, by the classical Greek philosophers. De-Hellenization has been pursued on behalf of the free person, and de-Christianization on behalf of impersonal science. They have been operating simultaneously and at cross-purposes.

The truth is that our world is in some ways more personal and more impersonal, more Christian and more Greek, than ever. The distance between our personal experiences and what we think we know through science has never been wider. Without admitting it, we've abandoned the true goal of science, which is to give an account of the way all things, including human beings, are. We don't really believe we can reason about the true situation of the only being in the world, the human person, who is open to the truth about nature. We think we can know everything but the being who can know. We don't deny that such a personal being exists, whatever our scientists may teach. We don't even begin to try to lose our puny selves in some impersonal system or pantheistic reverie. Such denial is for Buddhists, with their amazing self-discipline. For now the phrase "Western Buddhist" remains an oxymoron.

Beginning . . . A Catholic Understanding of the Story of Creation and the Fall (Eerdmans, 2005); and most of the writings and speeches contained in *The Essential Pope Benedict XVI*, ed. John Thornton and Susan Varenne (HarperCollins, 2007). Particularly important in shaping my argument here from *The Essential Pope Benedict XVI* was "On the Theological Basis of Prayer and Liturgy" (chap. 19) and "Truth and Freedom" (chap. 35).

It's especially clear that we Americans see ourselves both more personally and more impersonally than ever. Virtually all sophisticated Americans claim to believe that Darwin teaches the whole truth about who or what we are. For Darwin, the individual human being exists only to serve the human species. Even our super-smart species has no enduring significance in the accidental evolutionary process. It's true both that I'm nothing but species fodder and that what I, in particular, do has less than negligible significance for our species' future. Natural selection depends on the average, anonymous behavior of a huge number of members of any particular species. The individual or person and his illusory concerns about his personal significance mean, or are, nothing. Even the genes that I so dutifully spread are soon dispersed into insignificance.

The same sophisticated Americans who pride themselves on being whole-hog Darwinians speak incessantly about the freedom and dignity of the individual and are proud of their freedom to choose. The particularly modern source of pride remains personal freedom from all authority, including the authority of God and nature. Our professed confidence in the reality of that freedom may be stronger than ever today. Even our neo-Darwinian scientists, such as Daniel Dennett, who think there's no foundation for the idea of human dignity in what we know through science, admit it would be a disaster if they could really convince us to stop taking our dignity seriously. Certainly one piece of evidence that we're not living in genuinely reasonable times is that most sophisticated Americans seem unable to join Dennett in recognizing the laughable contradiction in their official self-understanding as autonomous chimps.

We Americans, in fact, are so unscientific that we don't even try to account for what we can see with our own eyes. Culturally speaking, we're divided into Darwin affirmers and Darwin deniers, into those who say that his theory of evolutionary natural selection can explain everything and those who say it explains nothing. Anybody should be able to see that the truth lies somewhere in between those two extremes.

The Darwin affirmers provide the best evidence around today that what Darwin teaches couldn't possibly be completely true. They tend to think of themselves so thoroughly as autonomous individuals that often they don't seek the natural fulfillment that comes through spreading their genes, through having kids. They're not doing their duty to their species by generating their replacements. They're even doing everything they can in the most scientific way not to have to be replaced. They think being itself will be extinguished if and when they die. Can Darwin explain why healthy members of a species enjoying the most favorable of environments would suddenly and quite consciously just decide to stop reproducing? It seems that members of a species smart enough and curious enough to have discovered the theory of natural selection are acting to make that theory untrue.

Meanwhile, our evangelical and orthodox believers come much closer to living the way nature intends for our species to flourish. They pair-bond or marry, have lots of kids, raise them well, and then step aside for their natural replacements without inordinate resistance. What the evangelicals and orthodox believe is better for our species' future than what the neo-Darwinians believe. Examining this behavior, a neo-Darwinian genuinely concerned for our species' future might insist that evolution not be taught in our schools. Nor can our sociobiologists explain why those Americans who believe that, as persons made in the image of a supernatural God, their true home is somewhere else are most at home in this world as citizens, friends, neighbors, parents, and children.

Still, our evangelicals tend to join both those who speak of their autonomy and our Darwinians in believing that there's no support in nature at all for their purpose-driven lives. If it weren't for the absolute truth of the Bible, they assert, something like aimless or relativistic naturalism would be true. They often present the human choice as between two competing worldviews, and reason has little to say about how to make that choice. Our evangelicals often give themselves far too little credit. Their criticism of both our libertarian autonomy freaks and our Darwinians would retain plenty of force even if they lost faith in the God of the Bible.

Our libertarians, our Darwinians, and our evangelicals all agree that there is no science of theology. Reason, they insist, can't give us any understanding on who or what God is in a way that would provide actual guidance for our lives. They don't believe that we're hardwired, so to speak, to know the *logos* who, or which, is the source of our freedom and our openness to the truth about all things. Libertarians and evangelicals both believe that the free person is real, but they don't believe that there's any support in nature for his existence. Darwinians, quite unrealistically, deny what anyone can see with his own eyes about personal or individual behavior. Because we all refuse to believe in the possibility of a science of theology, we all lack a way of talking reasonably about the real lives of particular human persons.

We don't live in a very reasonable time because we're governed by a particular cultural or historical choice to limit the domain of reason over our lives. This modern self-limitation, as I'll explain, was quite understandable. But we now know from experience that the simultaneous attempts to free faith from science or philosophy and science from faith have produced undignified, self-mutilated lives. Most fundamentally, we seem not to be courageous enough to live well with what we know. The truth is that the modern view of reason is quite questionable. It is, thank God, far from the last word on what we can know.

The Science of Theology:
Hellenic Christianity vs. Classical Philosophy

To free us from the delusion that we have that last word on reason, we return to the first words about the relationship between Greek philosophy or science and Christianity spoken during the period of Hellenic Christianity. Then, the Greeks and the Christians agreed that we're hardwired as beings with minds to think about who or what God must be and that we're animated by *eros,* or love, to seek the truth about God. The idea that God is *Logos* is what allowed the Greeks and the Christians to use both argument and mockery to collaborate against those religions that are obviously unreasonable and man-made. God is neither cruel nor arbitrary, and the truth about God must correspond to what we can know about ourselves and the rest of nature according to our best lights. Both the Greeks and the Christians contributed to genuine enlightenment, to the liberation of human beings from the confines of merely civil or political theology, from a world where the word of God both was used as a weapon and justified the use of weapons.

Through reflection, Aristotle attempted to grasp God as the object of every human desire or love. He understood God only as the *object* of love, as a wholly self-sufficient or unerotic or unmovable being, not as a person at all. Aristotle's God is certainly not a "relational" God, one who cares or even knows about the existence of particular human beings. According to Aristotle, our pursuit of divine knowledge, or what God knows, becomes progressively more impersonal. The pursuit of philosophic or scientific truth requires that the individual philosopher die to himself. The Socratic drama of the pursuit of wisdom is the particular being losing himself in his apprehension of anonymous or impersonal truth.

From this view, we approach divinity, or what is best in us, through our perception of the *logos* or rational causality that governs all things. We see past every anthropomorphic claim for personal intervention or personal causation that would disrupt that *logos*. From this liberated view, the idea of a personal God is an oxymoron. It is, in fact, a repulsive denial of the responsibility of theological science and science generally.

The Christian criticism of Aristotelian theology is that it doesn't account for what we really know about the human person. For the Greek philosophers, the realm of human freedom, finally, is a mythical idea, one that must be rhetorically supported but for which there's no scientific evidence. The only freedom is the freedom of the human mind from anthropomorphic delusions about natural causation. The Christians respond that human longings and human action display evidence of personal freedom, and the person must have some real foundation in being itself. What we do know, they say, points in the direction of the creative activity of a personal God. The personalities of God and man can't be wholly or irredeemably unrelated. The possibility of the free and rational being open to the truth depends upon the corresponding possibility of a personal, rational science of theology.

The classical philosophers were, of course, perfectly aware that human beings are "manly," that they need to feel important. Such self-confidence is required to make self-conscious life endurable and great human deeds possible. But according to their science, all assertions of human importance are unrealistic exaggerations, and the philosopher gently mocks without obviously undermining the aspirations of particular individuals to self-sufficiency. For the Christians, however, even science depends upon the possibility of personal significance, and Christian theology criticizes both the civil theology and the natural theology of the Greeks and Romans for their inability to account for personal freedom—for the being who is not fundamentally merely part of a city or part of some necessitarian natural whole. According to the Christians, not only do particular men and women need to feel important; they are, in fact, important. The Christians add that the unrealistic exaggerations of their magnanimous pretensions need, in fact, the chastening of the truthful virtue of humility, the virtue of ineradicably relational and lovingly dependent beings.

That there's a ground for personal freedom in an otherwise seemingly necessitarian cosmos does, in some ways, offend the mind, but to understand all that exists in terms of impersonal causation suggests that Being itself is constituted by an intelligence that is incapable of comprehending itself. The being who can understand Being, the human being, seems to be an inexplicable or chance occurrence in a cosmos that has no particular need for and is seemingly distorted by his existence. The appearance of the human person, even the philosopher with the name Socrates, necessarily offends the human mind in some ways, but as far as we know, the human mind can only appear or function in a whole person. The real existence of the whole philosopher or the whole physicist can't be accounted for in any mathematical or certain, necessitarian physics. So in some ways it might offend the person's reason less to affirm an account of the whole person, the precondition and ground of being open to the truth about Being or all that exists. The world, in the final analysis, is more love than mathematics, and the particular human person is more significant and wonderful than the stars.

The Greeks focus on the eternity, the Christians on the loving creativity of God. For the Christians, the God who is the ultimate source of our being is animated, as we are, by *logos* and *eros*. The source of our being is someone who can't be reduced to mind or will or even some theoretical combination of the two. Made in his image, we personal, erotic, and knowing beings can't be reduced to mind or will or body or even some abstract combination of the three. One aspect of the reasonableness of faith is its perception of the intrinsic link between God's love and the whole reality of human life.

The philosophic or scientific understanding of the world in terms of impersonal necessity or eternity alone can't account for the real existence of persons, of beings open to the truth and defined in this world by time. The eternal God of the Greeks has no relationship to the temporal, and the dependence and incompleteness of time-bound beings mean nothing to him. Insofar as human beings are moved by his existence, it is in pursuit of self-sufficient freedom from who they really are. If time and eternity really are infinitely distant from one another, then we can't understand why human beings can know God or anything eternal.

Classical monotheism, in truth, denies the real relationships between God and man and between eternity and time. It may, in fact, culminate in the conclusion that the only thing a human being can know for certain is that he's not eternal, that he's some kind of chance occurrence soon to be extinguished in a necessitarian cosmos. Greek philosophers clearly distinguished the personal illusion of religion from the philosophic science of theology, showing that, for the most part, at least the lives of particular men are as unreal or as insignificant as the personal gods they invent. For the Greeks, religion was useful for the regulation of lives, but it has nothing to do with the truth.

From the Greek view, the early Christians seemed like atheists. They rejected the whole world of ancient religion and its gods as nothing but empty custom or contrary to what we can really know. That's because the Christians agreed with the Greek philosophers that traditional myth must be rejected in favor of the truth about Being, and the Christians added that all human beings are called to regulate their lives in light of what they can really know. Only from the perspective of a personal *logos* can the truth affirm and guide human freedom. The Christians, by discovering a transformed understanding of the *logos* at the ground of Being, showed God to be a person concerned with persons. The Christians show why divine truth can't be separated from personal morality.

From the perspective of the distinctive reasonableness of Christian faith, man's inner openness to God comes from what he knows about himself as a relational being, as a person who knows and loves other "whos." The philosophical view of God is that our thoughts or minds alone are divine, and the mind detached from the whole human being is less a who than a what. The Christian view is that we're made in God's image as whole rational and erotic beings; not just thought but love is divine. The standard of moral judgment is what we can't help

but know about our personhood or creatureliness, about the responsibilities that flow from personal awareness of loving dependence.
Sin flows from the denial of the truth about our freedom, from the
madness that flows from the aspiration to be as autonomous or self-
sufficient as some thinkers imagine God to be. The sin described in
Genesis flows from the false separation of divine wisdom from personal or "relational" morality.

In the Hellenic world, the science of theology was always reasonable without achieving rational certainty. The truth is that both the
arguments for the Christian and the Greek accounts of the *logos* at
the ground of Being have problems. Christianity's view that what we
can know about the human person reasonably points in the direction of a personal *logos* doesn't eradicate the apparent *mystery* of personal freedom in a world seemingly governed by natural necessity. If
the mystery is real, the Greek philosophers argued, science becomes
impossible. The Christian response that without that mystery there
would be nobody to know scientific truth doesn't completely answer
that objection. Nor could the Christians dispel all questions about
why a wholly self-sufficient and rational God completely ungoverned
by time and chance would become a Creator. How can it be that such
a God is erotic or animated by a passionate sense of incompleteness?

And, of course, some Christians wondered whether the Hellenizing
of Christianity through the emphasis on God as *logos* chained him, in
effect, to natural laws that weren't his creation. The emphasis on either
God's love or God's reason can easily seem to compromise the freedom
of his will and so the omnipotence on which our hopes for personal
salvation rest. Arguably that emphasis also undermined the freedom of
the will of the persons made in his image. The limiting of the willful
God with either *logos* or love seems to undermine his personal significance, and so ours.

Modern Nominalism

It's understandable why there were Christian efforts to liberate God
from science, from the constraints of reason. The most obvious efforts
came from late-medieval nominalism. Words, the nominalists asserted,

are names, nothing more. Our speech, or *logos,* doesn't give us access to the way God or nature is. The word of God is pure will, and the word of man, who is made in his image, is also pure will. Words, for us, are merely weapons because we're not hardwired to discover the truth about God, nature, or each other through reason. This nominalist conclusion was, in effect, affirmed by the leaders of the Reformation. They, too, meant to free the personal experience of the living God from the cold constraints of reason. Our direct (really, private) personal experience of his will and his love eludes every impersonal system. The living, giving God, the Reformers believed, is nothing like Aristotle's God.

By freeing the person from *logos,* the combined effects of voluntarism and the Reformation were to deny the possibility of a science of theology. And so they also freed science from any concern with God, allowing it to focus exclusively on what we can know with certainty, the mathematically expressed laws of matter in motion. To know with certainty is to know without any personal distortion. Modern science becomes more openly impersonal than its ancient predecessor because Aristotelian theology left too much room for science's personal distortion and directed the mind toward uncertain speculation. The aim of modern physics, ultimately, is the same as that of ancient physics, to show that the world is the home of the human mind.

Now we can finally turn to how the nominalist denial of the science of theology shaped the early modern liberalism, the Lockeanism, that, in turn, shaped both the American Founding and the individualistic dynamic of American history. For Locke, we experience ourselves as free individuals or persons, but there is no divine or natural support for our personhood or individuality. Nature is utterly indifferent to my personal existence, so I have to establish my personal significance, my very being as a free individual, in opposition to that indifference. From my individual view, nature is worthless, and according to nature, I'm worthless.

The detachment of the person from nature or from *logos,* in the name of freedom and in the name of science, allows us to experience ourselves as pure freedom or pure selfishness. There's no evidence, in fact, for an active or giving Creator, no evidence that God or nature provides for the person in any way. Our personal freedom, like God's, is utterly mysterious: there's no evident natural or divine foundation for *me*, for my being. So I have to establish and expand my freedom—my very being—on my own, through my own willful work. I have to create or constitute myself out of nothing, as God allegedly created the whole world.

Like the Christians and against the Greeks, we Americans assert that each particular person is equally and infinitely significant. From the perspective of the person, from *my* perspective, nothing is more important than *my* security, significance, and happiness. Each person or individual exists for himself, not genuinely in a dependent and loving relationship with others. Love of God or other human persons is for suckers. It's undignified for me not to tell the truth about how contingent and self-determined my own being is.

The idea of God remains in Locke in the form of Deism, which was, in part, a revival of the ancient rejection of an active, personal God. Locke's "Nature's God" is a past-tense God. Deism also has some connection with the Pascalian view of the mysterious hiddenness of God. Certainly Locke's God is not quite the impersonal God of Aristotle, because Locke's affirmation of the reality of the mystery of the free human person points in some sense to a mysterious Creator. But that Creator does not show himself as a person to us. We act as suckers when we think of ourselves as creatures, as in some way gratefully dependent on or personally connected to his providence. Our Lockean Declaration of Independence, we remember, speaks of a Creator but never of creatures.

For Locke, words, our capacity for reasonable speech or *logos,* don't give us any access to the truth about nature or God. There is, in fact, no science of theology. Words are the weapons we use to secure our being against nature and without God. Words are the weapons we use to make ourselves progressively freer or progressively more real. Locke's state of nature, for example, was not meant to be an empirical account of the way human beings are. It distorts and exaggerates our personal or individual freedom. The state of nature was a tool used by Locke to liberate the individual from nature and from other individuals.

The Lockean individual is itself a weapon, a willful invention abstracted from the whole, relational truth about the human person. Proof of our freedom is our power to make that abstraction more real over time. Locke himself was all for limited government, but his project was hardly limited to government. He aimed, with great success, to reconstruct every human relationship and institution with the free or selfishly calculating individual in mind. As the Supreme Court said in *Lawrence v. Texas,* our Framers deliberately gave the word *liberty* no definite, stable content so that it could be used as a weapon for each generation of Americans to advance the cause of individual liberation or autonomy. What seems like necessary and proper limits to liberty to one generation of Americans seems like despotism to the next. Marriage, we now are coming to think, is a free contract between any two individuals for any purpose at all; it has been freed from any necessary connection to our biological purposes and limitations.

Locke's individual is free to view the wholly impersonal or mathematical nature that the scientists can comprehend and control as a resource for their personal disposal. He is even free to think of his own body in that way. His view of his freedom from nature even allows him to be critical scientifically of the impersonal pretensions of science. If it's true that there's no necessary connection between the free, willful individual and the natural order, then there's no reason to believe that we can comprehend the order of nature except by bringing it under our personal control.

Locke to Marx: History Replaces Nature

Freeing the person from nature necessarily personalizes what we can actually know about nature. We can only know what we have made in our own image. The purpose of our reason is to will personal reality into being. So all science, all human knowledge, must finally be technological; technology or History, the names we give to what we have made for ourselves, even seem to be all there is. The detachment of the person from nature frees the individual to impose his desire for personal significance on nature. We are free to replace impersonal natural evolution, which means nothing to us, with conscious and volitional evolution, human effort with the indefinite perpetuation of each infinitely significant individual in mind. And the science of theology, which aims at orthodoxy, is replaced by orthopraxis; there is no truth but who and what we have made for ourselves.

It's a pretty small step from Locke to Marx, from the view that the individual is free to constitute himself, to the "Historical" view that he's free to constitute all there is. The detachment of science from all concern with theology eventually seems to lead to the replacement of natural science by Historical science, to Marx's description of the impending total victory of human freedom over nature and God. The separation of eternity (impersonal natural science) from time (the free person or individual) at the beginning of the modern world is resolved, according to Marx, by the victory of time. Human freedom or History frees each of us from the tyranny of the indifference of eternal necessity.

There are many problems with this conclusion. To begin with, if History is a *science,* then *logos* once again seems to reign at the expense of the freedom or significance of particular persons. It doesn't matter what I really intend to do; my personal actions only have significance as part of a whole, a historical future, beyond my comprehension and control. Those who really believed History is a science were all too ready to sacrifice today's individuals for a historical perfection nobody now living will ever see or enjoy. From a Lockean view, those who gave their lives to History were suckers, and those who were murdered on behalf of History were denied their personal dignity.

The tyranny of Marxists can be traced to the detachment of the abstraction "History" from the lives of particular persons or individuals. As History became a scientific replacement for modern natural science, it became just as impersonal or systematic as modern science. Hegel and Marx even wrote of "the end of history," of History as a time-bound *logos* of temporal beings. The great Marxist/Hegelian Alexandre Kojève explained that the end of history would have to be the end of "man properly so-called," the disappearance of the personal being free from nature's domination. The end of History, according to Kojève, would be the victory of eternity over the temporary aberration of time. The human species would be reintegrated into nature with all the other animals, and there would be no one left to know the truth about the impersonal natural necessity that would once again be the truth and nothing but.

To be fair to Marx (as opposed to being fair to Marxist tyrants), he, quite incoherently, thought that the end of History or communism would be the free flourishing of individuality unconstrained by natural necessity or any other form of alienation. It's hard to know why Marx called communism *communism,* because in such a society we would be completely free from all relational obsessions, such as love, that would limit our freedom. The freedom won by human beings from nature and from each other under capitalism would remain, with the addition of liberation from the division of labor, from being compelled to work for others. Under communism, freedom would be just another word for nothing left that we *have* to do.

Our most astute libertarians today are beginning to see that Marx is their friend once he is stripped of insane and dangerous hopes such as the inevitability of revolution and the actual end of history. The world he worked for is the one today's libertarians celebrate as having largely arrived—the one with a huge and ever-expanding menu of choices for liberated individuals. Marx thought capitalism liberated women to be wage slaves just like men. Our libertarians tweak that observation by saying women are now free to seek self-fulfillment however they please, just like men, and the opportunities for work from which they have to choose are often challenging and enjoyable. There is no denying, in fact, that the achievements of modern technology in liberating lots of ordinary persons from scarcity and drudgery are wonderful revelations about what free beings can do here and now to improve their conditions.

Marx and our libertarians agree that the technological conquest of scarcity liberates the individual for "a menu of choice." But that liberation from God, nature, and even other people means that the person is deprived of all guidance about how to choose. All choice that doesn't concern survival becomes a preference, a whim, so our freedom becomes nothing more than anarchy or pure indeterminacy. I can be anything I want to be, I say, but nothing I choose has genuine weight or significance. So the person, as the existentialists whine, comes to be seen as nothing more than an absurd leftover, an accidental aberration, from the impersonal natural necessity that governs the rest of existence.

The truth is that the person can't constitute himself out of nothing, and the abstract individual Locke invented with that capability always falls short of becoming anywhere near completely real. We can't remake all of reality in our image; the more we comprehend through control, the more we're aware of the infinite spaces that continue to elude us. The more we experience ourselves as free or disconnected individuals, the more we experience the mysterious contingency of our very beings. We still have bodies and we still die, and in fact we're more death-haunted than ever. We still can't help falling in love, though we Lockeans and Darwinians and Marxists have no idea how to talk about love. All our personal efforts to secure our beings have made us too anxious and disoriented, too lonely and personally insignificant, to be at home in the technological world we have created to replace our clearly inadequate natural home.

Nihilism or Relativism

Without any connection to a personal reality, a personal *logos*, beyond his own making, sometimes it seems that the free being can't endure. Today, we allegedly autonomous persons are so conscious of the limits of our biological existence that we seem incapable of creating anything that can stand the test of time. And in our time, Marx's historical science has been replaced by nihilism or techno-relativism. We can't even pretend to speak more than whimsically about anything that doesn't contribute to our futile efforts at survival. The only real morality we have left—morality reduced to safe sex or, more generally, safe choice—has nothing to do with the significance of the person's existence. Our proud claim that something real distinguishes the person from natural necessity seems more questionable than ever.

Nihilism is the view that what distinguishes me from the rest of nature means or is nothing. It means that "I," the particular person, am nothing. The time after the discrediting of Locke and Marx should, from one nihilistic view, belong to Darwin or to the revelation of the complete truth of his impersonal science. Sober Darwinians agree with whiny existentialists that the Lockean individual is absurd. There's no natural or real evidence for his existence. Surely it's ridiculous to claim the individual was somehow just dropped into nature to go to war against it like some crazed parasitic predator. The Darwinian adds that nature really does intend all animals, even us, to be basically happy or content. So we've acquired through natural selection instincts that produce pleasure in us when we do our duties as social beings; we have a natural moral sense. If we really were to detach ourselves from those instincts, we would condemn ourselves to the futile pursuit of happiness that ends only in death.

The Darwinian concludes that the Lockean individual—the individual free from nature—is nothing but a misery-producing delusion. Surely the Darwinian is right that nature provides us lots of guidance when it comes to happiness. It's still the case in our individualistic time that most people claim they're happiest as members of families, and our natural longings really do point most of us in the direction of doing what it takes to keep the species going. So thoughtful Darwinians claim that they have the antidote to the nihilism of individualism. Nature gives us guidance concerning the point of our lives, and we find fulfillment and happiness in doing what we're inclined to do by nature.

But the Lockean can reasonably respond that Darwinism is nihilism. The impersonal truth is that I exist for the species, not for myself, and what I do as a particular individual means or is nothing. Darwin can't explain why members of only one species can think so abstractly and imaginatively that they conceive of themselves as individuals. Nor can Darwin explain why members of only one species are in full technological rebellion against nature. In Harvey Mansfield's analysis, the conviction that Darwin might teach the truth about the chance and necessity that govern every life might well have been the main cause of the "manliness run amok" of the twentieth century, just as it might be the cause of the biotechnology run amok of the twenty-first. People are more concerned than ever about their personal significance, their importance or status, their very being as particular persons, in our officially egalitarian time.

What we know is that the Lockean criticism of Darwin from the perspective of human freedom contains much truth. And the Darwinian criticism of Locke from the perspective of the natural goods connected with our embodiment is also largely true. Both these criticisms are true because the Lockeans and Darwinians both think too abstractly. They share the error of unrealistic abstractness because they agree that there is no natural support for human freedom. They also agree on what human nature is; what the Lockeans call human freedom has no natural or real support at all. Words are not meant to give us any access to the truth about nature. For the Lockeans, they're weapons for individual preservation and flourishing, and for Darwinians they're for the preservation and flourishing of the species. We're certainly not hardwired to know any personal reality that we didn't make for ourselves, including, of course, God.

The American Need for a Science of Theology

We are, despite our proud enlightenment, much more a willful than a reasonable people. We believe that we're perfectly free to deny what we can know and even or especially to deny that we know it. We claim to be free to find it comfortable to believe that we're really autonomous chimps. We're free, we believe, to choose personal reality over scientific truth, distorting science to serve a freedom that our scientists don't acknowledge as real. But one sign of our true dignity, our true freedom as rational, erotic, creative, and relational beings, is that we still know that it's degrading to prefer comfort to truth. Our attempts to live without being moved by love and death (because they're more trouble than they're worth) mainly produce not some less-than-personal apathetic passivity but chaotic, angry disorientation.

Our Founders, our political Fathers, clearly privileged personal reality over impersonal science, and so they built better—they were more Christian—than they knew. They sometimes thought of themselves as proponents of the light of science and "Nature's God" against the monkish ignorance and superstition of Christians. But for them science served, above all, human freedom. And that freedom is nothing like the Epicurean serenity that Jefferson claimed to have privately enjoyed or his allegedly rational acceptance of nature's indifference to Jefferson's personal significance. Our Fathers' service to the significance of the person or the individual is what saves them from all charges of capitalism, materialism, atheism, and so forth. Surely most of our Fathers would have laughed at the Epicureans, or Marxists, or Darwinians who claimed that they were, in truth, slaves to forces beyond their personal control.

Americans may justly be criticized for sometimes regarding even other persons as natural resources to be exploited. But they're rarely so materialistic as to forget that a free being is doing the exploiting. They can also be criticized for alienating themselves even from their own bodies, but that's because they think of themselves as something other than bodies. Our pragmatism isn't materialism, because it depends on our conviction that our freedom is somehow real. The free being who secures himself as something more than a body is the one, as Alexis de Tocqueville (author of the best book on Americans) explains, who freely pursues enjoyment but never takes time to surrender to actual, instinctual enjoyment. Americans, in a way, exhibit the extreme opposite of nihilistic behavior: They work hard to avoid the conclusion that their very being *is* nothing.

Not only that, our Fathers deliberately didn't make it clear whether the person they served is the creature described by Protestant Christians or the free individual described by Locke. Either way, they served the dignity of the person free from natural and political domination. Our Lockeans and Protestants ally against the impersonal natural science that denies the free will or free choice of the particular person or individual. Whether Protestant or Lockean, we understand ourselves as mysteriously free from nature. And either way we're way too sure that there's no science of theology.

Whether Protestant or Lockean, we can't really claim that our way of life is particularly reasonable. As Tocqueville explains, our Christianity saves us from the manliness run amok producing the view that anything might be done for some futuristic historical utopia. It also teaches us that we have moral duties in common and even that we were made for more than mere survival. But religion achieves these beneficial goals, Tocqueville adds, only by being exempted, without discussion, from our habitual critical scrutiny. Americans, in the name of moral freedom and just sanity itself, decide not to think about the most important questions concerning personal significance, including, of course, about God. So, in some deep way, both our religion and our incessant labor to secure our being seem to be diversions from what we really know. They both oppose human freedom to what we can know through science.

But what we know through science also seems to be a diversion from what we experience about our freedom. Our physicists can explain everything about the cosmos but the strange behavior of physicists. And our neo-Darwinian biologists don't even try to begin to explain their joyful discovery of the truth about all things as merely the product of tools for species flourishing. Everyone knows our scientists are self-forgetful and that they have little real to say about who human persons are. Certainly they can't explain why the Americans who believe that their true home is somewhere else are the ones most at home in this world or why those who say they believe that they are as at home here as members of any other species are most in rebellion against their social instincts and biological limitations.

Americans are caught between incompatible diversions because de-Hellenization has defended our freedom, our autonomy, so well against impersonal science and de-Christianization has emptied our freedom of any real or "transcendent" content. The result is that we live in unstable, disorienting, narcissistic, degrading, and impersonal times, and we wonder whether the freedom our Fathers worked so hard and well to secure is either real or worth defending. But our return to the time of the Hellenic Christians reminds us that the sundering of the person from *logos* was a very questionable historical decision, one that artificially and futilely limited the scope of human reason. As far as we can tell, *logos* must be personal; only persons are rational, erotic, and relational enough to be open to the truth about all things, and only persons have the significance that comes with living freely, responsibly, and lovingly with what they know. A wholly necessitarian or impersonal world of minds and bodies wouldn't be known by anyone at all. The modern diversions are the results of thinking unrealistically or abstractly about who we and God really are. It really is true that the beginning of the cure for what ails us Americans is more science, not less. Our Holy Father points us in the direction of the theory, culminating in the science of theology, adequate to the great success of the experiment in freedom of our political Fathers.

8

BUILDING BETTER THAN THEY KNEW:

JOHN COURTNEY MURRAY'S AMERICAN, CATHOLIC VIEW OF THE TRUE FOUNDATION OF OUR COUNTRY

John Courtney Murray (1904–67) was a member of the Society of Jesus. He taught at the Jesuit theologiate at Woodstock, Maryland, and was editor of the Jesuit journal *Theological Studies* from 1941 until his death. He became a leading American public figure—the subject of a 1960 *Time* cover story. He was known mainly for his work on the relationships between the Catholic Church and American political life, his interpretation of the American view of religious liberty, and his resolutely Catholic view of the true ground of that liberty.[1] His affirmation of the basic continuity between the Catholic and the American views of human nature and human liberty led to tensions with and even his silencing by the Vatican Curia. But something like his view of religious liberty was affirmed by the Second Vatican Council.[2] His most celebrated book, *We Hold These Truths: Catholic Reflections on the American Proposition* (1960), reflects, even in its title, his order of priorities.[3] The American Constitution, for an American Catholic, can only be affirmed as intrinsically good if it recognizes each person's freedom for participation in the moral community or "order of culture" (WT, 35) that corresponds to his or her deepest natural longing.

My purpose here is to illuminate Murray's enduring contribution to American political thought—especially we Americans' proper relationship to our political Fathers and our proper relationship to God.

Murray is surely America's leading "natural law" critic of the intentions of modern thought. He shows that from its beginning that thought was based on a willful and self-destructive atheism, while not denying the benefits of its destruction of unjust orders of privilege, including even the political privileges of an established church.

Murray shows that our Constitution and our Declaration of Independence—by placing the American people "under God"—are not to be understood as, in the most important respect, modern. He acknowledges that our leading Founders were, in fact, influenced by the modern theory of Locke more than anything else, but his theory, in truth, is not embodied in the political order they constructed. The American problem is that our political Fathers built better than they knew, or thought they knew, and so we have to know more or better than they knew in order to appreciate properly and sustain what they accomplished. If unmoderated, the theory that they affirmed is capable of consuming what they built. So the greatest gift an American Catholic citizen can give to his country, Murray claimed, is a theory adequate to its wonderful practice (WT, 10–11).

Murray quotes a key statement of the Third Plenary Council of Baltimore (1884): "We consider the establishment of our country's independence, the shaping of its liberties and laws, as a work of special providence, its framers 'building better than they knew,' the Almighty's hand guiding them." America's Catholic bishops rejected the theory but affirmed the results of our Fathers' work. God's hand guided them, whatever they might have thought. But Murray explains that what was providential was hardly miraculous: "The providential aspect of the matter, and the reason for the better building, can be found in the fact that the American political community was organized in an era when the tradition of natural law and natural rights was still vigorous" (WT, 30). Our Fathers, partly because of legislative compromise between Christian and secular currents of thought and partly because they and even Locke himself didn't think through all the implications of his theory, were more influenced than they knew by thought they believed they rejected.

This approach to defending my country and its Constitution differs in important ways from the exemplary constitutionalism of the great Harvey Mansfield. I do note, however, that Murray's understanding of

Locke's theory is much like that of Leo Strauss, highlighting the ways in which it works to the self-destruction of reason in modern thought and to endanger fundamentally liberty in the modern world. Mansfield, Strauss, and Murray all agree that American practice is better than Lockean theory, and that's, in part, because the accomplishments of our Founders are better than much of their theorizing. Mansfield shows, using Alexis de Tocqueville, ways in which America could be better understood using premodern or largely Aristotelian thought. Mansfield even adds that the depth of Tocqueville's understanding and ennobling of modern and American liberty owed a lot to the Christian Pascal. Strauss, of course, says that understanding our country as a mixture of premodern and modern—including Christian—currents in thought is not enough, because the premodern contributions are eroding in the absence of a thoughtful defense.

Our adherence to a universal morality, Strauss believed, is most deeply a matter of faith, one that we only hold to be self-evident, and so, in a way, we're stuck with the defense of self-evidence as a sort of dogmatism. The approach of Murray has the advantage of offering a realistic defense of what our Fathers built to defend and perpetuate liberty, while not resorting to Tocqueville's questionable approach of refusing to celebrate—of, in fact, ignoring—our Declaration of Independence. Our Declaration, it's tempting to say, is more Christian than both Jefferson and Tocqueville knew.[4]

Locke as Our Fathers' Theorist

The theory that seemed most self-evident to our American political Fathers was John Locke's. But we, Murray claims, can't take Locke "with any philosophical seriousness" today. The "eighteenth-century gospel" he inspired unleashed a "dynamism" of destruction based on "philosophical nonsense." Murray presents two ways—both partly true—of considering our Founders' view of that dynamic nonsense. The first is that they were theoretically superficial men who sometimes really thought Locke explained it all. The second is that they sometimes quite self-consciously knew that they were using Locke's theory as a means to level unjust orders. Their liberating efforts presupposed a different and truer view of nature than Locke's. In their eyes, to some extent, Locke's "philosophic weakness vanished before its performance of the political task" that they needed his theory to perform. Nobody can deny the Lockean achievement of "destroy[ing] an order of privilege and inaugurat[ing] an era of political equality" (WT, 311–19). Locke's emphasis on political consent, based on his denial that "the people are the great beast of aristocratic theory" (WT, 181), was, in fact, in accord with the Christian, Thomistic, natural law tradition.

Locke said something like words are weapons, nothing more. In some measure, our Fathers took him at his word, using his words as weapons, nothing more. For them, Locke's "theoretic dogmas" may well have been "false," but still "powerful." Murray's most nuanced judgment may be that Locke's theory couldn't "quite veil" from our Founders the natural law "imperatives of a human reason that has a greater and more universal power than was dreamt of in Locke's philosophy." Our Fathers, finally, were ambivalent Lockeans. Their own deeds were sometimes inspired by a more realistic view of the purpose of words than Locke's, but they pursued historical success with the weapon of Locke's theory in mind (WT, 311–20).

When and if our Fathers really believed that Locke taught the whole truth and nothing but, from Murray's view, they must have accepted two unempirical premises. The first is that we consent to government and every other human institution as radically free individuals. The second is that all human connections or relationships are to be understood as based on one's own self-interested calculation. That means, as Murray explains, that "all forms of sociality are purely contractual" or "have no basis in nature" (WT, 306). We aren't naturally social beings; we aren't hardwired, so to speak, to share a life in common. The idea that all "mutual relations" can be understood in terms of contracts that utterly free individuals enter into and dissolve according to their sovereign willfulness is, we can see, clearly "a false theory of personality."[5] But it is a theory that has the advantage of privileging one's own freedom over all established privileges. Locke's radically individualistic insight must lead to theoretical nominalism; our natural capacity for language or naming is not for the joy of shared discovery, which, of course, would point in the direction of shared duties. Words are for maximizing one's own individual power, and they correspond to no "metaphysical reality" (WT, 309). The "naked essence" of Locke's thought, Murray reveals, is that all human capabilities are for the generation of power. The "law of nature," from this view, is nothing but a name given to the self-interested decisions I make as a free individual to perpetuate my own being and enhance my comfort. The law of nature is nothing but a corollary of the liberty each individual has to act in his own self-interest rightly understood. Locke, Murray claims, said more "politely" what Hobbes said more "forthrightly." Man's natural condition is war, and every capability he has is a weapon of war (WT, 304).

Locke's most basic theoretical incoherence seems to be his effort to sustain both nominalist premises and at least the semblance of the realist epistemology suggested by the idea of the "law of nature"—the suggestion of continuity with the realist, Thomistic tradition of "natural law." Locke says that all free individuals can know that all free individuals are basically in the same situation. That seems to mean there are some truths about nature and liberty we can share in common. But it's also true that the truths each individual holds to be self-evident radically separate his thoughts and concerns from those of others, and the words he uses to communicate with others are not chosen with the truth in mind. What nature has given each of us, Locke explains, is pretty worthless, and that includes our natural inability to understand much of anything at all without freely imposing our will on it. What we can know is what we've imposed on nature; even truth is the individual's powerful creation.

Murray's best student, Francis Canavan, shows with admirable precision that Locke, "famous as an apostle of human rights," also taught an "epistemology and metaphysics" that "did not furnish an adequate foundation for a political philosophy founded upon a common human nature." Locke wrote that "universality belongs not to things themselves, which are all of them particular in their existence." There, Canavan contends, "Locke makes a basic move; only individual things exist, *therefore* only individual things are real." All "general ideas," Locke adds, are "inventions and creations of the [individual's] understanding, made by it for its own use." So words really are just weapons—as the nominalist says—for the basically hedonistic goals of separated individuals; there's nothing real that corresponds to the artificial or abstract common life that is the invention of individuals allied in pursuit of their separate interests.[6] And even Locke's epistemology seems deduced from the free individual who has been invented or abstracted from the real existence of particular human beings. Epistemology and metaphysics themselves are weapons wielded by invented individuals.

Murray suggests the paradox that Locke's realism isn't very realistic, and even that Locke knows that. Locke's attempt to feign continuity with the philosophical tradition has to be understood, for the most part, as one means among many he used to maximize his power (WT, 309). His "state of nature" doesn't seem to be a real place. It's a name he's given to a myth—a "fictitious" "abstraction"—he's invented to maximize our power and freedom. It certainly doesn't correspond to what we know about our natures (WT, 305). Locke's views of nature and liberty are less descriptions than transformational weapons meant to become truer over time. They, like all other words, are tools for individual liberation. Locke's denial of realism in the name of freedom has worked to some extent, but, from one view, the fantasy of the modern world is that it could work completely. It has, most powerfully, worked, contrary to Locke's intention, to undermine what freedom we really do have. Our Fathers and even Locke himself were genuine liberals—or for limited, constitutional government—only because they "did not draw out all the implications from his theory" (WT, 308).

The Jacobin French revolutionaries, Murray explains, actually understood all the implications of Locke's theory better than Locke himself. If all human questions are to be resolved through power, then the individual has, in truth, no perspective, either theoretical or practical, by which he can resist the power of the state. The naturally contentless individual is defenseless against superior power. The French project was the "monism" or politically imposed unity of their revolution, and the omnipotent and so omnicompetent "totalitarian democracy" that was the prelude to the much harder totalitarianism of the twentieth century. The French, inspired by Rousseau, attempted to reduce particular human beings to citizens and nothing more, and religion to "civil religion"—or yet another instrument of political power—and nothing more (WT, 308–9). Locke's nominalism led them to conclude that there are no real limits to the state's power to shape human beings according to its political requirements.

Locke's intention was to free the individual from political, natural, and divine determination. But because the freedom he promoted was merely negative or destructive, it didn't really empower the individual to constitute himself against the powerful forces surrounding him. "The logical outcome of Locke's individualistic law of nature," Murray contends, "was the juridical monism of the . . . French Republics." Every communal or social or purposeful reality—"the pluralism of social institutions"—between the "individual" and the "state" was abolished (WT, 308). Lockean theory, in the eyes of the French revolutionaries, asserted "the absolute autonomy of individual human reason." That means that "[e]ach man is a law unto himself," and everything "is a matter of individual choice." No obligations are imposed on particular human beings by God or nature, and there is no foundation for any political authority but the will of the individual. Reason makes us all equal, but reason gives no content to our freedom. So what there really is "by nature" is "an absolutely egalitarian mass of absolutely autonomous individuals." Society can only be constituted by "the people," and that public power is as unlimited as that of the individual human being, who lacks what it takes to resist or even differentiate himself from the homogeneous whole. Because "the state, like individual reason, knows no God," it knows of no authority above its own popular will.[7] Government becomes "the political projection of the autonomy of reason," and so it becomes "the Supreme Judge" of even "religious truth."[8]

Locke's wholly indeterminate freedom has no middle place between anarchism and slavery, no place for genuinely limited government based on particularly human purposes.[9] Locke's effort absolutely to free human beings from natural and divine determination subordinates them completely to the will of man as expressed in a wholly conventional or simply willful Rousseauean social contract. The view that there's nothing higher than the will of man, for Murray, eradicates every barrier to the particular individual's totalitarian determination by the will of other men.

Lockean destructiveness, it's easy for us to see, went beyond the establishment of a kind of limited, consensual equality toward a comprehensive egalitarianism that took aim at the root of human liberty itself. We now know that the modern experiment, Murray observes, will never "erect an order of social justice or inaugurate an order of freedom" (WT, 319). So Murray viewed his task as defending our real, natural freedom and openness to order and justice against promiscuous, willful leveling, to show that America is dedicated to more than groundless equality or impersonal public opinion.

We certainly have more evidence than even Murray did that our Framers—and maybe Locke himself—were naive in believing that the full destructive or isolating impact of Locke's radical individualism and nominalism could be contained over time. Our lives, in fact, continue to be progressively more informed by a theory we know to be abstract or incomplete or, in some very important respects, just not true. The theory, as Murray explains, was not meant to be true, but to become true, to become the basis of a redescription of all of human life. Our pragmatist Richard Rorty, in a way, just echoes Locke in his confidence that human life could be improved slowly but, eventually, quite dramatically, in terms of freedom, prosperity, and the reduction of cruelty through the right use of those tools or weapons called words. Although it appears not to be enough to show Locke is wrong, Murray thought it might do some good, at least, to highlight the ways he's been discredited on the level of theory.

Darwin, Freud, and Marx as Devastating Critics of Locke

Locke's theory, Murray says, need not be refuted by us. It was demolished by his theoretical successors. "[T]he Lockean idea of man," he observes, has been "destroyed completely" by "the genuine and true insights" of "Darwin, Marx, and Freud" (WT, 309). That doesn't mean, obviously, that Darwin, Marx, and Freud teach anything like the whole truth. Each, Murray is clear, in his "monistic" way denies what we really know about human liberty. Their denials of liberty flow naturally, so to speak, from Locke's abstract, nominalist separation of liberty from nature. Marx's radical view that we're nothing more than what we've produced in the economic history of the division of labor— that we're wholly historical and wholly economic beings—depends on Locke's anti-natural view that free individuals reveal themselves to themselves through their work to transform nature. Darwin's view, that we are, by nature, qualitatively no different from the other species depends on Locke's seemingly unscientific or unempirical detachment of human freedom and purpose from all natural guidance. The Darwinian says that everything that exists is natural, and the Lockean claims that our freedom is not natural. And so the Darwinian reasonably concludes that what Locke calls freedom couldn't really exist.

Marx's criticism of the anxious and miserable individuals invented by Locke is not so different from that of a Darwinian sociobiologist. They're distorted by experiences characteristic of beings unnaturally alienated from their true home. Marx wasn't wrong to notice that Locke's capitalist ideology had to some extent worked to detach individuals from their natural, social ties, and Marx exposed the real "loss of freedom" that came with the success of that "empty nominalism" (WT, 311). Marx, of course, exaggerates the effects of that detachment. The lives of individuals haven't been reduced to nothing but whimsical playthings of the market; women haven't become nothing but wage slaves, just like men, and of course the great mass of people haven't become no more than cogs in a machine. But all those exaggerations contain some truth, and contemporary life is full of the anxiety that comes with the experience of being emptied out of properly human content. Those exaggerations correspond to what the modern individual would become if Locke's theory could become wholly true, and the fact that they seem more plausible than ever suggests that a false theory continues to display transformational power.

Marx, everyone now knows, offered no real remedy for the human misery he described. "Communism," Murray writes, "is political modernity carried to its logical conclusion" (WT, 211). From the most obvious view, totalitarianism is the logical, wholly political antidote of the emptiness of the Lockean individual. But when Marx himself describes life under communism, of course, it's the very opposite of totalitarianism. It's even, in a way, the very opposite of communism; the particular human being is free from alienating social or communal duties. The state, the family, and the church will have all withered away. People will, quite unobsessively, be able to do whatever they want whenever they want. Everything we do would become undistorted by any real experiences of God, truth, love, or death. Without such alienation, man would no longer be "a stranger to his own will."[10]

From Murray's view, Marx's theoretical communism would merely radicalize—or make more modern—the loneliness and boredom and the alienation of one human being from another that existed under Locke-inspired capitalism. And under communism, of course, people would be deprived of the "opiate" of religious or revolutionary hope. For Murray, theoretical communism can't become real, because it can't eradicate who we are by nature. That's the deeper reason why the pursuit of theoretical communism produced its opposite—political or totalitarian communism. The logical conclusion of modernity is a political war against who we really are, against what we can't help but know. Murray unreservedly endorsed America's political struggle against modernity's logical culmination, but with the suggestion that the real or spiritual foundation of our struggle couldn't be wholly modern or Lockean.

What's most true, for Murray, in Marx is expressed more deeply or psychologically by Freud. The modern conquest of nature depends on expanding the realm of the "techniques of conscious reason" and "renounce[ing] the forces of instinct." The result is that our natural sources of happiness and satisfaction are increasingly repressed, and so our most basic needs are denied gratification. The success of the Lockean project doesn't bring "self-fulfillment and happiness, but psychic misery and loss of personal identity." Freud rightly replaces the economic misery of the Marxian proletariat with his own "Freudian proletariat, chained in neurotic misery amidst material abundance," and without, obviously, the solace of religious or revolutionary hope.[11] Freud has, of course, an unrealistically monistic or reductionistic or merely sexual view of human *eros* and happiness. But he is right that we are miserably anxious or disoriented when we deny or repress the truth about who we are by nature, and he's right to dismiss the merely economic or historical accounts of who we are by Marx and others that make the revolutionary overcoming of our alienation from nature seem inevitable or even possible. Freud "shattered forever the 'angel-mindedness' of Cartesian man"—the idea that we are essentially other than natural or embodied beings. And so it shattered forever "the brittle rationalistic optimism" based on the idea that our bodies are machines to be manipulated at will by free beings (WT, 310–11).

The Marxian and Freudian view that the Lockean war against nature or instinct is an error that has made us more unhappy than anything else is shared by Darwin. Murray's realistic affirmation of what's true in Darwin strikingly anticipated the sociobiological criticism of social constructionism in the wake of both the fall of communism and the naive social experimentation of the Sixties. Darwin's "principle of continuity in nature" shows that we are like the other animals in many ways and share some purposes with them. Evolutionary theory expresses a partial but very real truth about our being: "man is solidary, by all that is material in him, with all of life." "Purified of its monistic connotations," Murray writes, the Darwinian principle of natural continuity "is compatible with a central thesis of Christian anthropology," which is "the law of solidarity of both flesh and spirit." Our social natures connect us as both material and spiritual beings, and so it's not realistic to disparage our bodies on behalf of our spiritual freedom. "Evolutionary theory," Murray adds, "is not compatible with Lockean individualism," which views all solidarity with and dependence on others or nature as worthless illusions that can and should be overcome. Evolutionary theory, in truth, dealt a "mortal blow" to that atomistic individualism (WT, 310). Darwin is right both that we're social animals and that what we're given by nature is both good and, in the most important respects, inescapable, despite our best efforts.

Darwin's alleged naturalism or empiricism achieves its allegedly comprehensive explanations by abstracting from everything that essentially distinguishes particular human beings from the rest of nature. The Darwinian abstraction is, in a way, a mirror image of the Lockean abstraction: Darwin exaggerates—while Locke denies—the continuity between members of our species and members of all the others. The Thomist observes that our self-consciousness—as well as our singular, erotic openness to the truth about ourselves, other persons, and all that exists—transforms even the natural ends we share with the other animals. But he never denies that our longings or ends have a natural foundation. He incorporates what's true and rejects what's false in both Darwin and Locke, while adding more.

Darwin shares Locke's unrealistic nominalism. Words don't give us access to self-evident truths; they're tools we've been given by nature to aid in the survival and flourishing of a species. The truth is not genuinely self-evident to us, contrary to the claim of our Declaration of

Independence, because we're not hardwired to have selves or souls—or personal freedom—at all. Locke is surely wrong to think words alone could possibly sustain us against the impersonal forces of nature or the arbitrary will of tyrants.

The Modern Will to Atheism

Darwin, Freud, and Marx are astute critics of the empty unreality of the Lockean individual, but Locke remains right about the reality of human liberty. Locke can't defend individual or personal freedom from monistic destruction because he's detached that person from his real natural ends, from the truth about who he is. Murray's criticism of Locke, finally, is a criticism of the modern decision for atheism, and all the monistic tendencies of modern thought are efforts to eradicate the personal, social longing for God as a natural explanation for who we are. All modern thought attempts to understand us as less than who we really are by nature, and so all modern thought is self-consciously scientistic or willfully reductionistic.

For Murray, the "original act of freedom" that produced modern thought was "the will to atheism." The absence of God from modern theory flows from the prior "intention that he be absent." Murray's "own proposition, derivative from the Bible, is that atheism is never the conclusion of any theory, philosophical or scientific." It is, instead, "a decision, a free act of choice that antedates all theories."[12] That means, in Murray's eyes, "ignorance of God is not a want of knowledge or even a denial, it is a free choice of a mode of living."[13] God has given man the freedom to choose to live without him, but that doesn't mean that man can realistically—or unwillfully—say that he doesn't know of God. Leo Strauss, for what it's worth, agrees that modern philosophical atheism—as opposed to more genuinely philosophical skepticism—rests on "an unevident, arbitrary, or blind decision."[14]

The original modern intention was to "explain God away," to show that "God can have nothing to do with the order of intelligence." He is "to be relegated to the order of fantasy," to become an imaginary projection for which there is no evidence. That's why the key modern dogma is that religion is merely a "private matter" that exists nowhere but in "the individual conscience" and has no juridical or "public status." Public life or the reality human beings share in common is godless. The church or any religious community has no official or legal presence.[15] The modern will to atheism *is* the will to complete autonomy—or freedom from God and nature. Murray explains that "man fell in love with himself," that is, "with his own creative powers." He fell in love, in fact, "with the dazzling brilliance of his own creations." The will to atheistic freedom is based on the thought that nothing creatures have been given is either good or lovable, and so only an "anthropocentric" or self-created universe could do justice to who we really are. The modern, technological will has, in fact, "altered the face of the earth," and nature has been "made to feel in her very being that man is the master." That will, at its beginning, was, in fact, "rational and purposeful," to create a world worthy of genuinely autonomous beings—beings who have no need of God.[16]

The original modern will Murray calls "aristocratic atheism." The philosophical elite worked to understand all there is—including who we are—without God. Its lack of definitive success caused it to be succeeded by "bourgeois atheism"—the effort to show that people can prosper or be happy and comfortable without God. Because bourgeois life, as Marx and particularly Freud explained, turned out to be in some ways more restless and miserable than ever, it was succeeded by increasingly insistent "political atheism"—various attempts, inspired by Rousseau, to reduce human beings to secular citizens and nothing more. The movement of modern atheism from aristocratic to political is a move from theory to practice, from understanding to imposition, from scientistic abstraction to relentlessly forcible destruction.[17] Despite the logic of that movement, aristocratic, bourgeois, and politicized atheism, of course, all operate simultaneously in the modern world. The collapse of political atheism with the fall of communism, Murray wouldn't be surprised to see, led to an intensification of bourgeois atheism—shown in the efforts of our libertarians and our "bourgeois bohemians"—and of aristocratic atheism in the popularized, basically Darwinian science of our so-called "new atheists."[18]

For Murray, the whole modern experience is evidence that the Christian discovery of the truth about our freedom can't be expunged from any genuinely empirical account of "natural law"—about who we are according to nature. The misery Marx, Darwin, and Freud described is our misery in the willed absence of God; we now know that misery has no historical/political or economic or technological cure. We also know there's no returning to, for example, the Aristotelian or classical account of nature and human nature. For Aristotle, "man in the end was only citizen, whose final destiny was to be achieved within the city" (WT, 155). Aristotle, in truth, did not know of each human being's freedom from political life—discovered by the Christians and displayed in an unrealistically extreme and reductionistically distorted way by Locke. It's unclear, to tell the truth, whether Murray regarded Aristotle as primarily ignorant of God or choosing against him. But his choice, in any case, was clearly less willful than the characteristically modern one.

Murray explains that "Christianity freed man from nature by teaching him he has an immortal soul," which apparently he would not have known by natural means alone. That teaching revealed to man that he longs to be more than a biological, species-oriented being, that he has singular purposes not given to the other animals. So Christianity "taught him his own uniqueness, his own individual worth, the dignity of his own person, the equality of all men, and the unity of the human race" (WT, 192). Christianity freed human beings from what seemed to Aristotle to be the limits of their natures. That revelation about the real truth about who we are has survived every modern effort to distort or suppress it. We continue to know, despite the best efforts of the secular civil theologians and other ideologists, that "every fatherland" is, to some extent, "a foreign land" (WT, 15). *The* political truth that the Christians discovered is that "the whole of human life is not absorbed in the polis" (WT, 333), and that human dignity is not primarily "civil dignity" (WT, 52).

That's why the integrity of the political order can't be restored in post-Christian times except by "totalitarian" means. The modern secularist must make inauthentic denials that the pagan secularist—such as Aristotle—didn't have to make. It's inevitable, Murray observes, that any post-Christian "unification of social life" is both more "forcible" and takes place on "a lower level" than Aristotle's (WT, 133). The attempt to restore the monistic *polis* in the modern world is never really a political restoration, because the Christian criticism of civil theology, being true even if the personal God doesn't exist, can't be eradicated from the world. The revolutionary totalitarian democrats might have thought of themselves as guided by a republican "myth of antiquity," but they were really about the reactionary negation of the true discoveries of "Christian civilization," the true sources of egalitarian political and spiritual freedom.[19]

Every willful attempt to exaggerate the autonomy of reason ends up denying the reality of the genuine transcendence—or orientation in the direction of God and personal moral responsibility—of human freedom. In thinking about the "imperatives" of his own nature, Murray says he knows that "my situation is that of a creature before God" (WT, 32). And he called the modern denial of the human situation "a basic betrayal of the existential structure of reality itself" (WT, 215). What Murray himself knows, he claims, the "common man" also knows, "instinctively and by natural inclination" (WT, 204).

The decision for natural teleology and against willful atheism depends on the affirmation that the highest purpose of human beings is to seek, know, and love God. And on the basis of that decision, our self-understanding becomes more in accord with who, by nature, we are. The choice for God is at the foundation of "natural law" and can be validated on genuinely empirical grounds. The choice for God is a choice for a being who is not, essentially, "a solitary, separated individual," but a social, loving being essentially embedded in a community while retaining his own, personal identity.[20] The authentically postmodern choice is not for revelation against reason, but against wholly "autonomous reason" and for reasoning about who we are as whole natural beings. There is no such thing, Murray observes, as "abstract reason, but only reason as it exists in men," and it's willful fantasy of abstracted or utterly autonomous reason that unrealistically abolishes the distinctions between true and false and right and wrong.[21]

Our Nation Under God

Our political Fathers' will, Murray claims, was not fundamentally atheistic. He follows Lincoln, most of all, by showing that our Fathers, despite their Lockean theory, built "a nation under God." He does so, first of all, in opposition to the strict separationist jurisprudence that emerged in the 1940s. According to this view of constitutional interpretation, derived from the theory of Jefferson and Madison, government and religion are to have nothing to do with each other, and religion is to become a purely private, individual affair.

In absence of some recognition of the social and socializing function of churches or institutional religion, Murray feared, too much emphasis will be placed on the public schools as the country's only unifying factor, as the only way of overcoming the natural fact of individualistic divisiveness. The same "powerful and articulate philosophy of 'American education'" that would deny all juridical or public status to religious schools, he warned, is about the business of developing "a concept of the 'historic unity' of the American people and a rather mystical concept of democracy."[22]

The idea of democracy becomes a sort of fuzzy or almost pantheistic substitute for civil religion, and the American alternatives could either become being a part of the democratic community or withdrawing into "protest schools" that perniciously prevent children from being incorporated into the civic brotherhood. The result would be an impairment of the parent's right to encourage the genuinely free exercise of the religious dimension of his children's lives, and religious concerns would be viewed as necessarily conflicting with those of citizenship. Today, we also have more evidence than ever that the Court's primary intention has been to promulgate and expand the reach of a kind of secular public reason that is, in its effect, Lockean. The result, of course, is the unnecessary alienation of both our best Christians and our best citizens.

"For Madison as for John Locke, his master," Murray explains, "religion is of its nature a personal, private, interior matter of the individual conscience, having no relevance to the public concerns of the state."[23] Religion is completely separate from the public world constructed through the institution of government, and the state takes no interest in—or even has no awareness of—the relationship between the individual man and his private God. So the state has no jurisdiction over churches because churches have no juridical status at all. The freedom of religion is, from this view, for "religion without a church," for a phenomenon which is socially irrelevant or totally excluded from civic affairs or any public educational mission. The result is the same juridical monism that was characteristic of the omnicompetent politicization of the revolutionary French. The deep Lockean thought here is, of course, that individuals don't have social natures and words are just weapons, and so there's nothing natural pointing human beings in the direction of God.

The result for Madison is not civil religion but real secularism or a more perfect political atheism. Government, in the interest of individual liberty, has to get by without God, and there's no denying that the unamended Constitution of 1787 is silent on God. Because Madison, in Murray's view, didn't think through all the implications of his radical individualism, he views it as a violation of liberty for government to impose or even rely upon a civil religion. But that's at the cost of reducing conscience to nothing but a private fantasy. Locke, in the French revolutionary view, made civic unity too much of a merely self-interested construction that leaves too much intact of the solitary emptiness of the natural individual.

The Supreme Court, Murray shows, avoided this conclusion only by taking its constitutional bearings from Madison's personal opinions without embracing his theory. Murray imagines the "legal howling" that would have been the result of the Court taking its bearings from "natural rights" derived from a "pre-social" state of nature. In the world of twentieth-century theory and practice and in the midst of a welfare state sanctioned by the Court, Madison could confidently say that "the radically individualistic concept of religion . . . is today quite passé."[24] Mere jurists might, in fact, be entitled to detach the law's original intention from any claim for its theoretical truth, and so they can contribute powerfully to Locke's transformational intention without reflecting on the realism of what he actually says about who we are. So Murray dissented from the Court on our political Fathers' original intent—on the Constitution's history—in order to suggest a better or more realistic theory.

Our Fathers as statesmen, the evidence shows, did not intend the First Amendment to aim at strict separation of church and state, but only to prevent the national establishment of any particular religion. Madison, the statesman pursuing legislative compromise with the more Christian members of Congress, was far less ambitious in practice than he was in theory. Nonestablishment is subordinated to religion's free exercise, and there's no mention of the rights of some isolated conscience or even any concern for the option of atheism. Religion is viewed as a positive, institutional good, and it's the religion clauses of the First Amendment that are the key evidence that our Constitution presupposes the existence of a transpolitical God.

Murray shows that the establishment of religion was understood uniformly in the Congressional debates in "its proper, technical sense" of displaying no favoritism or preference to any particular organized religion—such as the Church of England. So the Constitution establishes the "political equality" of all churches and other religious institutions. Freedom of religion ended up meaning, contrary to Madisonian or Lockean theory, freedom of churches. And so religious equality is "the equality of differences," and those differences are much more than a whimsical variety of private fantasies.[25]

The anti-ecclesiastical tendency of the eighteenth century—which reduced religious liberty to the sanctity of the privatized conscience—didn't make it into the actual Constitution. Our Constitution presupposes that we are social, religious beings open to the supra-political truth about God, and that capacity of our natures that leads inevitability to organized religion is meant to be an effective limit on the omnipotence and omnicompetence of the state. Our Constitution, through the compromises that produced the religion clauses of the First Amendment, ended up being more Thomistic than our political Fathers knew. The legislature of Virginia, as Murray observes, seeing the somewhat un-Lockean nature of the political compromise, regarded the protection afforded to the consciences of individuals as inadequate. But, in the spirit of compromise, the legislature eventually—after almost two years—ratified it.

Our Constitution, Murray concludes, "was a great providential blessing" for Catholic American citizens. Because it points in the direction of the community called the church, Catholics as Catholics can be good American citizens. The liberty it protects is religious liberty in the sense of freedom for religion, the freedom to orient one's will with others toward the truth about one's situation as a creature. The American Constitution, because it is about the free exercise of religion, doesn't require civic theological affirmations from its citizens—affirmations no Christian can make with "conscience and conviction" (WT, 43). Murray was and still is criticized by conservative Catholics for his "Americanism"—for identifying American political solutions with ultimate or religious truth.[26] But Murray's inclination was, in fact, in exactly the opposite direction.

The key providential fact about our Constitution, for Murray, is that "the distinction between church and state, one of the central assertions of the [Christian, natural law] tradition," found its way into our Constitution. Our Fathers understood that separation as "the distinction between state and society," which they, following the tradition, thought of as society composed "of a whole area of human concerns which were remote from the competence of government." For our Fathers, it was emphatically not true that there was "nothing above the state" (WT, 58), because they presupposed that we are, by nature, more than isolated, contentless individuals. Among those natural societies to which government, properly speaking, is both ministerial and incompetent are the churches.

As others, such as Tocqueville, have noted, the American Revolution was limited; it didn't aim to reconstruct religion or the family or even local government. So our Fathers held that government can't "presume to define the Church or in any way supervise her authority in pursuit of her own distinct ends." Religious freedom is accorded not only to the individual but also to "the Church as an organized society with its own law and jurisdiction." The social areas from which our Fathers excluded government "coincides with the divine mission of the Church" as the Church itself understands it (WT, 69–70), and so "there's an evident coincidence of the principles which inspired the American republic and those which are structural to the Western Christian political tradition" (WT, 30). The providential compatibility of America's political mission and the Church's divine mission was actually a coincidence based on a compromise. None of those involved in the compromise were thinking in terms of the Catholic Church's self-understanding, but that's no reason why the Church can't affirm the result as providential, as what our political Fathers really gave us.

The Declaration of Independence

Following Lincoln, Murray finds the source of our fundamental law's principles in the Declaration of Independence. The religion clauses of the First Amendment were meant, in a way, to constitutionalize that "landmark in political theory," the Declaration of Independence. The key assertion of the Declaration is that there's "a truth that lies beyond politics: it imputes to politics a fundamental human meaning. I mean the sovereignty of God over nations as well as over individual men" (WT, 28). The Declaration too was a legislative compromise, the most instructive of the Founding compromises. Let me turn to a Catholic author writing at roughly the same time as Murray to explain why that's so.

R. L. Bruckberger, a French priest who wrote a classic reflection— *Images of America*—on his visit to America in the 1950s, compares in some detail Jefferson's fairly purely Lockean "rough draft" of the Declaration and "the final text" as adopted by Congress. For the interpreter, Bruckberger claims, "nothing speaks as eloquently as corrections on a text."

There's no doubt, Bruckberger contends, "that Congress and Jefferson had different concepts of God," and they imply "two profoundly different philosophies." Jefferson's "Nature's God," which was retained from the first draft, was essentially no different from Voltaire's "Great Watchmaker" or Robespierre's "Supreme Being." That Being's impersonal, past-tense existence is no real constraint on human will, and he's compatible with real political atheism. There was, in fact, nothing in "the reigning philosophy of the day" or Jefferson's "own attitude" that pointed in the direction of recognizing God as a Creator, Providence, or Judge, as a personal being who guides and restrains human will.[27]

But the final draft of the Declaration ended up giving the God of Nature all those personal attributes. That's because most of the members of Congress admired Jefferson's literary skill "but did not accept his philosophy." For them, "Moses and Jesus" were more important than the latest theoretical currents (IA, 92). Men who read and believed in the Bible had a decisive influence not only on the Declaration's character and content but, despite themselves, even on its philosophy. Congress remained to some extent within the Puritan tradition, and that first American Founding had a decisive influence on the second. "The greatest luck of all," Bruckberger writes, "for the Declaration was precisely the divergence and compromise between the Puritan tradition and what Jefferson wrote." A Declaration "in the strictly Puritan tradition would probably not have managed to avoid an aftertaste of theocracy and religious fanaticism." And neither theocracy nor fanaticism are, in truth, central to the political tradition of the West. "Had it been written from the standpoint of the lax philosophy of the day," Bruckberger adds, "it would have been a-religious, if not actually offensive to Christians" (IA, 93).

The compromise between the Puritans and the Lockeans is, in fact, superior to either of its components, especially as philosophy. That Congress, working with Jefferson, built better than either of them knew was "luck . . . strangely fused with genius" (IA, 92–93). "The men who signed the Constitution," Bruckberger claims, "were better than the philosophy of their day," and "the Declaration itself is superior to the men who signed it" (IA, 99). The Declaration was, as Murray says, providential; it depends upon what the American people were given from a variety of sources. The combination of Judeo-Christian revelation with the philosophy of the eighteenth century produced a "philosophy that most manifests the equality of all men in their natural and supernatural dignity" (IA, 98–99). It is the source of the genius of a nation that, at its core, offends neither philosophers nor Christians and doesn't even place the God of the philosophers and the God of the Bible at odds. That the God of Nature *is* the God of the Bible is the philosophic thought, as Murray says, at the heart of the Thomistic tradition. So Catholics can both affirm and account for the truth of the compromise of the Declaration—its accidental Thomism—far better than the Calvinists or Puritans and Lockeans or political atheists who did the compromising.

Michael Zuckert, the most able defender of the purely Lockean view of the Declaration, admits that the passages added by Congress about God as Supreme Judge and his providence "appear much closer to the Biblical religions than to the natural theology dominant elsewhere." These references seem, in fact to "echo more sectarian religious sensibilities." But this acting God, Zuckert adds, acts to enforce nothing different from the laws of the God of Nature. The Declaration never "strays from the conviction that the principles of the political sphere are contained within the sphere of reason and natural theology and don't depend upon 'special revelation.'" And so the Declaration points to a society of people with "diverse religious commitments," united only by "the natural universal principles that govern the political sphere."[28]

But according to Murray, the additions make all the difference. They lead to the conclusion that our natural faculties point each of us in the direction of our personal God, and that some common knowledge of that God is a limit to our diversity. The final, corrected version of the Declaration points us away from the political atheism of the impersonal Deism (of Locke or Voltaire) characteristic of the eighteenth century. There is a personal will higher than of particular human individuals, and so human sovereignty is not unlimited or unguided. It's true that the Declaration has, as Bruckberger notices, no reference "to revelation of any kind, no reference to the Bible or to that Christianity with which America is so deeply imbued." But it's still a "religious"—without being an ecclesiastical or anti-ecclesiastical—document. It's self-evident that the Creator—without whom a universal political morality is seemingly impossible—is the source of equality and the inalienability of our rights (IA, 83).

Bruckberger, in effect, echoes Murray when he says that the American revolutionary repudiation of "divine right" on behalf of a free people was "infinitely more radical than the French." The revolutionary French transferred "all sovereignty" from "the person of the king to the nation," and so they recognized no divine claims other than that of politicized or civil theology. The nation was, in principle, as totalitarian as was the absolute monarchy—the unlimited will of the people in general replaced that of the particular person. The French recognized no limit to political sovereignty, because their radical individualism produced no alternatives to natural anarchy and political despotism. That's why Congress was right that Jefferson was wrong to believe that abolishing divine right only requires transferring full sovereignty to the people (IA, 102–3). The divine will can't be given to human beings in a limited government devoted to liberty. A free people have to be not only less but more—as social beings under God—than political beings. The particular human being is not created by nor is he essentially a creature of government. Being a citizen is part—and by no means the highest part—of being a whole human person.

America as Part of Christian History

Jefferson and Madison's theoretical will was moderated by the necessity they faced as a statesman operating in a somewhat Christian environment. One result was the Declaration's virtually Thomistic or "natural law" theory, a result that can't be found in or reduced to the will of any particular Father or founder. The compromise between Locke and Calvin produced something like the synthesis of St. Thomas. America, as Murray says, was "very superficially Christian" (WT, 317) in the eighteenth century, but it was Christian enough not to embrace the politicized will to atheism. From the beginning of "the authentic American tradition," Murray claims, parties and statesmen who "erect atheism into a political principle" are rejected. Jefferson and Madison might have privately been atheists, but their atheism has no public status. The Americans privatize atheism and have political institutions that point beyond themselves in the direction of God. In America, it's atheism that's the private fantasy that can't be openly affirmed by those in political life. Murray even quotes the Supreme Court as having said, "We are a religious people whose institutions presuppose a Supreme Being." It's because of that presupposition that there's no need for the Constitution to mention God. From the beginning, the Americans—and especially their political leaders—acknowledged their dependence on God without resorting to official civil theology (WT, 29–30).

Because our Founding compromises accommodated Christian concerns, they can be seen as "recognizably part of the Christian tradition." In that respect, Murray affirms the conservative view that "Christian history" prevailed in our Constitution over "rationalist theory." And so the man whose rights are protected by the Constitution "is, whether he knows it or not, Christian man." That is, he's a man who "has certain original responsibilities precisely as man, antecedent to his status as citizen," a man whose understanding of his "personal dignity" has an irreducibly Christian foundation (WT, 30, 36–37, 39).

This conservative victory of Christian history over Lockean theory has, of course, been eroded historically by the transformational power of Lockean principle. So it can't be defended today as providential, but only as corresponding to true or rational theory, to what, as the Declaration says, is genuinely self-evident, as corresponding to the way we really are.

The true foundation of religious freedom, Murray explained, is the natural status or "dignity of the human person." That moral dignity is "rooted in the given reality of man as man." Each of us is given the basic imperative to "act in accordance with his nature." And that imperative given to the true "moral subject" is the source of freedom from political determination each dignified person has when it comes "to the search for the truth, artistic creation, scientific discovery, and the development of a man's political views, moral convictions, and religious beliefs." We're free by our natural gifts for all these aspects of "the human spirit."[29]

The key truth we hold in common—what Murray calls "the essential idea upon which a democratic culture must be erected"—turns out to be "the dignity of human nature," which includes "man's spiritual nature."[30] It's because of that nature—properly cultivated or habituated—that we can conceive of the possibility of real freedom, which is the freedom of a virtuous people "inwardly governed by the recognized imperatives of a universal moral law" (WT, 36). That's why Leon Kass, for one, has written that an effective defense of life and liberty now depends on an explicit defense of human dignity. The defense of the pursuit of happiness with no consideration of what's worthy of who we are is too empty or too indefinite to be an effective guide for the challenges we now face.[31]

The Catholic Contribution to America

American Catholic citizens as citizens, Murray claimed, are especially well equipped to give their country what it most needs—a theory that adequately accounts for the success of its experiment in liberty. Our lack of such a theory has produced what the authors of our Declaration might call a crisis of self-evidence. That crisis has moved from

Locke through Darwin in one way and the Jacobin/totalitarian version of Rousseau in another to the pragmatic, relativistic conclusion that there's no reality we can know that corresponds to our experiences of self or soul or freedom. If that's the case, then our Fathers' dedication to the protection of our equality in human liberty really makes no sense.

Locke, Darwin, and the totalitarian secular civil theologians all share the nominalist view that words are nothing more than weapons. For Locke, words exist to secure the individual's power or survival; for Darwin they exist to secure the species' survival; for the totalitarian civil theologians they exist to impose civic unity on naturally anarchistic individuals. They all deny that we're naturally equipped to hold the self-evident truth in common.

We need a science or theory of natural law that doesn't exaggerate either our freedom from nature or our continuity with the rest of nature. We need a theory that doesn't make us so homeless that our freedom is displayed in nothing but absurd, anxious misery, but one that doesn't attempt to make us so at home that our real experiences of freedom and dignity are unrealistically denied. We need a theory that grounds our personal dignity in our natural openness to God. The God who is *logos* and *eros* made us in his image, and so there must be a ground for human freedom rooted in our natural capabilities for knowing and loving. The best present expression of that view of who we are is found in the thought of our philosopher-pope.[32] Our Fathers, in this view, chose our natural openness over a consistently Lockean individualism that would reduce religion—and finally all our experiences of freedom and dignity—to private fantasies with no common or public weight.

Our theory, as Murray summarizes, has to "be asserted within a religious framework" (or a choice for God), be "realist (not nominalist)"—or based on the truth that words aren't merely weapons but give us access to the way things and persons really are, be "societal (not individualist)"—because we are given the ability to hold personal truth in common, and "integrally human (not rationalist)"—because the truth is that the whole human being or person—the being open to truth, God, and the good—can't be reduced to either mind or body (WT, 320). What our country most needs from its Catholic citizens, in Murray's view, is genuinely conservative in two senses. It conserves the whole truth about who we are against unrealistic abstractions and empty nominalism. It also reinvigorates the American rational tradition through conserving a tradition both older and more rational—or at least more realistic—than our own.

I don't think, of course, that American politics today is likely to be animated by a Thomistic philosophical tradition that's no longer even persuasive to most American Catholics. But maybe it's true that things haven't changed that much since the time of the Founding. The implicitly Thomistic or genuinely realistic philosophy of the Declaration and the Constitution Murray affirms was the result not of our Fathers' theoretical reasoning but of legislative compromise between Lockean and basically Calvinist factions. Today, we have a resurgent religious faction in politics composed primarily of evangelical Christians, and we also have a more aggressive, elitist promotion of secular autonomy. Perhaps our best hope for reasonable policy is compromise between those two factions, compromises that might often be better than either party to the agreement knows.

That potential for judicious, salutary, theoretically defensible statesmanship is undermined most of all today by an aggressive Supreme Court pursuing what amounts to an agenda to Lockeanize more and more of American life. As the Court explained in *Lawrence v. Texas,* its job has become deducing all the individualistic consequences of the single word "liberty" in the Due Process Clause of the Fourteenth Amendment. "As the Constitution endures," Justice Kennedy explained, "persons in every generation can invoke its principles in their own search for greater freedom." The word of the Constitution, in other words, is nothing more than a tool of Lockean, nominalist transformation. As Canavan writes, Locke's "nominalist epistemology . . . is now accepted as dogma" by many of our legal scholars, and the influence of that uncritical thinking on our Supreme Court has turned "the due process of law into an instrument for an enactment of a liberal political agenda."[33]

Murray's reminder that the Constitution (or fundamental law) and the Declaration (or the source of our fundamental principles) both have the character of compromise should be used to curb the principled urgency our judges, bureaucrats, and professors on behalf of liberty understood as autonomy—or freedom from nature and God. Their theory doesn't correspond either to the practice of our political Fathers or to a realistic view of who we are. It is with authentic piety to our Fathers' intention that we take our bearings from what is realistically self-evident to us, and we turn to "better than they knew" studies.

9

SOLZHENITSYN ON THE CHALLENGE OF OUR TECHNOLOGICAL CIVILIZATION

James Schall, as far as I can tell, is a wonderfully happy man. He lives well—with incredible intellectual courage and deep faith—in light of what he really knows—of, as he says (usually with italics), "*what is.*" He's also a relentlessly bold and astute friendly critic of the political life of his country. There are few writers he admires more than the Russian novelist, historian, and essayist Aleksandr Solzhenitsyn, who died in August 2008. Solzhenitsyn, maybe more than any other man (certainly more than any other writer), was responsible for the West's great victory in the "ideological war" with communism, a war, as Schall says, that was "about what is a human being" ("Will to Truth: On the Death of Alexander Solzhenitsyn," *Ignatius Insight,* August 6, 2008).

Schall reports that what he most admires about Solzhenitsyn is his "intellectual courage, the courage to tell the truth when the regime, any regime, is built on a lie." Solzhenitsyn was courageous enough not to hesitate to criticize the West—including our country—for our political lies, which, it should go without saying, are much less insidious, monstrous, and comprehensive than those that animated communist regimes.

And he was bold enough to add, in a 1993 Address to the International Academy of Philosophy in Liechtenstein ("We Have Ceased to See the Purpose") that the defeat of communism in many ways left the West worse off.

There was no longer any "unifying purpose" to mask the deepening moral vacuum characteristic of modern, progressively more technological life as such. "All we had forgotten," Solzhenitsyn contends, "was the human soul." Our prevailing answer to what a human being is remains far from completely true. My purpose here is to build upon Solzhenitsyn's criticisms of our country today, with a particular emphasis on the challenges presented to us by our technological and biotechnological success. What we've been given, Solzhenitsyn explains, is "an extremely intricate trial of our free will." The good and bad news is that human beings always have been and will always be, as long as they exist in this world, faced with such trials. We should, in fact, be grateful for having been given morally demanding lives—lives which require that we display our courage and make possible both human responsibility and human happiness.

True vs. Technological Progress

Up until now, it seems that the cost of modern progress has been the neglect of souls. "We have," Solzhenitsyn observes, "ceased to see *the purpose*" of particular human lives; we no longer know who or what we're living for. True progress, Sozhenitsyn explains, is always individual, or personal, moral, spiritual, and truthful. It depends upon the individual's self-limitation with a purpose in mind he didn't just make up for himself. It involves humble submission to a real authority higher than ourselves, an authority that calls us to personal responsibility. Anyone with eyes to see knows that he's been given moral responsibility as a personal being who can't help but know and love.

"There can be," Solzhenitsyn writes, "only one true Progress: the sum total of the spiritual progress of individuals, the degree of self-perfection in the course of their lives." So a truly progressive society would subordinate technological progress to personal progress. Technology would be good as one means among many for the responsible pursuit of personal perfection. But that subordination, Solzhenitsyn observes, has so far seemed to have been almost impossible. The characteristically modern view has become that *all* human experience should be reconfigured in a technological way. The modern slogan is, he says, "All is interests, we should not neglect our interests." The being with interests *and nothing more* thinks he must devote every moment to securing his own being in a hostile environment. And he thinks he neglects his interests—his true self—every time he attends to his soul or even just falls in love.

Solzhenitsyn readily admits people gain a lot when they come to think of themselves mainly as beings with interests. The average person lives longer, more freely, and with more creature comforts, and there's nothing wrong with being comfortable in freedom for a very long time. Our techno-thinking certainly succeeded in correcting the otherworldly excesses of medieval spirituality. And it really is true that one responsibility given to free beings with bodies is to attend to one's interests. Anyone who thinks he's above or below being, among other things, a being with interests really is mistaken about who he is.

Our Lonely Howl

For Solzhenitsyn, what we've lost by thinking of ourselves as beings with interests overwhelms what we've gained. The "gifts" of our "technological civilization" have both enriched and enslaved us; we are in some ways materially more secure, but at the cost of "spiritual insecurity." As his own example shows, people certain of the *why* or purposes of their lives can live well with almost any *how*. Solzhenitsyn was happy in the squalor of the Gulag because he knew *why* he was there. And no amount of any *how* can replace the absence of the *why*—of some idea of "*what* we are living for." People in our country, he notices, are more lonely and disoriented than ever. And just beneath the surface of the happy-talk of our therapeutic pragmatism, it's easy for him to hear "the howl of existentialism"—the desperate expression of profound spiritual insecurity.

Beings with interests and nothing more think that words are nothing but weapons to pursue their freely chosen private goals. So they don't have the words to express their social, personal longings—their loneliness in the absence of love and their inability to live well with the prospect of death. They howl because they're so detached from other persons that they can't truthfully communicate their experiences to them. They howl because they think that they're nothing but accidents in a world so hostile to their existence that they're stuck with constantly securing themselves all by themselves. They howl when they think about their biological demise, which they think will be the end of being itself. For them—for us, "the thought of death becomes unbearable," because "[i]t is the extinction of the entire universe in a stroke."

Solzhenitsyn may exaggerate how much we're stuck with howling, but all serious critics in our country are compelled to exaggerate in typically futile efforts to get our attention. Our philosopher/novelist/physician Walker Percy wrote (in *Lost in the Cosmos*) that American writers suffer from "Solzhenitsyn envy." Solzhenitsyn was taken so seriously by the Soviet government that he was thrown into prison for over a decade and later just kicked out of the country; the Soviet rulers knew that his truthful words were a fundamental threat to the future of their regime. But no American writer is considered dangerous enough to be imprisoned; our writers' truthful words—no matter how penetrating and apocalyptic—aren't viewed as any real challenge. From Solzhenitsyn's view, we're much more recalcitrant students or slower learners than were the Soviet leaders. Even he has not really been able, despite many attempts, to get *our* attention.

All real exaggerations contain a lot of truth. Anyone can see that there's plenty of evidence of efforts in the West to reconstruct all human relations to maximize individual freedom or self-sufficiency. The narrative of our country's historical progress that makes the most sense is that of the liberation of the individual. As the Supreme Court pointed out in *Lawrence v. Texas,* what seem like necessary and proper limits of individual liberty to one generation of Americans seem like despotism to the next. The very word "liberty" in the Constitution, the Court contends, has no definite meaning; it was placed there as a weapon to be used by individuals to increase their freedom over time. Free individuals have, over time, successfully reconstructed marriage as an optional institution detached from all biological imperatives. Now it's all about rights, not duties. So same-sex marriage seems to have become a constitutional right, although it wasn't always one. If marriage is really between two free individuals, then we have no right to exclude gay Americans from its benefits. But can any human institution endure that detached from responsibilities shared in common?

It's All about Me

According to social critic Christopher Lasch (in *The Culture of Narcissism*), the increasingly common product of our effort to understand ourselves as free individuals with interests and nothing more is the narcissistic personality. To be narcissistic is to experience everyone and everything as existing for *me*. It's true, of course, that almost no one is completely narcissistic, but it's also true that we're more narcissistic than ever. People think, in fact, that they're stuck with being more narcissistic; they experience themselves as more on their own than ever.

The narcissistic person, Lasch observes, aims to be protectively shallow, so as not to lose himself or his interests in other people, deep thought, or love. He also has a fear of binding commitments and a willingness to pull up roots. He wants to maximize his emotional independence to keep his options open. He wants to free himself to judge every moment of his life according to his interests, or according to what's best for securing his own being.

Most of all, the narcissistic person is repulsed by an experience of dependence—on other people, on nature, and even on his own body. He opposes *himself*—his free existence—to any attempt to limit his freedom. Because he can't acknowledge his dependence, he's incapable of feeling or expressing loyalty or gratitude. He insists on defining himself by himself for himself. He can't even be a materialist, because he radically separates *himself* from his biological existence and its satisfactions. He's stuck with seeing himself disconnected in every respect from the world around him. He experiences himself as real, but empty. He knows that he's not determined, and that his being is somehow the opposite of nonbeing. He knows that he's not nothing, and so he can't be accused of nihilism. But that's all.

Consider the apparent incoherent way sophisticated Americans understand themselves today. They are, most of all, proud of their autonomy, and they're increasingly pro-choice in almost every area of life. But they also proudly say that they know that Darwin teaches the whole truth, and so we're qualitatively no different from the other animals. We're just chimps with much bigger brains. Surely there's little more ridiculous than thinking of oneself as an autonomous chimp.

If you look at the behavior of these self-defined autonomous chimps, it's clearer who they really think they are. They work to maximize their autonomy, their freedom. They know they're nothing but chimps by nature, but they don't really believe they're stuck with what nature gave them. Even if the reigning theory of natural evolution is true, they think, why should they be bound by it? More and more they refuse to act like chimps: They're getting less gregarious, refusing to spread their genes by having little chimps, and rebelling more insistently against nature's indifference to their particular existences. They act like they don't like being chimps and have freely chosen to do something about it. (Meanwhile, those Americans who don't think of themselves narcissistically and don't think of themselves as chimps—our evangelical and orthodox religious believers—act in a far more chimp-like way. They're embracing their natural social duties by spreading their genes [having lots of kids], taking parenthood seriously, and not being all paranoid about the inevitability of their biological replacement.)

According to the great thinkers of the premodern world, human beings are political, familial, and religious animals. Their mixture of reason, love, freedom, and embodiment leads them to give institutional content and communal form to their lives together. But the contemporary narcissist hates any formal limitation or direction to his freedom. So he does what he can to live without politics, family, and church. He tries to live nowhere in particular, because he experiences himself as being nowhere in particular. Being, he believes, begins and ends with his own being, and so he can't think of himself as a part of any whole.

Moods and Bodies as Natural Resources for Free Beings

Sociobiologists tell us that the narcissist is somehow deluded into thinking that he's better off severed from the natural, social sources of the happiness of human animals. Christians—not to mention Alexis de Tocqueville—say that his protective withdrawal is based on the mistaken judgment that love is more trouble and more dangerous than it's worth. Today it sometimes seems as if people have to choose between

either living happily by being suckered by others and subjecting themselves unnecessarily to various risk factors or living more securely for
a long, free, comfortable, and miserable time. It's true that, with the
help of their family physicians, lots of Americans hope to escape the
burden of that choice through artificial happiness provided by Prozac
and similar drugs. Chemically engineered happiness promises to be
free from both the dangerous unreliability of others and having to give
even a moment's thought to one's soul.

There is, of course, a tension between the technology of mood
control and the progress of real technology—what really promises to
sustain the free being indefinitely. If my mood becomes too "Don't
worry, be happy," then I might stop working really hard to secure my
real self. I might neglect to take my Statin or scientifically work out or
even take action to divert the asteroid about to pulverize our planet.
What we really seem to want are "designer moods" that reconcile happiness with productivity. We want to be, as David Brooks observes,
"bourgeois bohemians," to be both hyperproductive and enjoyably
self-fulfilled. But finally bourgeois always trumps bohemian, because
the truth is the narcissist knows of no standard higher than his own
productivity. So whatever the hard-working "bobos" might say, the
bohemian part of his life is always just around the corner.

A perfectly technological world would be one in which every natural resource was harnessed to maximize the productivity of free beings.
According to the philosopher of narcissism John Locke, my body is my
property—a natural resource that I might exploit at will. Because I am
not my body (or even the chemical reactions that produce my moods),
I am free to use my body like all my other property. From some undisclosed location, I'm free to give orders to and about my body (and even
my moods).

That technological insight is the source of our enthusiasm today
for cosmetic surgery and cosmetic neurology. Thanks to high-tech
medicine, I can—by nipping, tucking, botoxing, and so forth—make
my body seem younger, more pretty, and more pleasing—or more
marketable. I can also, with the right drugs, make myself smarter,
have a better memory, be more attentive, be less moody, and even have
more physical endurance. From the traditional standards of medicine,
surely the physician shouldn't turn a healthy person into a patient just

to make him more productive. And any responsible physician should have some qualms about the inevitably perverse psychological result of turning a perfectly normal memory or mood into an enhanced one. But those concerns are now trumped by the patient's autonomy—or freedom from and for bodily determination.

We still say we shouldn't do anything chemical or artificial to boost the performance of athletes. We want natural gifts to be combined with real self-discipline to produce authentic excellence. The home-run hitter who takes steroids increases his own value as a player, and so in a sense his productivity. But the money he gets comes from entertaining an audience, and the customer is going to be right when it comes to what sort of display of excellence will please him the most. Steroids or not, it's finally the customer's choice, and the athlete is pretty much stuck with conforming to the (always somewhat arbitrary) rules of the game either way. In another sense, of course, the athlete isn't productive at all; his job is for most people nothing more than a source of pleasant recreation. The world would be just as wealthy, powerful, and free—and my personal existence would be just as secure and comfortable—without him.

The choice for natural over artificial excellence has little relevance for areas of life where the standard of productivity is less ambiguous or more real. It's much harder to say, for example, that physicians should turn down safe and reliable enhancements that greatly improve their medical judgment and reduce medical errors. Nobody's going to say let's stick with the natural way at the cost of significant suffering and loss of life. Athletes just play games according to basically arbitrary rules; medicine is about *really* keeping free beings going. Somebody might say that the physician, as an autonomous being, shouldn't be compelled to use a drug that improves his memory or judgment or endurance. And there will be some who worry, quite rightly, about the effects of such drugs on the physician as a whole person. Maybe it'll also be the case that the enhanced physician might lose some bedside manner, some of the sensitivity required for the more intangible dimensions of caregiving. But it seems to me that productivity in the service of health and safety will easily trump autonomy and sensitivity. Physicians who fall short of the expected performance standards won't be kept on the job out of respect for their conscientious objection to being improved or their personal flourishing as parents and friends. The possibility of artificially enhanced performance will become a fact of medical life, and the selfless sacrifice of one's autonomy and maybe personal happiness for the good of the patient will be part of the professionalism expected of the physician.

Productivity will, in fact, trump autonomy in most areas of work. Consider, for example, the notoriously unproductive and autonomy-obsessed college professor. We used to tolerate moody professors who drove some students off and never got it together enough to publish much. We didn't think they could help it. But soon enough a professor won't be able to claim a right to his so-called natural moods if he could easily get himself down to the drugstore and get brightened up. Now a certain professor might really believe that bad moods are what lead him to truth or beauty or even to God. But from a technological view, moods are just collections of chemicals, and, if possible, we should choose the ones that are of the most use to us. Because I am not my moods, the thought is, I should give orders to my moods with my productivity in mind.

The same sort of thinking will probably determine the outcome of another important bioethical issue we now face: Should I be able to sell my allegedly redundant second kidney? Some say that it's undignified to reduce human beings to commodities. But the free individual responds: I am not my body, and I am especially not my kidney. My kidney is a commodity, it's true, to be used by me. Some say it's undignified to sell kidneys, but an act of love to give them to those in need. But the free individual responds: When I need a kidney, I don't want to be emotionally dependent on someone else. I don't want to be stuck with the tyranny of being grateful. If I buy a kidney, I can remain free. After I write the check, I don't owe anybody anything.

It'll be a new birth of freedom, the narcissist believes, when I can count my extra kidney as part of my net worth in dollars, and other people are free to do the same. It's my business if my doctor has turned me—a healthy person with a top-notch kidney—into a patient to dispose of my resource as I please. In doing so, after all, I benefit not only myself. I preserve the life—the very being—of another free being, without having him become in any way dependent on me. Entering the kidney market is one way among many I can find to enhance my productivity.

We do have to consider that, if we allow people to sell their kidneys, we might end up expecting them to. Why give a poor person welfare or educational financial aid if he is sitting around with a perfectly good kidney to sell? There are already some serious ethicists who say that, given the plight of the poor in our unjust society, we should free them up to improve themselves by marketing what is a very valuable—and until now an untapped—resource.

Productivity as the Standard for Beings with Interests— Both Old and Young

The standard of productivity is also the basis of our increasingly meritocratic society. These are the best times ever to be young, smart, pretty, and industrious. But the pressure is on like never before to be young, smart, pretty, and industrious. (Not that times were ever that good for the stupid, ugly, and lazy.) The preferential option for the young inaugurated in the Sixties turns out to have had a technological justification. The young are the most flexible and techno-savvy among us. We go to the youngest member of the family—certainly not grandpa—to find out how to use our own iPhones, iPods, and various other iThings. What do the old know that we need to know now?

Technology seems to obliterate the need for the traditions and for the craftsmanship that used to be prized for guarding and passing on. More generally, we're now stuck with this question: What are old people for? We tell them it's time for them to enjoy, but human life, to be either dignified or happy, has to be for more than enjoyment (not to mention that biological necessities set definite limits on how much the old *can* enjoy, even with Viagra and similar products). As Solzhenitsyn says, technology is an undeniable cause of a "rift" between the generations, often "dooming" the old to loneliness and abandonment and depriving them of "the joy of passing on their experience to the young."

Our technological standard of productivity increasingly favors the young. But our technological success is causing our population to age. Sophisticated Americans benefit from constant medical breakthroughs and attentive responses to every newly discovered risk factor. They're living longer than ever. And (except for religious observant Americans and certain immigrant groups) people in the techno-Western world are having fewer and fewer children—partly because they don't want to limit their options by thinking of themselves as parents. Insofar as I identify being itself with my being, I see no need to generate replacements.

It's very good news that people are living longer. There seems to be a new birth of freedom in the growing period between parenting and productivity and debility and death. That freedom, for prosperous Americans, seems to be for whatever purpose the free individual chooses. But, from another view, the individual is productive for a small part of his life, and a dependent for longer (as a child and as an old person). If freedom and dignity are intertwined with productivity, then it may not be so great after all to live a very long time. Will the shrinking number of productive young people be willing or even able to support the increasing number of the unproductive old? "The gift of heightened life expectancy," Solzhenitsyn observes, "has, as one of its consequences, made the elder generation into a burden for its children."

Certainly both the young and the old are aware of the individualistic, meritocratic principle that nobody owes anyone else a living. And we have plenty of evidence these days that love, all alone, is unreliable. It's no wonder that the old do what they can to mask the signs of their age to avoid loneliness and failure. As Locke himself told us, in an individualistic society the only reliable hold the old have on the young is money. It's more important than ever to be rich if you're going to get very old, as almost all of us hope to do. But pension systems are collapsing, Medicare is demographically untenable, health care and caregiving costs are skyrocketing, and the stock market's future is shaky at best. It's tougher than ever to have confidence that your money is going to last as long as you are.

I tell my students I want to enroll them in my two-point program for saving Medicare. First, they need to start smoking and really stay with it. Second, they need to start making babies, and I mean right now, this week. So far I haven't been persuasive enough to get them with the program. But members of the Greatest Generation, in effect, did. They had lots of kids and gave very little thought to risk factors. They often smoked like chimneys, enjoyed multiple martinis, and only exercised for fun.

The excellent TV series *Mad Men* (that's what advertising executives called themselves in 1960) displays the smoking and drinking of successful Americans fifty years ago for our horror. Don't you idiots know you're killing yourselves! They really did drop dead much more often in their fifties, without drawing a dime of Social Security and (after 1962) of Medicare, but not before generating several replacements to fund those programs for the future. Our whole medical safety net is premised on demographics that have disappeared and aren't likely to return, and that's because, for good and bad, we're more narcissistic than people used to be.

One downside of thinking of oneself as a self-sufficient individual too much of one's life really kicks in when you get old and frail. Nobody, it turns out, is stuck—out of love or at least familial loyalty—with taking care of you. The fastest growing demographic category is men over sixty-five with no children or spouse, and even having a kid or two might not help you much in our mobile and increasingly duty-free society. A piece of good news is that we're persistently pushing heart disease and cancer back. The corresponding piece of bad news is that more and more seem destined to die of Alzheimer's.

We can already slow down that already very slow regression to infancy and death, and we might eventually be able to prevent the disease's occurrence through genetic intervention in many cases. But nobody now seems to see the road to its cure. Imagine what Alzheimer's must be like for someone who has no one to rely upon who loved them prior to their getting the disease. We're going to have more and more old and frail, debilitating and slowly dying wards of the state, so to speak. And the care they're going to get, because they're really on their own, isn't likely to be good. The truth is we have no idea how we're going to afford it.

Productivity vs. Caregiving

So one big downside of our productive, high-tech, narcissistic society concerns caregiving. Thinking in terms of productivity and caregiving are two very different ways of looking at the world, and at the purposes of human beings. Productivity is measured in money, and that means that its benefits are diminished if shared. It separates us from one another, at least emotionally. It even turns friendship into networking. It's a standard that's tough on people motivated mainly by love. Caregiving is unproductive, can't be measured by money, is all about loving solicitude, and usually seems boring and easy to people obsessed with productivity.

We Americans—in accord with a deeply traditional view—used to have a division of labor based on the distinction between productivity and caregiving. There was a rough division of labor between men and women. Men took care of politics and business and women the home and the children. Roughly speaking, men were about the money and women the love. Men were about the pursuit of happiness and women happiness itself. And I'm not only thinking of married women. We can't forget, for example, the legendary Sisters of Mercy, tough, intelligent, and adventurous women who devoted their lives to the sick and the dying out of love.

The American view, as Alexis de Tocqueville described it in *Democracy in America*, was that what men and women did was separate but equal—really incommensurable. People need both to be productive and to be cared for, and it's impossible to rank one human good over the other. There's no denying, Tocqueville added, that American men often didn't really think that what women did was as important as what they did, just as men were reluctant to admit how indispensable caregiving was to their own happiness.

The division of labor was, in fact, unjust. Men did have all the public power. They had the option of contributing to caregiving, which they too rarely exercised. The more productive ways of living were simply denied to most women. Autonomy and productivity are not the whole of personal dignity, women know, but they can't help but think, especially in the modern world, that it's too undignified to live without either.

The most intelligent and admirable American women, Tocqueville reports, willingly endured that injustice on behalf of love. They knew better than men the true purpose of human life. Because they knew the "why," they found themselves remarkably able to live with any "how." American men, by comparison, were unerotic and whiny and always bragging, quite unrealistically, that everything they did could be comprehended by the doctrine of self-interest rightly understood.

Tocqueville couldn't help but subtly give his judgment that American women are superior to American men.

So it's hardly surprising and basically good that women eventually demanded their liberation in the name of justice. But, for the most part, they were liberated to be productive—usually to be wage slaves—just like men. Men and women, in justice, are now supposed to share equally in being productive and in being caregivers. But nobody really denies that women took to the men's traditional role far more readily than men did to the women's, proving, again, the superiority of American women to American men.

Women flooded the labor market and significantly enhanced our country's productivity. But real wages dropped. The family wage (supported by the Democrats through the 1960s) became an increasingly distant ideal. Families increasingly seemed to need to work more hours than one person reasonably could to live well. Women who wanted to remain unproductive out of love have had a harder and harder time defending their choice or being honored for it. That's surely one reason why the legendary Sisters of Mercy have virtually disappeared. And because men are more unreliable and more narcissistic than they used to be, any wife and mom who can't pay her own way now has a very risky existence. The explosion in the number of productive single moms has caused some to wonder whether men have become superfluous.

We shouldn't overdo the effect our increased emphasis on both individual liberation and productivity has had on caregiving. Something like 80 percent of long-term caregiving is still done voluntarily by women, and working parents still find quality time to lavish attention on their one or two kids. Almost all of us would quickly go nuts without lots of routine, voluntary care. All I'm saying is that caregiving is more misunderstood and underappreciated for what it is than ever, and the amount of voluntary caregiving seems bound to continue to decline.

More and more caregiving is done for money, by workers. We have health care workers for the sick and disabled, day care workers for children, and so forth. Insofar as such workers save and prolong lives with their technical skill, they're clearly being productive. Nurses, for example, are getting paid more and more, and we know why.

Those caregivers who do nothing but attend to the requirements of day-to-day existence, who are about the maintenance of life, have trouble getting paid much more than subsistence. What they do, after all, seems mostly boring and easy, and it doesn't require much formal training. What gives caregiving incommensurable value is loving solicitude or what makes life most worth living. But we can't expect someone we hire to feel that love, although, of course, sometimes they do. When caregiving is reduced to what we can measure with money, it seems like much less than it really is. Free individuals often brag they'd rather pay for caregiving, for the same reason they'd rather pay for a kidney. Once money changes hands, they owe the provider nothing more. We somehow expect workers to do what was once done out of love without having to give them any love.

People say—and usually really mean—that our extensive use of caregiving workers is an unfortunate necessity of our productive and mobile society. Working mothers would rather not put their kids in day care, and children are often consumed with sadness and guilt for how little they can do for themselves in caring for their elderly parents. Still, our health care system isn't sustainable without more voluntary caregiving—and more genuine appreciation of the virtues of caregiving—that we're likely to have in our techno-future.

Working to Stay Alive

The main reason caregiving languishes is that it continues to get tougher for increasingly productive and narcissistic individuals to identify themselves—especially lovingly—with anything but themselves. They think of themselves less and less as basically parents or children, creatures, citizens, friends, or even parts of nature, and think of themselves more and more as free individuals. The narcissistic individual is both certain that he's not a biological being, and that there's nothing real about him that survives his biological death. Death, for him, is meaningless total extinction, and that's why, Solzhenitsyn observes, what people in the West lack, most of all, is "a clear and calm attitude toward *death*."

Being so death-haunted explains our birth dearth to some extent; we get little solace from thinking about the children who will live on after us. Although we love them (when we have them) as the unique and irreplaceable beings they are, we think less about them as our replacements. Not only that, we think about them less and less as beings who will produce their own replacements. We raise them more to be able to sustain themselves as productive beings in a hostile environment than to be nurturing and caregiving persons who are, first of all, parents and children. In a kind of narcissistic way, we tend to think of both ourselves and our children as so significant and so irreplaceable that we're convinced that thinking of anyone in terms of being replaced is an affront to personal freedom.

Nor do we get much satisfaction from producing any accomplishments that will stand the test of time much better than we can as biological beings, and that's why there's so little building or writing for the ages these days. Being so death-haunted also helps to explain the extreme measures taken by the old to look young, not to remind us that they're dying. It's one reason why the old are increasingly separated from the rest of society, and their care turned over to workers. It might even have something to do with why physicians have less time for their dying patients, and why the best and the brightest medical students are choosing dermatology—which, as medical specialties go, has very little do with either birth or death. Because death and caring for the dying have less meaning for us, we're increasingly inclined to want to think of death less as a beneficial or inevitable necessity or just God's will and more as an accident we can avoid if we work hard and are very, very careful. As long as these trends continue, we're going to spend more and more on health care.

Our Health Care Crisis

Our most immediate health care crisis also has to do with productivity trumping caregiving. The system of health insurance largely being a benefit of employment is breaking down. One problem, of course, is that too many people—those un- and under-employed—are uncovered. A bigger one is that this system, supported by tax deductions for employers and employees, is incompatible with the requirements of our increasingly dynamic and competitive globalizing economy, as well as with the increasing pressure on ordinary people to be productive. Employers, partly because of rapidly escalating health costs, often can no longer offer that benefit and remain competitive. Both employers and employees can no longer afford to be loyal; fewer and fewer people are being protected by unions or will have a career with a single employer. People really don't want and often really can't afford to pass up a better job just because they fear losing their coverage. And employers want to be able to fire an unproductive employee with a really sick kid without feeling too guilty.

Our present health care system largely depends on the somewhat paternalistic employer being an intermediary between the individual and government. But it seems that the last vestiges of social paternalism are fading away. Health care, it seems, has to devolve either to the individual or to government. Some say that the government, in fact, has a duty to provide the best possible health care for every dignified human being. That conclusion might be supported by Christian or Kantian morality. It might even flow from the Lockean view that people consent to government to have their right to life protected. That might mean that government has the duty to employ all means available to keep *me* alive as long as possible. A thoroughgoing narcissist wouldn't hesitate to claim that every possible resource should be thrown into the technological project of indefinitely delaying his death. But I've already discussed the demographic realities, among other factors, that make it completely unclear how government can fulfill even a modest view of that responsibility indefinitely. Nobody really knows how to save Medicare, for example, for more than a few more decades. (It almost goes without saying that "ObamaCare" evades this real issue.)

The European idea of a paternalistic government caring for the health of everyone as a common good undermines, in fact, the personal caregiving indispensable for sustaining our system. People, in our country, still tend to believe that families are primarily responsible for the old and disabled. In countries with cradle-to-grave insurance systems, people think that responsibility lies with the government, letting family members off the hook. Well, it would be disastrous in many ways—including financially—to let our voluntary caregivers off the hook. Not only are we not going to get, but we really don't want a providential government assuming the burden of sustaining isolated individuals. That is surely what some liberal reforms now seem to intend, but any policy generated by that seemingly "humanitarian" urge will be unsustainable.

We can't really accept the simple view that government is concerned with the common good, while the free economy promotes individual selfishness. The European Christian Democratic parties had better reason for thinking something along these lines in the 1950s and early 1960s, when lots of Europeans were still recognizably Christian and people were having plenty of babies. Today, it's clear everywhere that public bureaucracies are far more likely than private concerns to be infused with the self-indulgent, narcissistic cultural excesses of our intellectuals. Certainly we wouldn't want those bureaucracies deciding about rationing or compelling abortions or even making hard calls about the profoundly disabled or those very near death. We wouldn't want to turn health care decisions over to those most contemptuous of the moral choices of the least narcissistic Americans.

Nevertheless, health care shouldn't devolve to individuals left simply to their own ingenuity and resources either. That would make the lives of already anxious ordinary Americans far too hard. We need to eliminate the insurance tax breaks to employers and employees—to eliminate what amounts to a very regressive tax loophole. We need to use the huge amount of increased tax revenue to fund tax credits and direct subsidies to those who can't afford private insurance. We have to mandate the purchase of insurance by everyone, while making it very easy to purchase adequate coverage. We have to encourage competition among private providers to keep health costs down, as we did with considerable success with the Medicare prescription drug benefit. And we have to make sure that insurance is available for the "uninsurable," for those particularly at risk to have very expensive health care needs. (McCain actually had a proposal something along these lines on his website during the 2008 campaign, but he never defended it in public. Neither candidate [nor President Obama now] was willing to educate the American people on the unsustainability of their employer-based plans.)

We're also going to have to do more to reconcile productivity with caregiving. It's certainly the job of government now to curb the narcissism of our time by enabling and encouraging people to act out of love. We need to support programs that help parents, children, friends, citizens, and creatures do what they're inclined to do in terms of voluntary caregiving. What we need to borrow from the European Christian Democratic parties is the principle of subsidiarity, which means that care should be given in the most personal way possible. A sustainable health care system is possible only insofar as productivity is balanced with love, or by the thought that each human being is more than a being with interests.

One example of such a program, in my hometown of Rome, Georgia, is a center that's sort of an outpost of a hospital still run by the Sisters of Mercy in Atlanta. Old and very frail people—many with early-stage Alzheimer's—can spend the day at a center staffed by a nurse and other caregivers. The center is mission-driven and personal enough that the staff members, although paid, think of themselves as a lot more than workers. This "day care" allows old people to stay at home with their families—or "deinstitutionalized"—without impossible or unreasonable sacrifices of productivity and ambition.

Here's a program premised on the facts that we're people with interests, but more than that too. It assists people in being as self-reliant as they can reasonably be. Health care would be more expensive and caregiving would suffer if this program disappeared, and these days it couldn't have a future without government help. But funding for this "faith-based initiative" was decreased under our compassionately conservative president and was not included in the stimulus package of our compassionately liberal president and Congress.

We want as little caregiving as possible to be done by government, which can't help but treat people as either isolated individuals or needy dependents. Big Government, obviously, can't be the provider of personal care. At the same time, we want people, especially the most vulnerable among us, not to be all on their own. We want to keep the lonely howling—some of which seems to be the unavoidable downside of our technological progress—down to a minimum.

Postmodernism Rightly Understood

Thinking about the very practical dilemma of the future of health care and even the future of one particular kind of government program reminds us that we're not in the thrall of some impersonal technological process bound to deprive of our humanity. Technological civilization really is a trial of our free will, and we really still can think and act as if human beings are more than beings with interests. We really have been given distinctive purposes, and we really still can live in love with what and who we really know. We certainly live in demanding times, with anxious insecurity and profound loneliness making being happy particularly difficult, but far from impossible. We've neglected the soul. The result, as Solzhenitsyn writes, is a "nagging sadness of the heart" in the midst of plenty. But souls are still there, and there's no reason why the enjoyment of creature comforts is altogether incompatible with spiritual development.

The most immediate intended audience for Solzhenitsyn's speech on our vacuum of purpose were those, in the early 1990s, who bought into the "naive fable of the happy arrival at 'the end of history,' of the overflowing triumph of an all-democratic bliss." That fable or lullaby, we now all know, couldn't really produce either human happiness or human "tranquility." At the end of history, we would be freed from trials of free will for living in peaceful contentment in the present. But the truth is that "the trials of the twentieth century" have been replaced by new ones. We see, more clearly than ever, that modern progress has not been humanly satisfying. So we should be more open than ever to coming to terms with the distorted incompleteness of the modern or allegedly "progressive" understanding of who we are.

Solzhenitsyn, in his 1978 Harvard Address, reminded us, that "if man were born only to be happy . . . , he would not have been born to die." That's not to say that he wasn't born to be happy. His happiness comes from fulfilling the purpose he has been given—"his task on earth," and that "evidently must be more spiritual" than "a total engrossment in everyday life." Thank God, that total engrossment is impossible for beings born to die, and we have no choice but "to rise a new height of vision, to a new level of life, where our physical nature will not be cursed, as in the Middle Ages, but even more importantly, our spiritual being will not be trampled on, as in the Modern Era."

Our thought and public policy must be informed by postmodernism rightly understood, by what we can now see with our own eyes about the truth about who we are. Our social and political vision that guides us toward progress, toward that new level, needs to be based on the true progress—the genuinely moral, intensely personal drama of the good's truthful, courageous, and often happy struggle against the evil of lies—that should constitute every human life. "In the end," as Schall explains, "ultimate things have to be rediscovered in each of our souls."[1]

10

OUR HERO, SOCRATES

Nalin Ranasinghe's *Socrates and the Underworld: On Plato's "Gorgias"* is one of the most able, eloquent, noble, profound, and *loving* books ever written on Socrates. It restores for us the example of a moral hero who inaugurated a moral revolution in opposition to his country's post-imperial cynicism and nihilism. What Socrates discovered about the human soul remains true for us in our similarly cynical and nihilistic time. Here's the truth: "Self-knowledge is both the cure and the punishment for evil." We *are* the beings who can't help but know the truth about ourselves and be open to the truth about all things. The truth is *real;* we lack the power to command or negate it. The truth has *authority* over us; we can't live well unless we see that it is the power that allows us to perform genuinely free and deliberate acts. The truth is *attractive;* it both draws us out of ourselves and is a sort of magnet that puts our souls in order. And the truth is genuinely moral or *beautiful.*

Each of us and the *cosmos* itself "is so structured that true happiness can only result from virtue." Both intellectual and moral virtues are required to be genuinely open to the whole truth, and so the view that one form of virtue is possible without the other is mistaken. The Socrates Ranasinghe presents us with is undeniable *personal* evidence that "philosophy still has the moral authority to sustain the soul's resilience and inspire virtue in times of moral strife and social chaos."

Socrates can be *our* hero, freeing us from the cynical deceptions that seem to have given us a time without heroes.

One characteristic of our cynical and nihilistic time is that many of our scholars are certain to object that Ranasinghe's presentation of Socrates is too edifying to be true. It's easy to foresee their charge that this author doesn't have what it takes to penetrate beneath the superficial and banal pieties Plato employed to protect philosophical skepticism from moral indignation. This author is suckered by Plato's *exoteric* moralism because he's not rigorous and sophisticated enough to get to the *esoteric* or genuinely philosophic dimension of Socratic dialectic. The esoteric Socratic teaching is all about rational liberation—liberation of the philosopher from moral dogma for the amoral truth about the human situation.

Socrates' true view, according to this skeptical interpretation, is that *the philosopher* is an *atheist,* and he uses morality or *ethics* to serve his selfish and hedonistic goals. From this view, the philosopher Socrates befriends the sophist Gorgias in order to learn the right sort of manipulative rhetoric that will serve him and his liberated friends. Genuine spiritual or philosophical liberation is reserved for a very few, and the liberated few are stuck with employing various sophistic deceptions to humor the moral many who threaten their private enjoyment. Plato, from this view, writes to preserve and improve upon morality not because it is true or good, but because there's no doing without it for most people.

This skeptical view that, for Socrates, *truth* and *morality* are fundamentally at odds, Ranasinghe shows, is itself based on a relatively superficial reading of the Platonic dialogues, one complacently satisfied at stopping before genuine spiritual enlightenment begins. The skeptical reading of Plato isn't *erotic* enough, because it tends to be based on the suspicion that *eros* or love itself is, deep down, an illusion. That's why, as Ranasinghe suggests, skeptical readers miss how radical Socrates' criticism of Thucydides' deterministic "realism" is.

For Ranasinghe, the deepest level of Socrates' teaching is the overcoming of skepticism and a philosophical justification of morality, a justification of our undeniable erotic impulse to have faith in *logos* as the foundation of friendship as genuine human community. Ranasinghe's reading of the *Gorgias* clearly establishes that genuine dialectic is the deadly enemy of sophistry; this means that the sophist Gorgias and the philosopher Socrates could never be friends. The pseudo-philosophical interpreters of Plato achieve their sham enlightenment by not really appreciating the radical distinction between Socratic dialectic and sophisticated manipulation. Socratic dialectic means to offer spiritual enlightenment to us all.

The deepest depth of the Platonic dialogue is a return to its surface, which is genuinely illuminating conversation about the moral or purpose-driven concerns we *really* share in common. We learn that the true purpose of the capacity for speech given to particular members of our species is neither *technical* nor *transgressive*. It is an error to view words as primarily weapons for either practical manipulation or for destroying the various articulations of the moral responsibilities given to social persons open to the truth.

Socrates finally confirms the goodness of all that we've been given as the beings with *eros* and *logos,* which means that all pretensions to solitary liberation or autonomous self-sufficiency are revealed, deep down, to be nothing but unnecessarily misery-producing illusions. Speech directed by reason and pulled toward reality by *eros* is, most of all, what keeps us from being alone. It also allows each of us to make genuine progress toward personal moral perfection. Our truth-inspired responsibilities are *both* personal and social.

"The crucial question," as Ranasinghe articulates it, "has to do with how seriously one takes Socrates' understanding of the soul as the seat of moral agency." Do we really know enough to be able to say with confidence, against the skeptics, that our perception of moral choice is real? Socrates' "knowledge of ignorance" is his awareness that omniscience is not a human possibility. We can't really resolve the question of human freedom through the study of natural science, and one condition of our freedom is our ability to know that we can't fully comprehend or control all that exists. We don't have the power, in fact, to make ourselves more or less than humans stuck between the other animals and God. Divine freedom or blind determination by impersonal necessity will never characterize us.

Do we still know enough to know that being good and being happy are really choices open to us? Do we really know that any effort to feel good—to be happy—without really being good is bound to fail us?

Socrates, Ranasinghe patiently explains, gives a *psychic* account of evil; good and evil are both profoundly *personal.*

I am evil, I can say, because I'm to blame if my soul is disordered, if I've been choosing against what I really know about myself. Evil *is* real and personal, and so it has a real and personal remedy. Telling the truth to myself as a rational and erotic being is the precondition for my choosing good over evil. That means that no radical social or technological transformation—no mega-effort to escape from the reality we've been given—can solve or even address the problem of evil. The Socratic way—the only way that respects the mystery of human freedom—is to proceed one soul at a time.

The Socratic teaching is morally demanding—the truth is we're not excused from doing the right thing by being victims or playthings of arbitrary gods or impersonal forces. But it is also reassuring. An ugly old guy trapped in an unhappy marriage turns out to be the best and the happiest Athenian of all. We can live well in the most adverse circumstances. Our happiness doesn't depend on happenstance or what's beyond our control, just as it doesn't depend on being a successful control freak.

Socrates, Ranasinghe shows, was no Stoic. The Stoics were also tough-minded men. They did their duty as rational beings in what they saw as a cold, deterministic world, and so they thought it was possible to keep one's own fate in one's own control. The Stoics actually thought life is tougher than it really is. In their self-understanding, there's no room for freedom or love or real happiness.

The world would be evil if the Stoics were right, and one appropriate response would be tight-lipped rational endurance of what can't be changed. The Stoics were unerotic because they thought the only way to think of themselves as happy was to think of themselves as *minds,* and not as whole human beings. But Socrates was actually happy in thinking about who he really was, because the pull of his *eros* was away from the illusion connecting rational self-sufficiency with happiness.

If the Stoics are right on the facts, then the Epicureans (or the Epicurean sophists) actually make more sense. The world is evil insofar as it's hostile to my very existence. Everything human is ephemeral and pointless, and so both hope and fear make me stupid. Such sophists argue that since evil isn't caused by me and can't be remedied by me, my proper response to worldly events is apathy. I might as well try to lose myself in imaginary pleasures, including taking some proud pleasure in being able to rise above the futile sound and fury that surrounds me. My personal assault on reality is, in fact, a value judgment on reality. I'm free to do whatever it takes to get me through this hell of a life.

But the truth is that I can't ever fully believe that my perception of reality is nothing but a private fantasy. I can't turn what I really know about my death into "death" or a linguistic construction amenable to reconstruction with my happiness in mind. In a certain way the Epicurean teaching is tougher than the Stoic position. Losing oneself is a full-time job; there's no real break from the pursuit of pleasurable diversions. There's no greater source of human misery, perhaps, than believing that nothing makes us more miserable than thinking clearly about what we really know. The fact that that thought is very un- or anti-erotic also helps to explain why Epicureans don't actually have much fun; they, like the Stoics, mistakenly refuse to go where their erotic longings could take them.

One of the most wonderful and genuinely useful features of this book is the large number of pointed and witty contemporary applications of the way Socrates reconciles truth, virtue, and happiness. Here's the Socratic good news for us: Our alternatives extend beyond fatalistic Stoicism (as practiced by our southern aristocrats), emotive religion (as practiced, say, by our evangelicals) aimed at opposing the loving will of God to scientific or empirical nihilism, and the unerotic and otherwise boring Epicureanism promulgated by our academic deconstructionists and animating the creeping and often creepy libertarianism that characterizes our culture as a whole.

Our lefty postmodernists and our right-wing free marketers, Ranasinghe shows, serve the same sophisticated cause of liberating us from any responsibility to moral truth. They think we'll be better off if we believe that what Socrates says we most need to know is unknowable and succumb to their cynical claim that even the bonds of love are for suckers. By causing us to flee from what we really know and thus from our real potential for virtue, our sophisticates lead us to think and act as less than we really are. But it's still possible to recover who we really are; we can still imitate Socrates' ennobling example.

One reason among many that Ranasinghe's Socrates is so attractive to me is that he draws him close to my moral/intellectual heroes at the time I write—Pope Benedict XVI (Joseph Ratzinger) and the great Russian writer and spiritual witness Aleksandr Solzhenitsyn. Ranasinghe says that part of his mission is to contribute to Ratzinger's effort to restore the proper place of *logos* in Christian thought. And we learn much from his Socrates to supplement both the pope's famous speech at Regensburg on *logos* and his first encyclical on love (which itself dramatically restored the place of *eros* in Christian thought). Ranasinghe shows us that the personal *eros* that animates Socrates' dialectic isn't really drawn toward the impersonal and unmovable God described by Aristotle. Through his insistence that there is support for loving moral freedom in the very ground of being, Socrates makes it clear that what we know through our minds both depends upon and doesn't negate the real existence of particular persons.

Ranasinghe also allows us to wonder whether even the Socrates he displays for our benefit gives a fully adequate account of the personal truth about either human *logos* or human *eros*. We wonder, for example, how Socrates could be so happy in an unhappy marriage, but we have to add that he was hardly a model of conjugal or paternal responsibility. It's not so clear that his *eros* culminates in love of particular persons—the most strange and wonderful beings imaginable.

Christians are allowed a soft dissent from the Socratic account of the cosmic order that mirrors a well-ordered soul insofar as it doesn't clearly have room for a personal God who is both *Logos* and Love. At the same time, Christians learn from the Socrates Ranasinghe displays that the *eros* and *logos* described by the early Church Fathers might be described as a correction of Socrates' thinking along lines he himself—through his erotic dialectic and his morally steadfast life—revealed. Ranasinghe does both philosophers and Christians the great service of showing that the hard distinction between reason and revelation—or the liberated way of the atheistic or agnostic philosopher and the willfully obedient way of the believer in the personal God—doesn't square with what we can see with our own eyes about our souls or the cosmos. Christian philosophy or, better, philosophical Christianity need not be an oxymoron.

Ranasinghe's navigation through many scholarly and liberationist prejudices brings us toward the insight that Solzhenitsyn *is* the closest person to a Socrates in our time. Both men faced death with an intransigent courage in opposition to nihilistic lies. Both defend the reality of personal or psychic good and evil against the various sophisticated deterministic and social constructivist illusions that pervaded their allegedly enlightened times. Each man, through his heroic, truthful example, exposed and authoritatively discredited the tyranny beneath the democratic pretenses of his country's form of government.

Both Socrates and Solzhenitsyn claim, in Solzhenitsyn's words from his famous Harvard Address, that "if man were born only to be happy . . . , he would not have been born to die." That means he's born *both* to die and to be happy. The secret to happiness is not his futile and degrading self-denial, but living well or morally with who he really is. What's most wrong with communism, in its ancient (as implicitly but radically criticized in the *Republic*) or modern forms (as described by Marx), is its inevitably totalitarian attempt to deny the invincible reality of personal death and personal love.

Ranasinghe leads us to wonder whether either the heroic example or account of the soul given by Socrates can quite account for Solzhenitsyn. Compared to Solzhenitsyn, it almost seems that prudent Socrates was a wimp. Although his dialectical boldness was constant, he spent only one day as an old man in open and impetuous defiance of his country's rulers, and he died comfortably in prison sipping hemlock with his friends around him. The Soviet Union's challenge to human freedom and personal truth, of course, was much more radical and far crueler than the Athenian one. There's nothing in Plato or Thucydides that is quite as demonic as the Gulag or the ideologically inspired murder of millions. Socrates' victory over Athens was purely moral and long-term, while Solzhenitsyn actually defeated the lie of ideology as a ruling principle, not only in his country but everywhere, with stunning speed.

Still, Ranasinghe shows us that Socrates and Solzhenitsyn would agree on the relevance of the challenge of the *Gorgias* for our time. The *Republic* was the dialogue that exposed in advance the angry denial of reality that produced communist utopianism. We Americans battled with admirable responsibility against the various totalitarian forms of what Harvey Mansfield correctly identified as the "manliness run amok" (or revolutionary hatred of an erroneous perception of our real personal insignificance) in the twentieth century. But the defeat of the ideological lie of communism exposed more clearly than ever the spiritual emptiness of the contemporary West. It's natural that our fascination with the just or unjust city of the *Republic* be replaced by our close attention to the *Gorgias,* the dialogue about the impossibility of either filling or negating the soul through technical manipulation.

The Cold War gave us a common purpose in defense of liberty, but now we're stuck with remembering that we have little idea of what all our power, freedom, and prosperity is for. Ours is a time characterized by the success of the technological manipulation of nature and each of us. We see ourselves as beings defined by our *interests,* and we think we display our freedom as individuals who use words to maximize our own comfort and security. We agree with the sophists that words are weapons in the service of one's own liberty, and not at all for knowing and loving a reality or real beings that exist beyond ourselves.

We can't say that all our technological progress has made us either happier or more able to live well with what we really know. So our success must be understood, as Solzhenitsyn puts it in his 1993 Liechtenstein Address as a "trial of our free will." Our nihilistic error in understanding all reality—including our own being—as fundamentally technological has so isolated and disoriented each of us that the main fact about the human soul today is an overwhelming loneliness. The technological means for living well are useless for securing our happiness if we don't believe we have a purpose or point worthy of beings who have souls. Ranasinghe is right that we can turn to the heroic Socrates for much of what we most need to know to act as rational, moral, and loving beings with *souls* today.

We've been given the technological gift of very long lives, but the old seem to have become useless and cut off from the young. While we live alongside more senior citizens than ever before, we don't appreciate their recollections of the past or the evidence they provide of what lies ahead of us. They seem to have nothing to offer the young to guide their basically technological futures, and we no longer think of wisdom in terms of enduring problems or cultural transmission. Surely Socrates is *the* model for how to live happily as an old man without strong family ties, and he offers for us all the perennial human wisdom that is a condition for replacing the feverish techno-pursuit of happiness with happiness itself.

Friendship has been diminished in the direction of networking, and so members of the same generation also regard each other with alienation and apathy. Increasingly we see one another only as *users*. Because we don't know how to think in terms of the reality of common responsibilities, we seem to live in the most unerotic or boring of times. But our erotic longings, in truth, persist. That's why Solzhenitsyn hears just beneath the surface of our happy-talk therapeutic pragmatism "the howl of existentialism." That howl, Socrates would say, is all we have left when we've lost confidence that our real experiences can be articulated and shared. The example of Socrates intensely and happily engaged in his characteristically intensely social and morally concerned activity can help restore our confidence that, as rational and loving beings, we're made for more than instrumental relationships.

And most of all, as Solzhenitsyn says, we lack a "clear and calm attitude toward death." Free individuals today tend to believe that being itself is identical with one's own being, and so *my* extinction is the end of *being itself.* We're the most death-haunted people ever, in part, because we spend so much time denying its inevitability. We end up dying no matter how astutely we attend to the various risk factors that surround us. We're also traumatized by death because we have so little confidence in the reality of love; the abstract individual we've constructed lacks the capability to be moved deeply by beings other than himself. Socrates' calmness in the face of death, which so astonished his friends and fellow citizens, came from never identifying being with himself, from regarding the point of his life as his responsible and loving participation in a reality beyond himself.

Ranasinghe shows us a Socrates old and beautiful, the hero most needed to remedy what ails an aging society consumed by image and vanity. He helps us to appreciate that Socrates is the antitechnological thinker most able to show us how to benefit from our technological progress. This Socrates gives us confidence that the best way to win friends and influence people is through truth and love. We can still be happy while learning how to die. My personal finitude is not only necessary but good, a small price to pay for being given *logos* and *eros,* as well as the demanding and joyful challenge of living virtuously with what I really know.

Ranasinghe is my new hero. But I haven't even begun to explain *how* he performed one of the most noble of deeds by using a single dialogue to display the riches of the Platonic presentation of Socrates. I wouldn't want to spoil the wonderful surprise you'll begin to discover by turning the pages for yourself.

11

STUCK WITH VIRTUE IN
OUR PRO-LIFE FUTURE

According to Daniel Callahan in *Setting Limits: Medical Goals in an Aging Society* (2003) and his other works, the possibility of indefinitely extending the duration of human life is a social threat comparable to the one addressed by environmentalist legislation. We can't let individuals use their natural surroundings as they please, because eventually human life as a whole will become unsustainable. And we can't let people live as long as they please, because social life will become unsustainable. Callahan's position differs from that of Leon Kass: Kass worries about how the obsessive pursuit of immortality or longevity will affect the quality of one's own life, and Callahan worries about the social consequences of indulging the individual desire to live as long as possible in a biotechnological age. Already, Callahan thinks, we're socially threatened by the existence of too many very old people, and we have to act before the problem becomes unmanageable.

Callahan and the environmentalists are both about the protection of nature against the free human use of technology. Technological efforts treat nature as simply a resource for the satisfaction of our needs, neglecting nature's own purposes and what's best for nature as a whole. Technology aims to transform our natural world into something better with each of us in mind. Similarly, biotechnology aims to overcome the limitations nature has, so far, imposed on every human life. Biotechnology aims, from this view, to transform our natural bodies into something better with each of us in mind, neglecting the benefits that come from living as natural—embodied, social, belonging, begetting, and mortal—beings in this world. If we manage to wander too far away from our natural lifespans, then our naturally social qualities will be distorted and damaged in ways that threaten the conditions of our lives together. So, what's best for a particular individual, at least in that individual's opinion, can turn out to be fatal for society, on which every individual depends for his or her flourishing.

Pro-Death Environmentalism

Callahan's understanding of environmentalism is refreshingly anthropocentric. He doesn't care about nature as such, but about what's required from nature to sustain human life. We can transform nature some, but not too much or in the wrong ways. His environmentalism is about human lives. The problem with the uncontrolled exploitation of nature is that it leads, contrary to its intention, to human sickness and death. My maximization of my power and profit can be at the expense of other human lives and even human life as such. Callahan's argument against extreme prolongevity, however, is not pro-life. Particular human beings must die earlier than they might in order to benefit society. I can be criticized for preferring the extension of my life to what's best for society as a whole. But I can criticize society for using me—for compelling my extermination—for its own good. This pro-death policy isn't enacted with *me* in mind; its premise is not that living for an indefinitely long time is bad for me. It's that my continued existence is bad for everyone else—or society in general.

Prudent, anthropocentric environmentalism is perfectly in accord with the American Constitution—or the spirit of modern liberalism. Human extinctionism, of course, is not. Even if nature would cheer if we humans were to disappear, we humans have every right to stay around. Each free human being, says the modern view, exists for himself—to secure his own being in a basically hostile environment. We don't exist as nature fodder or, for that matter, species fodder; nature exists for me. That means, among other things, that it's stupidly thoughtless for me to trash the nature on which I depend. It also means that when I think of nature, I think of what's best for me. Free individuals, it goes without saying, are bound to do some violence to what, without them, might well be a perfect natural order. To some extent, our modern view is that nature even has it coming. After all, nature—for example, the process of evolution—is either completely indifferent or hostile to my continued existence as a particular being. Human extinctionism is based on the perverse premise that I should, quite self-consciously, care about nature more than *me*.

From this modern view—the individualistic foundation of our form of government and our way of life—Callahan's proposal is a soft and selective form of human extinctionism. It's all about cutting my life short—doing me in—for reasons that aren't good for *me*. It's about turning me into society fodder or based on the perverse premise that I should care more about society than about me. The purpose of modern science—the core of which, as Descartes explained, is medical science—is to make each of our beings as secure as possible. That doesn't mean that every tax dollar has to be spent on pursuing indefinite prolongevity or anything like that. It certainly doesn't mean that we have a right not to die, as some transhumanists assert. It does mean, however, that modern science or technology will continue to achieve unprecedented breakthroughs in protecting the lives of individuals, and that one reason particular individuals consent to government is to avoid nonbeing as long as possible. I can't be understood to consent to a social policy that would aim at my avoidable death on behalf of the social fabric. A pro-death policy with a social ecological justification is a rather obvious and profound violation of rights.

It's true enough, as Callahan says, that some people are more concerned with indefinitely perpetuating their lives than others. Others think more in terms of a "whole" life with natural purposes and a natural end. And others still, he might have emphasized, believe that this biological life is not all there is for each of us. Why don't we let free or autonomous individuals choose for themselves concerning life extending treatments? The scientific research and technological development that indulges the preferences of some will be available to all. It will turn out to be very tough for any of us to choose against extension, and we'll all be stuck with the burden of those who choose for it. So, Callahan concludes, the choices of some can't help but transform the lives of us all.

The Social Threat of Enhancement

Callahan claims that indefinite longevity stands out among possible biotechnological developments in having this effect. He isn't strongly in favor of limiting individual choice for the common good in general. The example he gives of the harmless use of medical technology is cosmetic plastic surgery and similar sorts of physical enhancements. They are, he says, about personal vanity with minor social consequences. Giving into vanity is surely bad for one's soul, but it's part of the modern principle of autonomy that society doesn't tell individuals what's best for their souls.

It seems to me, however, that the available and especially the coming physical, emotional, and cognitive enhancements will probably have much more profound and troubling social consequences than the unlikely prospect of extreme longevity. Efforts to prolong lives serve, of course, the health of the patients, and so they are obviously in accord with the Hippocratic Oath. Death, Callahan tells us, is not a disease to be cured. But death is often caused by the diseases old age makes progressively more likely, and death, which is very bad for one's health, is the main enemy of medicine. The fact that death wins in the end in every human case might demoralize existentialist philosophers to the point of impotence, but physicians find their vocation in not surrendering until there's no other option.

Merely cosmetic or enhancement surgery, however, turns a healthy person into a patient—into a sick person—for reasons having nothing to do with health. Performing such surgery, in that way, is a clear violation of the Hippocratic Oath. We justify that exception by reference to the individual's autonomy; he is free to choose to become a patient. People enhance themselves for a variety of reasons, including vanity and rather singular conceptions of personal identity (a woman trapped in a man's body, for example). But the main reason for the choice of cosmetic enhancement—through surgery or neurology—is to make oneself more productive. The two distinctively modern views of human freedom and dignity—one coming from Kant and the other from Hobbes—are autonomy and productivity. People talk about their autonomy or self-determination more than ever, and our sophisticates—including, of course, the justices on our Supreme Court—seem determined to extend that self-understanding to every feature of our lives. We also, more than ever, live in a meritocracy defined by productivity. These are the best times ever to be young, smart, pretty, and industrious. But the pressure is on like never before to be young, smart, pretty, and industrious.

People nip, tuck, botox, and so forth to look younger or more pleasing and so more marketable. They enhance their moods, cognitive abilities, memories, and so forth for basically the same reason. The fact that enhancement is available and legal will put the pressure on everyone to take advantage of it to remain competitive. The predominant social effect may well be new forms of tyranny, as productivity trumps autonomy at every turn.

Consider the notoriously autonomy obsessed and characteristically rather lazy, moody, and unproductive college professor. He thinks he has reason to believe that he has a right to his moods, because they are the source of his creativity and his openness to the truth about our very being. Still, the dean might well call said faculty member in and say we'll keep you around if you get less moody, and there's now a safe and easy chemical remedy to your mixed student evaluations and poor record of publication. Studies show, the dean might go on, that moods are nothing more than collections of chemicals, and so we should prefer—and even call true—those that make us more productive. Even in the case of the professor, productivity trumps autonomy (as we see already, to tell the truth, in the promiscuous impetus toward the quantitative assessment of everything in education).

Callahan might say that there ought to be a law to protect the professor's autonomy, and it's always possible he could sell that idea. But consider the case of the physician. There may soon be ways that medical doctors can easily improve their memories, their judgment, their moods, their cognitive abilities, and physical endurance. The result would be, for the enhanced physician, many fewer errors and more lives saved. We might say that the physician should be able to choose to be a "natural doctor" in the name of autonomy or even in the name of personal sensitivity and bedside manner. But what sick person would prefer "natural" to "enhanced" diagnosis and treatment? And will there really be, in effect, a pro-death law protecting the "natural doctor" from unfair competition from the enhanced one? Where health and safety are involved, productivity will most clearly increasingly trump autonomy.

The various likely modes of biotechnological enhancement—beginning with better and better cosmetic surgery and neurology—are actually much more socially intrusive—much more potentially tyrannical—than extreme prolongevity. Because they correspond to the reigning standards of freedom and dignity and have strong pro-life implications, there's little reason to believe that "society" is going to be able to stop their development. We can only hope that we will develop the virtue to live well with and not abuse them. Similarly, we can't deny that Callahan is right that a rapidly aging society is full of challenges to human freedom and dignity and even to the very sustainability of social life. In view of the obvious benefit of living longer and longer—of fending off nonbeing—my view is that we're stuck with confronting and living as well as we can with its downsides.

The Downsides of Being Old

People, especially sophisticated people, are already living longer and having fewer children. With no additional longevity breakthroughs at all, we can see a future where fewer and fewer young people are responsible for more and more old and unproductive ones. We can also see that the prolongation of life in a mobile society full of autonomy freaks breaks the already tenuous connection between the generations, creating a class of lonely old people who find it more difficult than ever to find compensations for the misery of their mortality in love and work. The old, more than ever, are going to be a burden on the young, and the young are going to be disconnected enough from the old to be less ready than ever to embrace that burden out of love. And even if they've been prudent with their resources, the old have every reason to fear that their money won't last as long as they do. Not only that: The good news is that we're rapidly pushing back cancer and heart disease; the bad is that more and more people will die from Alzheimer's—which is the agonizingly slow and hugely expensive surrender of every human capability. The demographic dynamics we're facing seem to make Social Security and Medicare unsustainable, and we're going to need them more than ever.

Even modest increases in longevity, of course, accelerate the trend toward having a country basically ruled by the old. It might become a place dominated by people obsessed with holding on to life at all costs. My own experience, however, is that the very old are often grateful for just being alive and for any benefit or kindness they receive. They are less bitter or lonely than we think they should be, because they are less modern—less governed by the illusions of productivity and autonomy—than we are. A more real problem is that the old—even if they are healthy—lack the flexibility and openness to innovation required of a technological society, and they will become increasingly resistant to being replaced by the audacious and impetuous young who are open to the challenges of our techno-future.

The demands of technological productivity, in many ways, reinforces the preferential option for the young that began with the Sixties, while producing a rapidly aging society where the young may well have less and less political influence. The old will remain stuck with trying to look and act young to remain productive, making themselves, in many cases, more repulsive to those who are really young. Another real problem is that a country governed by old people with few children might become too risk-averse to do what's required to defend us against less techno-developed countries dominated by angry young men fathering lots of kids. The virtue of courage seems like insanity if lives seem to have an almost indefinite duration and if a mother only has a single son or daughter to send off to war. This fact, by itself, might be at least one cause of the death of the West.

We can also worry that in our efforts to free the human person from natural limitations, we might transform ourselves into merely determined or merely engineered beings, into being ignobly freed from being animated by the personal longings that flow from love and death. Can personal relationships (like marriage and parenthood) really be sustained for an indefinitely long time? Can personal virtue (such as courage) really be possible if death, debility, disease, and so forth disappear as ennobling necessities and become accidents that can be prudently avoided through constant attention to risk factors? Conceivably, we can imagine, every sacrifice of life will seem Christ-like—an optional death suffered out of boundless personal love. But would even Socrates have been up for that kind of sacrifice? His noble choice of death over dishonor occurred very near what he knew would be the natural end of his singular life.

The thought of Enlightenment thinkers such as Bacon, Descartes and Condorcet was that only indefinite longevity could transform the world in a genuinely humane way. Without it, the progress of modern science wouldn't be experienced as progress at all. Human lives are distorted by a fear of death, and that fear accelerates in the modern world with the atrophying of various illusions about personal immortality. That fear would recede, Condorcet explained, if human lives were long enough that it would be impossible to count their days. The individual would no longer be distorted by the prospect of dying, and the result would be an unprecedented birth of peace, freedom, and unobsessive enjoyment. The unalienated existence Marxists promised with the coming of communism could only be possible if people were no longer moved by a scarcity of time, by the fairly imminent prospect of no longer being at all. Indefinite longevity finally made sense as a real possibility with the coming of regenerative medicine, with the promise that perhaps every bodily part could be replaced by a new and even better one. The promise here isn't for immortality. An old body, like an old car, will eventually stop working, but not at any particular time. No matter how old you are, you won't experience any definite limit to how long you'll be around.

This modern promise is countered, of course, by plenty of premodern wisdom. Psalm 90, for example, asks God "to teach us to number our days" in the name of wisdom. The twentieth century critic of techno-liberation Hans Jonas wrote that "a nonnegotiable limit to our expected time is necessary for each of us as the incentive to number our days and make them count." Natural necessity used to be the source of that limit. Can we really replace natural necessity with a nonnegotiable, pro-death act of will? Leon Kass is surely right to say that the effectual truth of indefinite longevity will be to increase our hostility to our natural mortality. And so it's hard to see how or why our wills would suddenly shift to the side of "natural death." It's the natural "gradual descent into aged frailty," Kass writes, that "weans us from attachment to life and renders death more acceptable." But what is no longer inevitable and annihilates my very being can hardly be regarded as acceptable.

Kass also echoes Jonas in his claim that numbering our days is the source of our "creative depth" and moral seriousness; the scarcity of time is what causes us to rank our pursuits. Counting is what makes them count. The immortality of the Greek gods (and the quasi-immortality of today's vampires of films and TV) was the source of lives we have to regard as not worth living. But it seems to be above our human pay grade, so to speak, to be compelled to actually choose mortality as a condition of love, greatness, meaningful work, poetic genius, and living virtuously with what we really know. Even vampires, to say the least, continue to be quite conflicted over this superhuman choice.

The Individual vs. the Species

From one view, the source of the narcissism behind the prolongevity project is our perverse and futile intention to negate the intention of natural evolution. The secular version of the wisdom of the Psalm is coming to terms with the idea that we evolved, like all the other species, for reproduction and replacement and not for long lives. We autonomous individuals may wish to live for ourselves, but nature employs us as species fodder, like it or not. Lots of evolutionary biologists believe that nature has imposed ineradicable constraints on how long any particular member of our species can live. There's a natural ceiling on life spans that even the most ingenious humans can't reasonably hope to break through. It's not so much that nature aims at the death of each of us. It's just that there's no species-based reason why nature should have selected for the extended operation of particular animals. Nature doesn't care about my particular being after I've done my natural duties. From this view, Callahan just shouldn't be worried.

Some scientists, such as Carl Sagan, have suggested that we conceive a human immortality project consistent with what we really know about nature. We should come to consciously serve the indefinite perpetuation of our species. Our species, like all the others, is destined for extinction unless we bring the planet under our control. Because natural climate change will eventually make the natural existence of our species unsustainable, we need to work hard against natural unpredictability and for controlled stability. And because eventually (and we can't really tell when—what with those rogue asteroids and all) our planet will become uninhabitable no matter what we do, we should disperse ourselves to other planetary environments to increase our odds of survival. The earth may be our natural home. But Mother Earth is unreliable enough to make it prudent for her conscious children to develop other plans.

Modern technology, proponents of species immortality say, should serve the species, not individuals. Individual immortality is impossible and undesirable; we need to be replaced by better models for evolutionary progress to continue. The trouble with that way of thinking is that it's contrary to the nerve—expressed by Bacon and Descartes—of the modern way of thinking. We're out to conquer nature, to replace impersonal or cruelly indifferent natural evolution with conscious and volitional evolution—evolution with me, with each of us—in mind. The conscious individual doesn't serve the species; he serves himself and other persons. Nature may push him to do species-perpetuating stuff, but he uses technology—his freedom or autonomy—to push back in his own direction. The unprecedented breakthroughs of modern technology give us reasonable hope that we can alter nature's intention for each of us. If we start to live long enough, we might even say it's reasonable that evolution might lay off on pushing us to reproduce. We don't know, at this point, to what extent we can willfully decide to hang around and, in effect, refuse to be replaced.

Personal Hope

There have been a variety of modern efforts to get the individual to identify himself with a whole greater than himself—with nature, society, the nation, history, a pantheistic God, and so forth. Every attempt to absorb the contingent, ephemeral person into an enduring or immortal whole has failed. "People just aren't satisfied," Carol Zeleski observes, "by an eschatology that focuses exclusively on social justice; they are not convinced that individualism is the root of all evil; they are starved for transcendence, hungry for miracles, and sure of only one thing, if life is to be truly meaningful, death must not be allowed to have the last word." Extreme prolongevity, the reasonable view is, is still nothing in light of eternity, and its pursuit shouldn't become so obsessive that it displaces our belief in a personal God, or even what real immortality we can achieve through those we love or though our accomplishments. Callahan's main ground for hope should be, it seems to me, that the personal God—who sustains each of us in our personal identity—is still so alive in his country.

There's even some hope, I think, in parental love. The relational bond between parent and child (and certainly between mother and child) resists technological and biotechnological destruction. It gets stronger in some ways (as in the case of the increasingly common lonely and anxious single mom) as other social, relational bonds atrophy. People are, it's true, self-obsessed enough these days to bother less and less about creating new persons. They think of all persons, beginning with themselves, as irreplaceable. But things change, of course, when they loosen up (or screw up enough) to generate actual replacements. The loving anxiety about the very being of the gift of the child, of course, is some combination of existentialism and high technology. We're more moved than ever by the contingency of personal being in an indifferent universe. And we're more aware than ever that there are steps we can take to reduce personal contingency and enhance personal control.

Still, what spooks parents most of all about the possibility of "designer babies" is that children might become too enhanced—too different from them—to love them and be lovable. We want our children to be more secure than we are and certainly live longer than we do, but we don't want them made into gods. Nor, of course, do we want them reduced to beings to be controlled like automatons. There are loving, personal limits we routinely assume and readily affirm, when we think about it, to equipping persons with or subjecting persons to "rational control." Parents, out of love, don't want their children to be perfect or immortal. They know well enough that, except in the case of the personal God, perfect person is an oxymoron, and they want their children to be good persons. So parents do worry about what techno-relativism does to their children, and they're open to at least some of what Callahan says about the social downsides of the pursuit of prolongevity.

Modern technology has, all along, caused massive social disruptions to which human beings have adjusted. They have become more powerful, secure, and free even as they experience themselves, in some ways, as more impotent, anxious, and determined by forces beyond their control than ever. The secret to human happiness will remain in being virtuous—or living socially and responsibly in light of what we really can't help but know about love and death. Our efforts shouldn't be directed toward futile attempts to stop the pursuit of extreme personal prolongevity, which may well never come anyway. It's surely contrary to our rights-based way of life and elementary considerations of human love and dignity to regard the old as a social threat. Our efforts should be toward thinking about how to practice virtue in the, in some ways, unprecedented circumstances in which we will find ourselves. Callahan is wrong to be pro-death, but he's right to say that to live well—or for society to have a real future—we have to care about more than mere life.

12

THE FUTURE OF LIBERALISM AND THE FUTURE OF NATIONS:

REFLECTIONS ON SCIENCE, THEOLOGY, PHILOSOPHY, AND THE HUMAN PERSON

What's the relationship between liberalism and the nation? Does liberalism threaten the very existence of the nation? Can liberalism have a future without the nation, without a definite and limited political form? Do we have to choose between being liberal and being national or political? Can a free person be a citizen?

From the beginning, liberalism and political devotion have, of course, been in tension. The nation—or nation-state—is the modern form of the *polis* or political community. The *polis* came into existence when human loyalty stopped being wholly personal or despotic. Loyalty shifted from the personal rule of the despot to the way of life—the system of justice—of the place. Personal loyalty can be nomadic; it can travel with the despot. Political loyalty is to a community occupying a particular territory. The *polis* or nation inspires and depends upon political loyalty. The citizen, strictly speaking, finds his or her identity as a part of a political whole. He or she is formed by the "cave" or the process of "political socialization" of a particular *polis*. The citizen exists, we now say, to serve the cause of his country—a reality much bigger and greater than himself.

The virtue of the citizen is loyalty—even unquestioning loyalty. Liberalism seems to have its origins in opposition to that comprehensive understanding of citizenship. Each particular human being—the person—is not part of a political whole. The person him- or herself is a whole, with personal responsibility and a personal destiny. A person can still be a citizen of course, but being a citizen expresses only part— and not the highest part—of his or her being. I have the freedom to form or integrate myself according to what I can see for myself about who I am, both in terms of my capabilities and limitations and about what and who I know and love.

Christian Liberalism

Liberalism begins, at least on a big scale, with Christianity. St. Augustine, for example, criticized the serious theologies of the Greeks and the Romans from a liberal view. Civil theology was about the polytheistic Gods of Athens and Rome, who existed to give divine sanction to the city's (*polis's*) view of justice and to the loyalty of citizens. Civil theology, Augustine explains, doesn't give people the security for which they long. The city, so to speak, doesn't care about you the way you care about the city. If you live for your city, that means that you're really city fodder. There can be no adequate political recognition of your unique and irreplaceable being as a particular person.

Civil theology, Augustine goes on, is obviously untrue, and it's degrading to believe it's true. As cities get more sophisticated, intelligent and sophisticated people, for good reason, stop believing. Polytheism is an offense against the human mind. The truth is that every human being is more than a citizen. We're not born to be stuck in some "cave" or another; we're all equipped—we're all free—to be open to the truth about who we are.

St. Augustine also criticized the sophisticated—or philosophic— natural theology of the Greeks and Romans. According to natural theology, we're all part of nature or some impersonal process. Aristotle's God, for example, is not a person, but a principle. Our moral pretensions and desire for personal significance, it turns out, have no natural support. The natural theologians—philosophers and scientists—are incapable, Augustine claims, of seeing the unique and irreplaceable existence of every particular human being. They are incapable of accounting for our personal desire to be more than merely biological beings. That's our desire to be, to be personally significant, to be known and loved as persons. Our irreducible personal longings—which exist in every being born with both *logos* and *eros*—point in the direction of a personal God who knows and loves us as persons. When each of us "relates" to that God, we remain a whole person relating to a whole person. We don't lose ourselves in God—or for that matter in nature or the city.

St. Augustine says that each human being is to some extent an alien or pilgrim in his or her earthly city. Deep down, the particular person can't understand him- or herself as a citizen or think of one's country as one's truest home. The person is also alienated, to some extent, from nature, because he knows nature is not his truest home either. Philosophers and scientists will always see me as a what—as a natural kind—but the truth is I'm a who, which is why it makes more sense to think of God as a who, and not a what.

So that's liberalism: Each unique and irreplaceable person is a whole, not a part. That doesn't mean, to repeat, that persons aren't partly natural, partly political, partly familial, and so forth, but the whole who is the person is more than the sum of the parts. That's not modern liberalism, though. Modern liberalism differs from Christian liberalism in its attempt to secure and defend personal identity without any reliance on a personal God and only minimal reliance on "relational"—including political—attachments.

Modern Liberalism

There is a sense in which modern liberalism did promote a return to the *polis* as a political form. Christianity in Europe detached people from political loyalties and gave Europe a common culture. One result of that detachment from civic loyalties was wars of religion, wars over competing views of what it means to be included in the community of the faithful. Europe's modern nation-states emerged in particularistic opposition to the universality of monotheistic, creedal loyalty. Europe was once again divided up into a large number of political or clearly territorial places. But political loyalty in the comprehensive, classical sense could not, thank God, be completely restored. The *polis,* we can say, was permanently and in many ways beneficially destabilized by

Christianity. Because of the enduring personal truth of liberalism, the modern nation can only truthfully aspire in a very incoherent and incomplete way to be a *polis*. The creedal loyalty to Christianity was sometimes even displaced by creedal loyalty to secular liberal principles, as in the American loyalty to the self-evident truths of the Declaration of Independence.

Modern liberal philosophers, such as John Locke, agree with the Christians that civil theology is untrue. We are by nature free individuals—whole or, in a way, emotionally self-sufficient beings, and we invent political life—we institute government—to serve our individual needs. I don't exist for the city, the city exists for me. And I can, in principle, withdraw my consent to be governed if I judge it's not doing me any good. I ask first what my country can do for me, not what I can do for my country. The modern separation of church and state is a not necessarily a religious way of expressing the Christian view that our deepest devotion is not to our country, and that our political obedience can be separated from love or profound emotional loyalty.

The modern liberals also agree that natural theology isn't completely true because it can't account for me for my freedom—the freedom of each of us. We're free from nature and dissatisfied with nature. We can and should use our freedom to master nature, to create a world more conducive to our longings as unique and irreplaceable beings. Nature stinks because it's out to kill me, and I can at least do something about its random acts of cruelty against particular individuals. Modern liberals use their technology to oppose nature or natural theology. Just because each person can't help but and should regard him- or herself as unique and irreplaceable—as a whole and not merely a part—doesn't mean there really is a personal God who lovingly provides for each of us.

There's no evidence for the existence of such a God, just as there's no evidence that any of us survives our biological demise. Anyone who lovingly trusts that God provides is a sucker. The truth is that we're all alone in a hostile environment and—God knows why—stuck with providing for ourselves. I'm not saying that Locke, for example, was an atheist. Let's say he was a Deist. That means he believed in an emphatically "past tense" God, who has left us alone to provide for ourselves. The God of the Deists may be different from the Aristotelian principle insofar as we can hold him to be a Creator mysteriously responsible for our freedom, but he's clearly not personally concerned with any of us in particular. He doesn't care about me. So the good and bad news for the modern liberal is each of us really is on his or her own. We're really, really free. We're really not part of anything larger, and we're stuck with satisfying our deepest personal longings ourselves.

The free human person brought into being the impersonal state. To maximize our freedom, we can't think of government as deserving of our personal love or loyalty, and patriotism must become much less instinctive, and much more calculating. I can see that government is part of what's good for me. But the territory and tradition that my political community occupy is much less important than its capacity to serve my personal interests. Except for a few loony libertarians, nobody's ever denied that the modern state still needs some loyalty. But the source of loyalty becomes more and more of a problem. As the modern world becomes more "Lockeanized," loyalty is the virtue that most obviously deteriorates. The "right of secession" is more consciously and deliberately applied to all the relationships that are parts of our lives. Even friendship becomes a temporary alliance or "networking."

The modern state has also suffered, since the beginning, from the growing contradiction between liberal personal longings and increasingly impersonal or mechanistic science. Freeing the person from nature and God had the cost of freeing nature and theology from the person. "Nature's God" becomes no guide at all for human thought and action, and nature seems more and more hostile to our personal existences. It seems tougher and tougher for each of us to be so alone, seemingly accidental exceptions to the impersonal laws that govern everything else that exists.

Modern Civil Theology

The problems of diminished loyalty and increasingly anxious loneliness were addressed by the effort to restore civil theology in the modern world. This effort was inaugurated by the philosopher Jean-Jacques Rousseau. According to Rousseau, each human being, by nature, is an unconscious part of a mechanical natural world. In a way, we're self-sufficient too; we don't need anything more than nature has given us. Each of us is unalienated and lacking in nothing, precisely because there's nothing unique or irreplaceable about anyone in particular.

But somehow we, in our freedom, have accidentally moved further and further from nature. The more free we get, the more miserably alienated we become. People living in big modern states are big messes. It may be true that they're wealthy, powerful, and free. But they are neither happy nor admirable because they have no idea who they are or what they're doing. They can't understand themselves as parts of some whole, but they don't have what it takes to become wholes or authentically integrated persons either.

We have to cure ourselves, Rousseau claims, of our anxious, displaced disorientation. We have to consciously and deliberately make ourselves into citizens, into parts of a political whole. Because we can't be parts of nature anymore, we have to understand ourselves as parts of a city or nation to be happy again. The state has to become a nation, or at least a nation-state.

So Rousseau invented nationalism, with various romantic and organic features, to gain our emotional attachment. Nationalism, as the English conservative Roger Scruton often explains, was a pathological form of human loyalty. While national loyalty properly understood is part of the natural social inclination to fashion a political home, the new nationalism rested on the idea that free individuals, in the absence of radically artificial reconstruction, are alienated, adrift, insignificant. What made nationalism pathologically aggressive and even "totalitarian" was the belief that there's nothing properly natural or traditional about having a political, territorial home. (And so nationalism as conceived by the French revolutionaries can be distinguished from the more natural or indigenous uprisings by people with shared customs and traditions against the great nineteenth century European empires.)

Nationalism flourished in the nineteenth century, and Christianity in various countries was largely subordinated to national purposes. Nationalism was the cause of the incredibly bloody First World War, for the nearly a million casualities during the Battle of Verdun alone. Huge, huge numbers of men were slaughtered who had come to identify themselves primarily as parts of their nation.

Then Hitler and the Nazis came along with a much more fanatical form of nationalism, including an insanely racist political religion. The trouble with thinking of yourself as merely part of a nation in the modern world is that it's so easy to see that it's not true. So Hitler employed all means necessary to make it true. The Nazis went much further than anyone ever had before in terms of understanding citizens and, really, everyone as merely expendable parts of a national whole. Everyone who's not a German lives and dies for the benefit of Germans. And every German citizen is nothing but cannon fodder and a reproductive machine for the Fatherland. Even Nazi racist exterminationism was mainly an aspect of that nationalism.

Nature vs. History

Probably the most fanatical attempt to resolve the contradiction between the liberal devotion to the unique and irreplaceable person and impersonal science and theology was History—History with a capital "H." This contradiction, remember, was expressed for a long while as History versus Nature. History is the name for what free persons have created in opposition to nature. It is the evidence of the real existence of human freedom. One modern goal—maybe the most deeply modern goal—was for History to reconstruct all of natural reality. Nature would come, in every respect, under human control. Our personal existences would become completely unalienated and secure.

With the complete triumph of History (as described by Marx), free persons would no longer be reduced to part of some larger whole alien to them. They wouldn't merely be cogs in a machine—as they were under any system of the "division of labor"—or citizens or parents or in the thrall of some otherworldly opiate. They would be able to do whatever they wanted whenever they wanted. Completely unalienated and unobsessed, they would be free to form themselves into whatever kind of personal reality they pleased. They would even be free to change who they are on a whim. For reasons unclear to me, Marx called this perfect personal liberation communism. Human persons would be free from all communal determination for self-determination. Communism, from that view, is not communism at all. In Plato's *Republic,* for example, communism is for making every citizen nothing more than a part of the political community, but at the end of History the liberated person experiences himself as not part of anything at all.

This vision of perfect personal liberation through historical transformation was the cause of the horribly cruel and murderous Communist totalitarianism of the twentieth century—embodied in nations such as the Soviet Union and the People's Republic of China. Those nations employed every means—however monstrous—they could to eradicate everything natural about human existence. These Historical efforts turned out to be radically depersonalizing in all sorts of ways. Here are two: They aimed to strip persons of any real content, of any individuality, and they ruthlessly sacrificed the imperfect persons of today for the radically liberated persons of tomorrow.

So History turned out not to be not so personal after all. We now know that it was the most pernicious of all the impersonal modern forces. History—like nature—doesn't really care about me. The twentieth century was a display of hundreds of millions of persons consumed as History fodder. Persons weren't viewed as who they really are—unique and irreplaceable wholes—only as perfectly expendable parts of History.

Humanitarian Fantasies

Most leading European thinkers now think they've learned the undeniable lesson of the world wars and the Cold War: The nation should have no future. The human rights and dignity of the person require our gradual surrender of both territorial democracy and political loyalty. There should no longer be any attachment to a particular people in a particular place, and nobody should understand himself as a citizen—or in any respect a dutiful part of a political whole. All power should devolve in the direction of an amorphous and rather apolitical European Union (which, having no clear territorial identity, is potentially a global union). That Union might be criticized as diminishing personal significance in the direction of impersonal, meddlesome, bureaucratic despotism; however, it seems that the most urgent thing is not to empower people to act as citizens but to save them from the destructive consequences of doing so.

Today's sophisticated devotion is to the cosmopolitan, humanitarian protection of human rights. Every human being, we still say, is unique and irreplaceable. Nobody may be sacrificed for another, or to some cause or ideal, because we know of nothing higher than each of our bare existences. We do what we can to protect each person from not being and nothing more, because each person is nothing more than the opposite of not being. We have to stop sacrificing present persons to some imaginary future—as the Christians did with their visions of personal immortality or the Marxists did with their vision of perfect Historical liberation. And we have to stop sacrificing the security and enjoyment of our biological existence to claims that we are for anything or anyone more than not violating the rights of others. So it would seem that the contemporary European—with unprecedented Enlightenment—has reconciled us to the truth that, for each of us, my bodily existence is all there is. Because it's better than not being at all, it's well worth holding on to as long as possible.

But this Enlightened view is full of contradictions. If bodily existence is all there is, why do we privilege human beings over the other bodies? Why is it that we alone among the animals have rights? One obvious answer, of course, is that we alone among the animals are disgusted with the limits of our natural existence. Each human person doesn't really think of him- or herself as just a part of nature, and especially today he can't help but hate the nature out to kill him or her—or extinguish his or her very being. When I die, as nature wants me to do soon enough, I'm gone; the fact that the matter that was an indispensable condition of me—but not simply me—becomes a tree or a dolphin makes no difference to me. I can't lose myself in some vision of an impersonal natural process. I wouldn't care about rights and all that if I really thought I was just one part of nature among infinitely many.

So contemporary Europeans seem to know that they're more than merely their bodies, although they don't seem to know who or what. The truth is that a person's content comes from realities outside him- or herself, which he or she integrates into a personal whole. So the extreme attempt—allegedly in the service of personal wholeness or self-sufficiency—not to be a part of anything at all leads to emptiness and solitary fantasies. It also leads, as Pierre Manent has often observed, to perhaps the most extreme hatred of one's body ever, because the person is unable to experience any social compensation for his or her bodily limitations.

The contemporary European can't be a pantheist or even a consistent Darwinian. He doesn't really find himself at home in nature, nor can he find himself at all at home in his country, his church, or his family. He or she tends to live, instead, in a sort of postpolitical, postreligious, and postfamilial fantasy. He hates, and thinks he can live without, the institutions that are reflections of his or her embodiment—institutions that human beings form as a result of having and coming to terms with their bodies.

The postpolitical fantasy is that the nation can wither away. The wars fought by nations can be replaced by humanitarian police actions aimed at deviant evildoers. The draft is an affront against human dignity and personal freedom. The truth, of course, is that liberalism can't free human beings from their political needs altogether. New national, despotic, and imperial challenges will inevitably arise; it will remain a dangerous world, with war always a possibility. Evidence of the European fantasy is the incomprehension of the illiberal challenge it is now facing from the Russian nation. The depoliticization of Europe through the European Union, it's increasingly clear, is making the devotion to human liberty impotent.

The protection of human rights may have seemed, for a while, to require the enlightened dismissal of the nation. But the Russians, Chinese, and Iranians have begun to remind the Europeans, we can hope, that the nation or some *polis* is the real human alternative to despotism and empire. Being a part of a nation or *polis* has to be a part—but not the whole—of any free person with a future. Anyone truthfully devoted to rights knows they can be exercised only within a political context. The perfected liberation of the cosmopolitan, humanitarian world dreamed up by Marx and many theorists today will never happen, and, if it did, the price for the absence of alienation would be a chilling human emptiness. People wouldn't know who they are or what they're supposed to do. The gradual centralization of European authority in Brussels seems to be based on the utopian illusion that it's possible to move beyond civic duty and political loyalty into a world

where experts resolve human conflict through technocratic deliberation and international agreements.

That illusion even seems to be based on the same Rousseauean
error about who we are that produced nationalism. If persons are, in
truth, apolitical, isolated individuals, it makes sense that they are fit
to be controlled by despotic experts. Politics should be replaced by
administration, and laws should be replaced by rules and regulations
that compassionately free people from having to deliberate about their
personal futures. This kind of "soft despotism," Tocqueville explained,
leaves persons alone in their petty lives and personal enjoyments, as
long as they don't think and act like citizens. The mean between the
despotic extremes of nationalism and apolitical administration, we
might say, is political life, although a political life chastened by the
personal insight that each of us is more than a citizen.

The postfamilial fantasy is reflected, above all, in birth rates below
the rate of replacement, but also in low rates of marriage and the
detachment of motherhood from marriage. A free person, conscious
that his or her death ends all, can't think beyond his or her personal
existence. And so he or she refuses to subordinate him- or herself to a
whole that includes family members who came before and after him or
her. He or she rejects the illusion that he or she can live on or through
his or her children. But the natural future of our species and the political future of a people requires replacements being born and raised,
and it's a perverse mark of our freedom that we seem to be able to
suppress the natural instinct meant to keep life going. People are refusing, more than ever, to be the social, species-serving animals described
by Darwinians, to be part of nature. The demographic crisis caused
by so many not thinking of themselves as parts of a family—as dutiful parents—may be the main reason to wonder whether Europe—or
excessively consistent, lonely liberalism—could possibly have a future.

The Europeans (and this is doubtless more controversial) seem to
me also to be living in a postreligious fantasy. Very few go to church
or think of themselves as dutiful members of a church. An unfriendly
observer might say they spend their leisurely lives sitting in cafes in
squares with beautiful churches that they regard as monuments to
some irrelevant past. And so, despite their technological prowess, they
don't have what it takes to produce their own testimonies to personal

longings and personal greatness. They actually are full of hostility to the various forms of repression caused by their nation's religious past. For them, religion is all about injustice, and so a multifaceted affront to the person and his or her rights. For a while, European intellectuals prided themselves in being full of existentialist anxiety in the absence of God, but that powerfully disordered passion was undeniably a source of murderous political recklessness. Personal anguish led to the slaughter of real persons.

So the contemporary European claims to be too enlightened to be moved, as a person, toward any kind of illusory transcendence. He or she refuses either to believe in God or be haunted by his absence. But that proud claim for self-knowledge is really an almost desperate attempt at self-induced lobotomization. There's plenty of evidence, after all, that all the longings that make a person more than a merely biological being remain just beneath the surface. The lobotomy, thank God, never quite takes. The person remains somewhat miserably disoriented in the perceived absence of the personal God.

The preponderance of evidence we have from Europe—and, of course, I'm guilty of instructive generalizations that omit many exceptions—is that liberalism has become toxic, if not yet fatal, for human imaginations that have room for nations or political life. Liberalism has always opposed itself to citizenship, and it has, along the way, made being a citizen both too calculating and too fanatical. And the modern oscillation between expecting too much and too little of citizenship, it's now thought, can only be brought to an end by bringing citizenship to an end. Modern personal life—in the absence of the personal significance that comes through being part of a family, country, or church (or through loving relationships in general)—might be too empty to perpetuate itself indefinitely. A real, whole person can only be constituted through a personal ordering of a variety of social parts.

The American Nation and the American Person

The American nation, we can also see, seems to have a much more likely future. There are many reasons for the American difference. The two world wars and the Cold War were clearly not as traumatic for us.

They, in fact, reinforced our national self-confidence. All the cruelty and murder didn't occur on our continent, and so the human cost of the monstrous twentieth century was quite manageable for us. Not only that, of course, but in each of these wars we, with very good reasons, think of ourselves as having been a force for good. Our successful purpose was the defense of personal freedom and human rights against insane evildoers.

We can also see that America has not really engaged in the effort to stabilize free, personal life in the absence of a personal God. The American view has never been either that God is dead—and so impersonal science and theology are clearly true—or that God should be reconfigured as the foundation of some American civil religion. Writers often talk about the American civil religion—but it's always described as some variant of Biblical religion with an active God.

From our very beginning, Americans haven't been stuck with the extreme contradiction between intense personal longings and impersonal science or theology. Consider our Declaration of Independence. The theoretical core of the Declaration—the part about self-evident truths, inalienable rights, and instituting government—speaks of a "Nature's God" who's a past-tense Creator. This Deist God is the source of the impersonal laws of nature, and how that God guides us as free persons is very unclear. But more specifically Christian members of Congress insisted that two other references to God be added to the very modern Jefferson and Franklin's draft. They're found in the rousing conclusion, which ends, of course, with "sacred honor." The Declaration's Creator-God is the Supreme Judge of us all, and he is the source of divine providence.

Due to a legislative compromise, the Declaration as a whole presents a · "Nature's God" who's a Creator and who knows and cares about each of us. We can say that through most of our history legislative compromises between very modern and Christian Americans have reconciled or at least considerably reduced the distance between Christian and modern views of the person's natural and theological environment. Americans always go wrong when they allow high Lockean principles to trump our national impetus to compromise—most recently, as in the case with abortion, as a result of judicial intervention. So Americans view political life, in part, as the free construction of self-interested individuals securing their material being in a hostile environment. But they also, in part, regard it as limited by the conscientious, social duties persons have to their personal Creator.

Political life is both dignified and limited by the real existence of dignified and limited creatures. And so, as Tocqueville explains, the Americans have always regarded religion as a limit to the spirit of social and political reform. Present persons can't be sacrificed to some vague historical future, although the Americans always have plenty of confidence in progress. Because the Americans don't really believe people are radically, miserably alienated from God and nature now, they don't think anything and everything must be done to relieve them of their misery.

The Americans, as our friendly British critic G. K. Chesterton observed, are a seeming oxymoron—a creedal nation. The American creed is that all human beings are created equal, because there's a center of significance in the universe that's the source of the personal significance of each of us. Everyone, in principle, can be a citizen of our country by accepting the "dogmatic lucidity" of our national faith. That faith informs the American understanding of citizenship by laying the foundation for the way of life shared in our national home. American citizenship is not merely a national or political construction, and so we are fully at home with the thought that the nation—though real—is not the real source of the significance of citizens. (Because the term "creedal nation" really is somewhat oxymoronic, we're stuck with having to think hard and make compromises when it comes to immigration.)

This view of America, which finds its strongest support among conservative Americans today, explains why America can remain a nation while never having succumbed to the excesses of nationalism, why History has never planted its depersonalizing roots (at least very deeply) here, and why there are credible Christian and secular accounts of our Founding that might be deeply irreconcilable but nonetheless are readily compromised in practice. Finally, it explains why the Americans are so confident (even unreasonably confident) that the nation is the form by which democratic self-government should take root everywhere.

The Americans, and especially American conservatives, are much more alert than the Europeans to what's required to sustain liberalism—or the way of life devoted to the true liberty and dignity of the human person. So the American conservative dismisses as hopelessly naive the various studies touting Europe as the exemplary "soft super-power" of the future, as leading the world to an unprecedented combination of freedom, benevolence, and social justice. American conservatives see that liberalism, from the beginning, was always deficient in sustaining the institutions required to conserve itself. These include, as I've explained, the nation (including patriotism and the duties of the citizen). Liberals, from the beginning, tried to reduce the state to nothing more than a useful contract for personal fulfillment, but that reductionism never did justice to the social and political dimension of who we are. And citizens have to be ready to sacrifice and die for their political home even to effectively secure their rights.

Conservatives have also aimed to sustain religion as an indispensable source of moral duty and of the true belief that there's something beyond our own puny efforts that sustains the unique and irreplaceable dignity of each of us. Liberals characteristically err by denying how dependent their conception of personal freedom and dignity is on Biblical/Christian religious capital and premises. And conservatives have reminded us that familial love and duty are always in danger of liberal or individualistic erosion; people aren't simply free individuals but men and women, parents and children, and so forth. The person, liberals often forget, is an intrinsically relational being. The main reason, for example, that the American birthrate still meets the demand of replacement is the social behavior of religiously observant Americans. That behavior, we might say, isn't strictly speaking liberal or individualistic. But where would we be without it? Persons aren't so unique and irreplaceable that they can do without biological replacements.

America's persistent national self-understanding is the main reason why we continue to fund a huge military establishment capable of projecting our power and influence everywhere. We're prepared to do what's required to defend our national home in the world today. The Europeans have chosen to have minimal military expenditures and reduced military capabilities. When they need airlifts, they turn to our air force, and they *rely* on our navy for keeping the open seas open. Much of Europe's relative depoliticization or denationalization is parasitic upon one nation in particular. The Europeans can afford not to do everything required to defend themselves precisely because we choose not to be like them. If we chose to live like them, who, in fact, would protect us? We seem stuck with being a nation, and the Europeans, it seems to me, ought not only praise our distinctiveness but also follow their conservative or Christian and national thinkers—such as England's Roger Scruton and France's Pierre Manent—in doing what they can to imitate us.

A Personal Postscript on Political Philosophy

If I had ended this book with a rousing defense of the American nation as the world's model, I might have seemed to come close to the rhetorical strategy of many of the students of Leo Strauss. But I've already made it clear enough to anyone who cares the many differences I have with those erudite and often brilliant and admirable writers. Their analysis of regimes is largely in terms of citizens, statesmen, and philosophers, and they aim to moderate the personal pretensions of Christianity, natural rights, and History with a return to the relatively impersonal sobriety of the natural right of classical political philosophy.

I obviously dissent from the fundamental need for some complete return to Plato and Aristotle by agreeing with Christian and even modern thinkers that the person is the bottom line, that no human being is most fundamentally either a citizen or a philosopher. That doesn't mean I'm a "historicist" or convinced that our self-understanding develops or changes radically over time. Tocqueville was right when he claimed that Jesus Christ had to come down to earth to show human beings the ways in which they are all equally free persons; he showed them more clearly what has always distinguished members of our species. And seeing this truth about who we are doesn't depend on what the Christians believe about who Jesus is or about the Trinity. Tocqueville himself, of course, didn't share those beliefs. Nonetheless, he was able to show at least something close to the true or personal relationship between magnanimity and humility and greatness and justice in the service of elevating democracy.

I also disagree with many students of Strauss in not promoting a civil theology based on veneration of the greatness—both theoretical and practical—of our Founders. Our Founders, I've said, built better than they knew. Our grateful and loyal appreciation of their enduring practical accomplishments as statesmen engaged in prudent compromise does not mean they should be beyond criticism as political thinkers. We may have to think better than they did about the foundation of our creedal nation. Their deliberation should be a model for ours.

Let me close, instead, with some provisional remarks that bring the thought of Strauss—perhaps the most impressive and among the most influential political philosophers in America's history—close to mine in other ways. Natural right versus History, or reason versus revelation, or philosophy versus law are surely rhetorically exaggerated as stark alternatives in Strauss's writing. America and Americans are impure—but strange and wonderful—mixtures of all those allegedly fundamental alternatives. Certainly our faith in the absolutism of the Declaration of Independence to which Strauss calls attention is partly grounded in a philosophical sense of self-evidence, partly in the revelation of a monotheistic personal God, and partly in grateful, traditional veneration for our law and our Founders. Our common faith, in fact, has its vitality in our refusal not to choose one form of extremism over another and in not regarding the truth we hold in common about who we are as some final solution.

Our Declaration's devotion to *nature,* Strauss (in *Natural Right and History*) agrees with John Courtney Murray, is compromised by Locke's proto-historicism (nature gives us self-creating beings nothing of value). Its devotion to *reason,* Strauss would say, is somewhat diluted by the legislative compromise that transformed the Nature's God of the philosophic Jefferson's first draft of the Declaration into also a providential and judgmental God. Strauss adds, however, that all universal moral law depends on monotheistic revelation—on an omniscient and omnipotent God who's willful (or creative) and loving (or, as Chesterton says, a center of significance who gives us all significance). The God of any law—even of what we call natural law—can't be a purely necessitarian "Nature's God."

So Strauss suggests in his criticism of John Dewey that he approved of the statesmanlike compromise in Congress between the Calvinists and the Lockean Deists that produced something better than the extremism of either of the parties to the compromise. It would be dangerous, Strauss even says, if our absolutism were simply philosophical absolutism. That sort of absolutism is the foundation of unscrupulous and extreme modern experimentalism encouraged by the philosophers driven by History. Our Founders did sometimes think of our Constitution as an unprecedented modern experiment, but they didn't think they were some modern equivalent of philosopher-kings. Strauss, I think, would not have regarded the defense by some misguided Straussians of the "Nature's God" of the Declaration as liberated from personal, creationist premises as a promising way of fending off either the progressivist or relativist versions of historicism. The standard Lockean version of what that philosophic deity gives us, for one thing, is finally only negative. That God is indifferent to the personal being of each of us, and we are free—as historical or self-creating beings—to transform what he gave us with our personal significance in mind. The nominalism—the idea that words are tools for individual liberation and nothing more—characteristic of modern thought is already present in our Founders' Locke.

Nor does it make much sense to justify our Founding, as some Straussians do, as embodying some classical idea of natural right; no law, Strauss makes clear, can do that. For Strauss, natural law is an oxymoron, and the Enlightenment effort to derive an effective morality merely from rational reflection on the interests we share in common is naive. Both Thomas Jefferson's confidence that our country could be graced by the effectual selection of natural aristocrats of wisdom and virtue to rule and *The Federalist*'s Machiavellian controlled experiment of employing enduring institutions with teeth to solve the problem of the unreliability of characters Strauss gently criticizes (as well as appreciates). Strauss's own view seems to be that public opinion informed by the moral absolutism of the Declaration of Independence, assisted by those strong institutions, might serve to contain the experimentalism of unscrupulous men, who, when safely checked, are often capable of producing good political results.

Many Straussians—to defend that civic morality—think they're stuck with the absolute defense of the American compromise as more than a compromise. Natural rights have to be exoterically defended in the esoteric light of natural right or what's best for philosophy as a way of life. But even the absolute defense of natural rights as universal moral law can't liberate "Nature's God," as the philosopher does esoterically, from the "exoteric" or civil theological creative and providential God. So Straussians are compelled not to write as atheists, but also not from the perspective of genuine believers. Too often they come off as seeming to believe more than is reasonable in America, with an incredible faith in our Founders as the wisest of men. They aren't so good in limiting government from the perspective of the person who is more than a citizen, whose political home is not his truest home. But the progress of our welfare state has showed us pretty clearly the unreliability of individual self-interest, by itself, as a brake on Big Government.

Those, such as the American Catholic Thomist John Courtney Murray, who defend the American compromise as the product of men building better than they knew, from Strauss's view, unreasonably believe that the Thomistic synthesis of Nature's God and the personal, creative God is actually reasonable. But we Thomists remember that Strauss also thought that impersonal Platonism and creative History are philosophic extremes, and that we can't know for certain that Being is anonymous or impersonal. We also remember with, I think, Lincoln (not to mention Chesterton—a huge admirer of Lincoln) that our belief in equal rights depends on a deeper belief in the equal significance of every human person.

It's far from clear, as I've explained, that personal—but not Historical—*logos* is an oxymoron. The rediscovery of the personal *logos* would be, for us, postmodern. It would combine the *realism* (as opposed to modern nominalism or constructivism) of classical political philosophy with what we can call Christian and modern *personalism*. The person, in fact, is not a Historical creation, and that's why, as a rational and erotic being open to the truth, he's stuck with virtue no matter how people transform their world. If we are persons by nature—as the beings hardwired, so to speak, for language or speech—then the good news is that the philosophers of History (including the Nietzscheans [including, at times, Strauss] who obsess about the possible coming of a Brave New World and its "last man") are wrong that we are given the freedom to make ourselves more or less than human—or more or less than persons. The bad news, in a way, is that we'll never be totally at home in the natural world, the political world, or some designed techno-world we create for ourselves.

Strauss was surely right that a somewhat vague idea of nature or natural right functioned well as a weapon against History, and Platonic philosophers, Lockean techno-individualists, and Biblical believers readily allied to defend natural human liberty against tyrannical efforts by the Communists at its Historical abolition. Personal destiny and responsibility, in fact, defeated the effort to reduce persons—including even philosophers—to History fodder. Neither natural right nor History can explain the personal, courageous responsibility dissidents such as Solzhenitsyn took for defeating the impersonal lie that was Historical ideology. The disappearance of History with a capital "H" was not the end of the free and responsible person. And it certainly was a defeat of the promise of modern atheism that we can create for ourselves a world so fulfilling or unalienated that God and religious longing would just wither away.

The defense of the goodness of nature, of course, becomes more urgent as the quackery of History is displaced by genuinely promising biotechnological efforts to alter our natures. And that defense can't be based, even esoterically, primarily on what's best for philosophers. In Huxley's *Brave New World*, for example, the alienated philosophers—"anybody who's anybody"—continue to dwell on the isles of the blessed (such as the Falklands and Iceland), while the great mass of people are reduced to subhumanity through the right mixture of mood-altering chemicals and intrusive socialization in the name of happiness, as opposed to the alienated Lockean's joyless quest for joy.

The Brave New World, the book suggests, might not be so bad for philosophers, who won't be compelled but might be able to rule. Rights—including, for example, our right to our natural moods— make no sense unless it's really possible for ordinary persons to be both free and happy while assuming the responsibilities we all share. And so it seems more true than ever that neither "natural right" nor "History" is the solution, because neither captures adequately who we are.

Strauss did well in countering creative History with impersonal nature, and he was right to oppose the tyrannical fantasies of those who thought that who we are or what we know depends in some deep way on our Historical success. But surely the idea that each of us by nature is personal—or has a unique, irreplaceable, rational, loving, moral, dignified, and creative destiny given to us by who we are as natural beings—deserves a new look as what's certainly most needed and what's most probably true in facing the post-Historical, biotechnological challenges of our time.

NOTES

Chapter 1: Modern and American Dignity

1. See Chantal Delsol, *The Unlearned Lessons of the Twentieth Century,* trans. R. Dick (Wilmington, DE: ISI Books, 2006), especially chapter 12.

2. The discussion of St. Augustine here is based on his *City of God,* especially books 5–8.

3. The account of the classical philosophic view here is defended by Thomas Pangle, *Political Philosophy and the God of Abraham* (Baltimore, MD: Johns Hopkins University Press, 2006).

4. See John Locke, *Second Treatise of Government.* Support for my view of Locke here can be found in the work of Michael P. Zuckert: *The Natural Rights Republic: Studies on the Foundation of the American Political Tradition* (South Bend, IN: University of Notre Dame Press, 2002) and *Launching Liberalism* (Lawrence, KS: University Press of Kansas, 1996).

5. The meaning of transcendence here is indebted to Harvey C. Mansfield, *Manliness* (New Haven, CT: Yale University Press, 2006). The present essay as a whole is an Augustinian reflection on manliness or a manly reflection on St. Augustine. What is it that causes human beings to claim the dignity of irreplaceable personal significance? Does that claim make any sense beyond human assertion?

6. Tom Wolfe, "The Human Beast," the 2006 Jefferson lecture.

7. See Leon R. Kass, "The Right to Life and Human Dignity," *Enlightening Revolutions: Essays in Honor of Ralph Lerner,* ed. S. Minkov (Lanham, MD: Lexington Books, 2006).

8. Kass, 130.

9. See Pierre Manent, *A World beyond Politics,* trans. M. LePain (Princeton, NJ: Princeton University Press, 2006).

10. See ibid., chapters 5–7, 11.

11. See Walker Percy, *Lost in the Cosmos: The Last Self-Help Book* (New York, NY: Farrar, Straus, and Giroux, 1983), 13.

12. See Charles Rubin, "Human Dignity and the Future of Man," in *Human Dignity and Bioethics* (Washington, DC: President's Council on Bioethics, 2008).

13. See the Tocquevillian/Pascalian reflections on compassionate conservatism and biology in chapter 5 of my *Stuck with Virtue: The American Individual and Our Biotechnological Future* (Wilmington, DE: ISI Books, 2005).

14. Aleksandr Solzhenitsyn, *The Solzhenitsyn Reader,* ed. E. Ericson and D. Mahoney (Wilmington, DE: ISI Books, 2006), 596.

15. Thomas Hobbes, *Leviathan,* especially chapters 11 and 18.

16. Alexis de Tocqueville, *Democracy in America,* trans. H. Mansfield and D. Winthrop (Chicago, IL: University of Chicago Press, 2000), volume 2, part 1, chapter 5.

17. Ibid., volume 2, part 4, chapter 6.

18. Ibid., *Democracy in America,* volume 2, part 1, chapter 7.

19. Delsol, *The Unlearned Lessons of the Twentieth Century,* 194.

20. Hobbes, *Leviathan,* especially chapters 13 and 17.

21. See Percy, *Lost in the Cosmos,* 73–79.

22. See my *Stuck with Virtue,* chapter 5, with the fate of Charlotte in the last chapter of Tom Wolfe's *I Am Charlotte Simmons* (New York, NY: Farrar, Straus, and Giroux, 2003).

23. See Mansfield, *Manliness,* 59–61, 220.

24. See Tom Wolfe, "Sorry, but Your Soul Just Died," *Hooking Up* (New York, NY: Farrar, Straus, and Giroux, 2001), with Mansfield, *Manliness,* 220–24.

25. Everything I know about Kant and human dignity and more can be found in Susan M. Shell, "Kant and Human Dignity," *In Defense of Human Dignity: Essays for Our Times,* ed. R. Kraynak and G. Tinder (South Bend, IN: University of Notre Dame Press, 2003), 53–80.

26. See Mansfield, *Manliness,* 59–61, 220.

27. See the work of Walker Percy here; an introduction is found in my *Postmodernism Rightly Understood* (Lanham, MD: Rowman and Littlefield, 1999), chapters 3 and 4, as well as in chapters 5 and 10 of my *Aliens in America: The Strange Truth about Our Souls* (Wilmington, DE: ISI Books, 2002). The best introduction to Percy's work for those with little patience for novels is his *Lost in the Cosmos.*

28. I think of myself as presenting simply a somewhat confused and complicated line of thought found in the work of Richard Rorty, our most able "cultural philosopher" today.

29. See Manent, *A World beyond Politics,* 191–96.

30. See my "McWilliams and the Problem of Political Education," *Perspectives on Political Science* 35 (Fall 2006): 213–18. This issue of *PPS* is devoted to the work of Wilson Carey McWilliams, the most profound defender of the connection between human dignity and egalitarian political community of our time. And also see, of course, part 1 of volume 2 of Tocqueville's *Democracy in America*.

31. This question is what animates part 1 of volume 2 of Tocqueville's *Democracy in America*.

32. Delsol, *The Unlearned Lessons of the Twentieth Century*, 194–95.

33. See Robert P. Kraynak, "'Made in the Image of God': The Christian View of Human Dignity and Political Order," *In Defense of Human Dignity*, 81–118.

34. See the chapters by Robert George and Gilbert Meilaender in *Human Dignity and Bioethics*. It can be wondered whether George's secular "natural law" argument depends on the not self-evident proposition of our creation by a personal God. And surely a shortcoming of Meilaender's argument—at least in terms of formulating American public policy—is his inability or unwillingness to connect his Christian and egalitarian view of dignity to our secular understanding of rights. See my discussion of this book in the next chapter.

35. The American view of dignity articulated here—one that aims to reconcile the doctrine of our Declaration of Independence and the true tradition of Christian realism—is indebted, above all, to G. K. Chesterton, *What I Saw in America* (New York, NY: Dodd and Mead, 1922). See also my *Homeless and at Home in America* (South Bend, IN: St. Augustine's Press, 2007), especially chapters 1–3.

36. Václav Havel, *Open Letters* (New York, NY: Vintage Books, 1992), 263.

37. Leon R. Kass, *Life, Liberty, and the Defense of Dignity* (San Francisco, CA: Encounter Books, 2002), 248.

38. The claims in this paragraph are supported through the use of the work of Walker Percy in my *Postmodernism Rightly Understood*, chapters 3 and 4.

Chapter 2: The Human Dignity Conspiracy

1. *Human Dignity and Bioethics: Essays Commissioned by the President's Council on Bioethics* (2008). A version was published by the University of Notre Dame Press (2009). I have an essay in the book—"Modern and American Dignity" (chapter 1 of this book)—but it does not figure in the analysis here. The book also includes my "Commentary of Meilaender and Dennett," from which I have borrowed a little for this article.

2. Steven Pinker, "The Stupidity of Dignity," *New Republic,* May 28, 2008.

3. See Pinker's testimony to the President's Council on Bioethics, March 6, 2003, available at www.bioethics.gov.

4. Pinker, "The Stupidity of Dignity."

5. The history of dignity presented here is indebted to the Council book as a whole, and particularly to Adam Schulman's "Bioethics and Human Dignity" and Daniel P. Sulmasy, O.F.M.'s "Dignity and Bioethics: History, Theory, and Selected Applications."

6. Tom Wolfe, *A Man in Full* (New York, NY: Farrar, Straus, and Giroux, 1998).

7. Hobbes, *Leviathan,* chapter 10.

8. Rubin, "Human Dignity and the Future of Man."

9. Kant, *Grounding for a Metaphysics of Morals,* trans. James W. Ellington (Indianapolis, IN: Hackett Publishing, 1981), 40.

10. Leon R. Kass, "Defending Human Dignity," in *Human Dignity and Bioethics.*

11. Susan M. Shell, "Kant's Concept of Dignity as a Resource for Bioethics," in *Human Dignity and Bioethics,* gives a more positive and arguably more nuanced view of Kant's possible contribution to our understanding of dignity than the one presented here.

12. Kass, *Life, Liberty, and the Defense of Dignity.*

13. The International Academy of Humanism's 1997 statement in defense of cloning research in higher mammals and human beings, as quoted by Leon R. Kass in "Science, Religion, and the Human Future," *Commentary,* April 2007.

14. Kass, "Science, Religion, and the Human Future."

15. Daniel C. Dennett, "How to Protect Human Dignity from Science," in *Human Dignity and Bioethics.*

16. Gilbert Meilaender, "Human Dignity: Exploring and Explicating the Council's Vision," in *Human Dignity and Bioethics.*

17. Robert C. Kraynak, "Human Dignity and the Mystery of the Human Soul," in *Human Dignity and Bioethics.* See also Kraynak, "Commentary on Dennett," in the same volume.

18. Daniel C. Dennett, "Commentary on Kraynak," in *Human Dignity and Bioethics.*

19. Patrick Lee and Robert P. George, "The Nature and Basis of Human Dignity," in *Human Dignity and Bioethics.* I have attributed this argument primarily to Council member George simply because it is mainly identified with him.

20. Diana Schaub, "Commentary on Meilaender and Lawler," in *Human Dignity and Bioethics,* with Schaub, "Commentary on Nussbaum, Shell, and Kass" in the same volume.

Chapter 4: Delsol on Human Rights and Personal Dignity

1. These books were published by ISI Books in 2008, 2006, and 2003 respectively.

2. Delsol doesn't actually use the phrase "negative Platonism," although it's central to Patočka's thought. See Johann P. Arsonson, "The Idea of 'Nega-

tive Platonism' in Jan Patočka's Critique and Recovery of Metaphysics," *Thesis Eleven* 90 (2006): 6–26.

3. Tocqueville, *Democracy in America*, 407–10.

4. See Thomas L. Pangle, *Leo Strauss: An Introduction to his Thought and Intellectual Legacy* (Baltimore, MD: Johns Hopkins University Press, 2006).

5. See Václav Havel, *Open Letters* (New York, NY: Knopf, 1994), and *The Solzhenitsyn Reader*.

6. Percy, *Lost in the Cosmos*, with my *Aliens in America*, 51–74, 251–72.

7. See especially Solzhenitsyn, *The Solzhenitsyn Reader*, 561–75, and chapters 5 and 9 of this book.

8. Thomas Hobbes, *Leviathan,* ed. C. B. Macpherson (New York, NY: Penguin Classics, 1982), chapter 10.

9. See Tocqueville, *Democracy in America*, 407–10, 425–26, 66–73.

10. Delsol, *The Unlearned Lessons of the Twentieth Century,* 195.

11. See chapter 8 of this book

Chapter 5: Tocqueville on Greatness and Justice

1. On all the points made in this paragraph, see Mansfield, *Manliness,* and Wolfe, *I Am Charlotte Simmons.* I say more in chapter 7 of my *Homeless and at Home in America.*

2. This section is nothing more than a reading of what Aristotle says about the magnanimous man in book 4 of the *Nicomachean Ethics* in light of what he says in that book as a whole. It is very indebted to secondary sources that go beyond that book to Aristotle's other writings for clarification on this man's character. My debts to these sources are too numerous, subtle, and doubtless unconscious in some ways to be adequately acknowledged in particular notes. So let me just list them with gratitude: Carson Holloway, "Christianity, Magnanimity and Statesmanship," *Review of Politics* 61 (Autumn 1999): 581–604; Larry Arnhart, "Statesmanship as Magnanimity: Classical, Christian, and Modern," *Polity* 16 (Winter 1983): 263–83; Susan D. Collins, "Moral Virtue and the Limits of Political Community in Aristotle's 'Nicomachean Ethics,'" *American Journal of Political Science* 48 (January 2004): 47–61; and Jacob Howland, "Aristotle's Great-Souled Man," *Review of Politics* 64 (Winter 2002): 27–56. My greatest debt turns out to have been to Mary M. Keys, *Aristotle, Aquinas, and the Promise of the Common Good* (New York, NY: Cambridge University Press, 2006), chapter 6; it took a good Catholic woman to drive home what should have been the obvious point that Aristotle's character is just unrealistic, and Thomas employed Christian psychology to make him more genuinely self-conscious and so more genuinely virtuous. I have agreed and disagreed with all these sources and have employed them in a selective and probably distorted way to provide a "coherent narrative" that would be a suitable prelude to Tocqueville.

3. Mansfield, *Manliness*, 221–23.

4. As Keys reminds us; see her *Aristotle, Aquinas, and the Promise of the Common Good,* 156–58.

5. Numbers in parentheses are page references to Alexis de Tocqueville, *Recollections: The French Revolution of 1848,* ed. J. P. Mayer and A. P. Kerr (Piscataway, NJ: Transaction Books, 1987). For a somewhat different and expanded discussion of the theme of greatness in these *Recollections* (or *Souvenirs*), see my *The Restless Mind: Alexis de Tocqueville on the Origin and Perpetuation of Human Liberty* (Lanham, MD: Rowman and Littlefield, 1993).

6. Three numbers separated by commas in the text refer to volume, part, and chapter of *Democracy in America*. This first reference, for example, is to volume 2, part 2, chapter 1.

7. On the general context of Tocqueville's thought and its relation to Pascal, see my *The Restless Mind.*

8. See Keys, *Aristotle, Aquinas, and the Promise of the Common Good,* 197.

9. See Harvey C. Mansfield and Delba Winthrop, "Tocqueville's New Political Science," *The Cambridge Companion to Tocqueville,* ed. Cheryl B. Welch (New York, NY: Cambridge University Press, 2006), 84.

10. See ibid., 86.

11. Mansfield, *Manliness,* chapter 4.

12. See Mansfield and Winthrop, "Tocqueville's New Political Science," 86–92.

13. Delsol, *The Unlearned Lessons of the Twentieth Century,* 194–95.

Chapter 8: Building Better Than They Knew: John Courtney Murray's American, Catholic View of the True Foundation of Our Country

1. The two best introductions to Murray's life and thought are Robert W. McElroy, *The Search for American Public Philosophy* (New York, NY: Paulist Press, 1989), and Thomas P. Ferguson, *Catholic and American: The Political Theology of John Courtney Murray* (Lanham, MD: Rowman and Littlefield, 1993).

2. Murray's disappointment with the weak foundation for religious liberty found in the Council document *Dignitatis Humanae* is described by Francis Canavan, S.J., "Religious Freedom: John Courtney Murray and Vatican II," in *John Courtney Murray and the American Civil Conversation,* ed. R. P. Hunt and K. L. Grasso (Grand Rapids, MI: Eerdmans, 1992). One way Murray tried to spin what the document actually says in the direction of his own view is described by Russell Hittinger, "The Declaration of Religious Freedom, in *Dignitatis Humanae,*" *Vatican II: Renewal within Tradition,* ed. M. Lamb and M. Levering (New York, NY: Oxford University Press, 2008).

3. John Courtney Murray, *We Hold These Truths* (Lanham, MD: Sheed and Ward, 1960). Subsequent references to this book are found in the text (WT).

I have borrowed here and there throughout this chapter from two earlier chapters of mine on *We Hold These Truths* in my *Aliens in America* and *Homeless and at Home in America.*

4. See Harvey Mansfield, *America's Constitutional Soul* (Baltimore, MD: Johns Hopkins University Press, 1990), with his (with Delba Winthrop's) introduction to his translation of Tocqueville's *Democracy in America.* For an incisive recent analysis on Strauss and America, see Leora Batnitzky, *Leo Strauss and Emmanuel Levinas: Philosophy and the Politics of Revelation* (New York, NY: Cambridge University Press, 2008). For more on view of Strauss, see my "What Is Straussianism? (According to Strauss)," *Society,* forthcoming.

5. John Courtney Murray, S.J., *Bridging the Sacred and the Secular,* ed. J. L. Hooper (Washington, DC: Georgetown University Press, 1994), 111.

6. Francis Canavan, "Rights in a Federalist System," in *Defending the Republic,* ed. B. Frohnen and K. Grasso (Wilmington, DE: ISI Books, 2008). The quotes from Locke are from *The Essay Concerning Human Understanding,* book 3, chapter 3, subsection 11.

7. John Courtney Murray, S.J., "The Church and Totalitarian Democracy," *Theological Studies* 14 (December 1952): 525–63.

8. John Courtney Murray, S.J., *Religious Liberty: Catholic Struggles with Pluralism,* ed. J. L. Hooper (Louisville, KY: Westminster/John Knox Press, 1993), 70.

9. Murray, "The Church and Totalitarian Democracy," is his most extended defense of this claim.

10. John Courtney Murray, S.J., *The Problem of God: Yesterday and Today,* (New Haven, CT: Yale University Press, 1964), 110.

11. Murray, *Bridging the Sacred and the Secular,* 158.

12. Murray, *The Problem of God,* 85, 95.

13. Ibid., 77.

14. Leo Strauss, *Natural Right and History* (Chicago, IL: University of Chicago Press, 1953), 75.

15. Murray, *The Problem of God,* 90–99.

16. John Courtney Murray, S.J., "St. Ignatius and the End of Modernity," in *The Ignatian Year at Georgetown* (Washington, DC: Georgetown University Press, 1956).

17. Murray, *The Problem of God,* 86–87.

18. David Brooks, *Bobos in Paradise: The New Upper Class and How They Got There* (New York, NY: Simon and Schuster, 2000); Edward Feser, *The Last Superstition: A Refutation of the New Atheists* (South Bend, IN: St. Augustine's Press, 2008).

19. Murray, "The Church and Totalitarian Democracy," 545.

20. Murray, *Bridging the Sacred and the Secular,* 113.

21. John Courtney Murray, S.J., "How Liberal Is Liberalism?" *America* 75, no. 6 (April 1946).

22. John Courtney Murray, S.J., "Laws or Prepossessions?" *Essays on Constitutional Law*, ed. R. G. McCloskey (New York, NY: Knopf, 1954), 332.

23. Ibid., 325.

24. Ibid., 328.

25. Ibid., 332.

26. This sort of anti-Americanist criticism is found throughout Donald J. D'Elia and Stephen Krason, eds., *We Hold These Truths and More* (Steubenville, OH: Franciscan University Press, 1994).

27. R. L. Bruckberger, *Images of America*, trans. C. G. Paulding and V. Peters (Piscataway, NJ: Transaction Publishers, 2008; originally published 1959). Subsequent references to this book are found in the text (IA).

28. Zuckert, *Launching Liberalism*, 215.

29. John Courtney Murray, S.J., "The Declaration on Religious Freedom: A Momment in Legislative History," in *Religious Liberty: An End and a Beginning*, ed. J. C. Murray (New York, NY: Macmillan, 1966), 40–41.

30. Murray, *Bridging the Sacred and the Secular*, 108.

31. Kass, *Life, Liberty, and the Defense of Dignity*.

32. See chapter 7 of this book.

33. Canavan, "Religious Freedom: John Courtney Murray and Vatican II," 171.

Chapter 9: Solzhenitsyn on the Challenge of Our Technological Civilization

1. Ratzinger, Joseph. *The Regensburg Lecture*, St. Augustine's Press, 2007, 129.

INDEX

259